Mind
Over

Psychological Self-Improvement for Boys

Gene L. Warner

Copyright © 2008 Gene L Warner, Grand Haven, Michigan 49417 USA – All rights reserved.

Published in the United States by

www.boysmindbooks.com

Book Description: Happiness and success in life depend on something nobody teaches you anything about – your mind. Most of the time brains just free-run, doing whatever they want with the inputs they receive, and taking us wherever they happen to drift, which often turns out to be places we would rather not be. Instead of letting an out-of-control brain be your master – a "monster" that constantly works against you – you can decide to take control, making your mind think rationally and constructively to provide a highly successful, abundantly happy and richly rewarding life.

Publishers Cataloging in Publication Data
    Warner, Gene L.
        Mind Over Monster
        Psychological Self-Improvement for Boys
            First Edition Published July 2008 (Rev Sept 2017)
        p. cm.
        Includes index
        ISBN: 978-0-9797896-2-5
        1. Self-Help/Personal Growth. 2. Child Psychology. 3. Personality. I. Warner, Gene L. II. Title

BF721.W37   2008   BISAC: SEL03100
155 – dc22   LCCN: 2008906290

Author Website Address: www.boysmindbooks.com

To Imago

~

A Special Boy

What Is a Neurotic?

"Basically, an adult who consistently acts illogically, irrationally, inappropriately, and childishly. Neurotics, then, make themselves unreasonably or unnecessarily bothered or bewildered. They bring on more pain or anxiety than they, theoretically, need experience. Many of them have more than enough wherewithal – good looks, high intelligence, and fine talents – to get along successfully in this world. But somehow they don't."

Albert Ellis
How To Live With a "Neurotic"

Contents

1. Introduction 1
2. Mind or Monster? 11
3. Your Beautiful Mind 21
4. Personality 35
5. The Three A's 51
6. Straight A's 89
7. Bad Habits 123
8. Venery 145
9. Abuse & Neglect 163
10. Depression & Suicide 209
11. A Practical Faith 221
12. The Good Life 277

Index 279

Chapter 1
Introduction

Yes, introductions in books are usually boring. That's why readers often ignore them. I want you to read this one. That's why I've called it "Chapter 1."

Who Is This Book For?

If you are a boy who is at least ten years old, and who is beginning to think about who you are and how you fit in, this book is for you.

Why Only for Boys?

Because I was one for many years – thirteen years, eighteen years, or possibly longer, depending upon what one considers "a man." I have had no experience being a girl and, contrary to today's popular opinions, there are differences between males and females, which go way beyond physical features.

A person's gender has a lot to do with their natural interests, attitudes and emotions. People therefore expect males and females to look different, think differently, and act differently. Some people think this is unfair and wrong, and call it "sexist," "sexual stereotyping," "male chauvinism," and so on. But, like it or not, this is how things are right now.

Girls who act boyish are acceptable to most people. There is a cute name for them – *tomboys*. Boys who act girlish, however, are likely to be targets for ridicule and abuse by other boys, and even girls.

There is no cute name for them. Effeminate boys are called *homos* or *gay*.

I believe that the *gender roles* of men and women are different by nature, rather than nurture. I am therefore sensitive about women who try to teach boys about how men should think and behave. I think it is just as inappropriate for men to think they know what is best for girls. That's why what I write is intended just for boys.

Girls are certainly welcomed to read this book. It might be well worth their time if they come away with a much better understanding of what makes boys tick.

Why Ten?

Have you noticed that there are a lot of unpleasant and unhappy people in the world? Have you wondered why they are like that, and how they got that way? That is what this book is all about. Its purpose is to tell you some things about that, so you will be able to avoid what makes a boy grow up to be an unpleasant and unhappy man.

If you are still a young boy, a pre-teen or even an early teen, you are probably still usually pleasant and happy as long as you get enough sleep and nobody is picking on you. After a boy has entered the second decade of his life, that often begins to change.

It so happens that *puberty*, the physical process that turns a boy into a man (at least physically), also occurs around this time in a boy's life, usually sometime between ages ten and fourteen. But that is not what this book is all about. As you go through that time in your life and begin to become a sexually capable male, there are obvious physical changes. Along with them come changes in the way you think about things. That is a big deal, but that is not what causes the emotional problems that cripple so many unhappy adults.

Kids are usually simple people. As a kid, you accept what you see, hear and feel, without doing much thinking about the significance of events, the meaning of things other people do, or the purpose of your life. It is usually not very hard for others to know what you are thinking. Your behavior usually shows what you are thinking or feeling. You are emotional, rather than intellectual. In other words, how you feel as a kid usually depends upon what is going on around you at that moment, not upon how you think you should feel. Kids are simple minded for a very good reason; the brain is still developing and is not yet capable of doing much deep thinking and reasoning.

Sometime around the age of ten, and this is different for every person, your mind has developed to the point where you become able to think more deeply about things. As a simple example, if you believed in Santa Clause when you were little, you began to sense that certain parts of that story did not really make sense. You eventually realized that it was all made up; that there is no Santa Clause, except in the imaginations of little children. Your thinking might go even beyond that, realizing that your parents fooled you into believing in Santa Clause, and you might wonder what other tales they've been telling you, and why.

As you begin to think about things this way, your thoughts begin to create feelings. This is different from how you were as a younger child, when your feelings were mostly a result of what was happening to you at the moment.

So I would like to get this book to you around the time this begins to happen, so you can learn how to avoid turning yourself into an unpleasant and unhappy man. If that happens, it can take years to fix. Often it never gets fixed at all, and those men spend the rest of their lives thinking it would have been better if they had never been born.

The late Albert Ellis was a well-respected but hard-nosed psychologist famous for saying things like "Neurosis is a high-class word for whining." He believed that the second decade of life is the time when people who are screwed up got screwed up. Lee Iacocca was an engineer, not a psychologist, but during his career, which ended with his being president of two of the biggest auto manufacturers in the world, Ford and Chrysler, he learned a lot about what made people tick. Referring to general education in his book *Where Have All The Leaders Gone?* he said, "I've always believed that the ten-year span from five to fifteen is the make-or-break time."

So that's "why ten?" It is a critical time in every boy's life; a time when every boy has a chance to get the rest of his life started on the right foot.

Not ten? Eighteen, twenty-one or forty-four? Feel free to read this kid stuff anyway. Having been the way you are for a long time does not mean you have to stay that way. It's never too late to become a happy, successful and popular person. Tomorrow can indeed be "the first day of the rest of your life."

You're Just a Boy. What Do You Know?

Most adults think kids are not very smart, especially kids who are still fair complexioned and cute, full of energy, and who still speak in sweet, high-pitched voices.

It is true; you are obviously much less knowledgeable than an adult. That is simply because adults have been exposed to many more years of experience, and have had the opportunity to learn all sorts of things the hard way. You will eventually have all those same experiences, and will learn all sorts of things that people usually do not or cannot learn at home or in school. But adults usually make the mistake of judging a book by its cover. Because kids appear to be ignorant and naïve in many ways, adults wrongly assume that kids are totally innocent, and are incapable of serious thought or responsible decision-making.

You and I know that is not true. A ten-year old boy once told me, "We know a whole lot more about a whole lot more than most people think we do." I knew this boy very well, and I knew what he meant. Knowing him that well helped me remember what I was like when I was ten. I was just like him; I knew a lot of things too. However, many of those things were not things I would have been comfortable discussing with my parents, or any other adult. As a result, most adults probably believed that I was ignorant and naïve. It is easy to understand why they thought so. But they were wrong in thinking that my brain's capabilities were so limited.

Writers are often advised to adjust their work to the reading level of an average nine-year old. That seemed especially appropriate for this book, and I originally planned to do that. It is not really a big deal, just a matter of using short sentences and avoiding big words.

But I changed my mind. I would rather believe what my young friend said; that kids are a lot smarter than people usually think they are.

The idea of dumbing down my book seemed rather condescending. I am not comfortable doing that. My intention is to tell you what a wonder your mind is, and what great power it has. Writing down to you would not help promote that idea. It would also make the book boring for anyone whose reading level is higher than that.

I would also rather just be myself. My writing usually comes out somewhere between the seventh and eleventh grade levels anyway, corresponding to ages twelve to sixteen. If you are ten and earnest enough to be reading this book, you are probably already at that level anyway. If you find some parts a bit of a struggle, I am sure your wonderful mind will be able to figure things out and learn from the experience.

So, "You're just a boy. What do you know?" Whatever your age – ten, twelve, sixteen, or twenty-one – I am writing this for you. By the time you are done with this book, you surely *will* know a whole lot more about a whole lot more than most people expect – or even than most people.

And you are certainly not "just a boy." One of the best things about being born male is that you get to be a boy for a while. Boys are wonderful.

And you are also a gold mine of potential!

Who Am I

When you read books written for any purpose other than entertainment, you should ask, "Who is this person? What does he know, and why should I believe anything he says?" If the book has a jacket, you can usually find out about the author on the back inside flap. It will tell about his educational achievements, what he does for a living, what other books he has written, and so on.

I am nobody. I have only a high school education. I have not previously written any other books of this kind. However, I am over two-thirds of a century old now, and during those sixty-eight years have experienced much of what life will present to you as you continue to grow up.

When I was a boy, between the ages of about six and eighteen, I was growing up in a very unhappy family, so I became a very difficult and unhappy young man. That lasted until I was well into middle age. After the best part of my life was past – "best" in terms of good looks, physical fitness, energy, enthusiasm and opportunity – I finally began to get my head on straight, and became a happy person. During all those earlier years, I spent a lot of time trying to figure out what was the matter with me, and read many books that seemed to promise answers. Because of that, I suppose I could claim to be well studied or self-educated in psychology, neurology and human behavior.

You would probably expect the author of a book like this to be a shrink, or at least someone with a college degree. There are lots of books like that. I have read lots of books like that. Does that make me an expert?

No; of course not. And especially not, because over the years, ever since Sigmund Freud published his fascinating thinking about what makes people behave the way they do, psychological theories and fad therapies have come and gone, one after another. What is hot on the talk shows and bestseller lists is always soon replaced by something else, and usually by something much different. Nevertheless, each new scheme is hyped as the final truth, its inventor being worshiped as the new guru, and newly recruited believers flock to lectures, bookstores and hip therapists with money in hand and high hopes.

Today, most of the ideas previously promoted by yesterday's "experts" have been discredited and dismissed. That means that in spite of their impressive credentials, their thinking turned out to be incorrect, or at least less useful than whatever came along next.

I suggest you look upon me not as an expert, but as a practical grandfatherly figure who has learned some important things the hard way, and wants to save you from wasting the best years of your life repeating my experience.

About Your Parents

Do your parents know that you are reading this book? Did they buy it for you? If not, what will they think when they find it hidden under your mattress?

If you are less than eighteen years of age, you are under the age of majority in most U.S. states. The age of majority is the age when the law says you can be considered an independent adult, and are no longer legally under the control of your parents. If you are underage, your parents have the right, and a legal responsibility, to know what you are up to.

This book contains some rather explicit talk about personal things, like your relationship with your parents and others in your family. It talks about politics and religion. It also talks openly about love and sex. Would your parents approve of your reading this kind of material?

This raises a hard question. It is a classic question of intellectual freedom vs. censorship – your right to read what you wish, versus someone else's right or responsibility to control the kind of material you are exposed to.

Here is the rub:

If you are reading this book because you are finding life difficult and you are very unhappy, your parents are probably an important part of your problem. Their problems have become your problem. If they had been able to solve their problems, you might have no need to read this book. If they have not yet been able to do that, then it is important for you to know that their problems are *their problems*. You do not have to inherit them, or otherwise let those problems wreck your life.

Much of what is in this book could be considered "parenting." Some of it is political, some of it is moral and some of it is religious. If it conflicts with what certain authority figures in your life would have you believe, you will have to decide what the best thing to do is, given the nature of your family, and the feelings you have about yourself. Life is full of decisions like this; situations where you need to think about how what seems best for you might not please someone else. Doing what you want is not always the best answer. Neither is self-sacrifice.

Why is This Book (Not) So Small?

In the beginning, I thought I would be able to say what I thought I wanted to say in less than a hundred pages. Living life successfully as a happy person is not really complicated or difficult. People who are not happy usually do not believe that. They think their problems and disadvantages are special, and they feel helpless about fixing them. Worse yet, people often know that, but choose not to believe it. Rather than accept the responsibility for their own life – for making themselves happy and successful – they choose the role of "victim," blaming their situation on others or on circumstances that were beyond their control, and which supposedly left them with deep-seated and highly complex problems.

Thick books have been written for people who think they have big problems. Until recently, those books usually told their readers just what many of them wanted to hear – that their problems were excruciatingly complex, somebody else's fault, and very likely to prove amenable only to a lifetime of medication and counseling. If you continue reading this book, you will find out that is pure nonsense. Newer ideas, called *Cognitive Behavior Theory* and *Rational Emotive Behavior Theory*, greatly simplify things and remove much of the mystery. It would not have taken a lot of pages to explain how anyone who is willing to accept these new ideas could change their mind and swap their problems for happiness and success in life.

In the process of writing, however, I came to realize that there are special challenges that every boy has to come to terms with, and I thought these were worth talking about in more detail – what to do about school, religion and sex, for example. Much has already been written about such things, but most of it represents predictable adult attitudes.

The information age we live in is changing things just as dramatically as other historical paradigm shifts, such as the Renaissance and Industrial Revolution. Many of the ideas cherished by the adult world are proving to have always been invalid, or have become at least significantly less valid for your generation. I thought it would be useful to write about some of these things, showing how new ways of thinking can simplify what have, in the past, often caused lots of headaches and heartaches.

Most people do not like to change their minds after having believed something for a long time. Others have a vested interest in keeping things as they are. I am therefore certain that some of what I have to say in the following pages will be roundly criticized by some, leaving a few others absolutely enraged and furiously angry. That is not my intention, but in anticipating hurt feelings, I have written at length about certain things that you will be challenged to explain, should you decide to accept my point of view.

That is why my book turned out to be (not) so small.

Chapter 2
Mind or Monster?

This book is about neurology and psychology. It is about how the mind works, and how it affects your feelings and behavior. It is about how you can make it always work for you, and keep it from becoming your worst enemy.

The Mind

Neurology is a medical science dealing with the nervous system and its physical disorders – the brain, spinal cord, nerves, and nerve clusters.

The brain, the central processor, is extremely capable and powerful, with three main functions:

- *control* - regulating the physical body functions,
- *storage* - its memory, and
- *thinking* - reasoning, problem solving, etc.

From this point of view, the brain seems similar to your personal computer. But, unlike your computer, the brain is also capable of intellectual functions, such as:

- evaluating the meaning of everything your senses take in (sights, sounds, smells, feelings, etc.),
- coming up with ideas on its own,
- making plans and carrying them out, and
- producing emotional states, or "feelings".

Because of these functions, we usually refer to the brain as our *mind*.

We have also learned that the brain is wired like a vastly complex network using nerve cells, and that it functions by virtue of electrical impulses in some sort of organic chemical domain.

That's about it.

Experiments have indicated that the brain remembers everything that ever happened to you, but nobody understands how it does that. Nobody understands how our mind operates in its reasoning mode – how it comes up with ideas and solves problems. Nobody understands how or why it produces feelings.

Minds sometimes break down. The control system, for example, goes haywire. Hands shake and are no longer capable of delicate work; that's called Parkinson's Syndrome. In Alzheimer's Syndrome the memory system begins to fail, so the mind loses its ability to recall facts and use that information for reasoning and problem solving, and eventually even forgets how to do things like swallowing food. Defects such as these are thought to be chemical, although there are no cures.

More strangely, minds sometimes seem to receive bogus inputs from the senses. They see things that aren't there, or hear voices which really do not exist. Destructively delusional mental activities like that are actually very uncommon, all together affecting fewer than one in one-hundred.

Most of the time brains work just fine, physically. Their output however is often not so good. Here is where a computer analogy does work – "garbage in/garbage out."

Psychology – Subduing the Monster

Psychology is often thought of as a science. I am not comfortable with that, because the word science suggests a careful process of learning facts about the world we live in. So far, we know very little about exactly how the mind does what it does.

Although the mind seems highly resistant to disease and physical problems, *neuroses* are very common. This is actually a misnomer, an incorrect or unsuitable name for conditions also sometimes called emotional problems. About 236-years ago, a doctor in Scotland (William Cullen in 1769) guessed that these problems came from "a general affection of the nervous system," so he called them nervous, or *neurotic* problems. Today, we understand that was a catch-all category for problems doctors of that day were not able to blame on any obvious physical cause. The same thing happens today, when doctors diagnose some slight problem as "probably just some sort of virus," and prescribe an antibiotic – which has no effect on viruses at all.

Neurotic can mean anything from "a little bit upset" over something to being in the depths of a disabling or suicidal depression. Nobody likes to be called a neurotic. That sounds a lot like *psychotic*, which is the medical word for "insane," "nuts" or "looney-tunes." Yet, when asked, about fifty years ago, what percent of the population he considered neurotic to some extent, Dr. Albert Ellis, a leading psychologist and author, replied, "Oh, approximately ... 100%."

That is a lot of trouble and unhappiness, which creates a huge market for mind repairmen. Over the last three-hundred years, a variety of solutions have come and gone. Each one, in its turn, comes on strong with the promise of it being the answer, only to fade quickly away as the next big idea becomes popular. Today, there are three different approaches to fixing the problems:

- *psychoanalysis* – the idea that emotional problems come from thoughts and feelings that are sealed off deeply inside the mind. The reason might be that they were things that hurt so badly, the mind pushed them out of sight to stop the pain. Another reason might be that the thoughts were so mean or vulgar that they caused severe feelings of guilt and shame, so the mind hid them hoping to stop those bad feelings. This faction believes that analysis by a highly skilled therapist can eventually discover these things hidden in the subconscious part of the mind, and will then be able to explain how they cause the person's emotional problems.
- *behavior therapy* – is based upon the idea that one's problems are the result of, simply put, "bad habits." The idea is that you have developed inappropriate, but fixed ways of dealing with certain ideas and situations during your past experiences. How or why that happened is not considered important. You may, or may not realize this is the problem, but in either case this faction asserts that it will be difficult or impossible for you to replace these bad habits with better solutions without professional help.
- *neuropsychiatry* – in a nutshell, this faction assumes that emotional problems have a physical cause. In other words, the brain is not working right because of some physical injury, disease or chemical imbalance. Medication of some sort is prescribed as a solution, sometimes even surgery.

What these three ideas have in common is the notion that without professional help, you are stuck with your problems; that on your own you won't be able to figure out what the problems are, much less do anything about them.

Does this really make sense?

The mind is a very, very powerful machine. It got that way through millions of years of practice. Man has survived to your generation because he has been able to solve his problems successfully up to this point. Of all the living creatures from bug to beast, man has the largest brain, and the most highly developed mind. Our technical and intellectual achievements are actually awesome. Does it make sense to believe that we are capable of doing all things, yet not capable of controlling our attitudes and emotions?

It is easy to see that the above approaches do not work very well. For one thing, there are still lots of screwed up people around – and people who are still screwed up and unhappy in spite of being treated by these methods. For another, they apply only to people who are already screwed up, and are not very helpful in keeping people from getting that way.

With these things in mind, psychologists began to look for better ideas about how people become mixed up and unhappy, how to keep that from happening in the first place, and what to do about it when it does happen.

In 1955 a Dr. Albert Ellis came forth insisting that anyone could learn how to straighten themselves out. He called his ideas *Rational Emotive Behavior Theory*, or "REBT." He asserted that our emotions are caused by our thoughts and judgments about events and people – especially ourselves. He said that we can learn how to control our emotions by taking control of our thinking and judging, just as easily as we learn how to do anything else.

This did not go over very well with his fellow psychologists and psychiatrists, because it did not agree with what they had been taught, and had been practicing, perhaps for many years. Further, Dr. Ellis insisted that his approach was so logical and simple that anyone who wanted to could quickly learn how to do it, so long-term therapy or treatment was just a waste of time and money. That was a very unpopular idea with just about everyone. It threatened the income of therapy providers, and also put the monkey on the patient's back, identifying them as the cause of their own problems, and making them responsible for fixing their own problems. As a result, Dr. Ellis' ideas were not eagerly accepted.

Like earlier treatment ideas, Albert Ellis' approach was for people who were already disturbed, and did not have much to say about how they got that way, or how to keep people from getting screwed up in the first place.

Then a psychologist named Aaron Beck came up with an idea he called *Cognitive Behavior Theory*. That was a new, very simple idea about how and why the mind creates incorrect ideas, or *cognitions*, that disturb people. "CBT" quickly took off as a new and better way to help people overcome emotional and personality problems. It also really helped make sense of Dr. Ellis' approach.

This resulted in a fourth approach to psychology; a common sense approach combining the ideas of REBT and CBT. It says that emotional problems (neurotic thinking and behavior) result from incorrect interpretations of things that happen to you during your life, that you are aware of those faulty cognitions, and that you can fix them using the same skills you ordinarily use to solve any of life's other problems.

It also says that you can learn how to avoid these sorts of problems in the first place by learning about how your mind works, and how to take control of what your mind is doing, rather than letting it just do whatever it will.

Men have traditionally been resistant to seeking help with neuroticism. Men with "emotional disorders" or "mental problems" were apt to be thought of as wimps or nuts by other men. That was usually enough to keep them away from shrinks, and if they did get involved, it was usually a well-kept secret.

REBT and CBT changes that by replacing ideas about deep-seated emotional issues or possible brain problems with ideas that are a lot easier for men to swallow. You do not have to be nuts anymore, just somewhat mistaken in your thinking about certain things. Since most people think it is an admirable thing when a man is able to admit that he is wrong about something and change his mind, this new approach can be seen as an exercise in self-improvement, rather than therapy.

I chose the title "Mind Over Monster" because monsters is what minds usually become when left to do whatever they want. Unless you take control of what your mind is doing, your mind is likely to become your worst enemy – a monster that keeps you from being happy and being whatever you can be. Unfortunately, this happens to a lot of people, as you can easily see by looking around at the way others behave.

Just as your mind has the power to become a monster, it is equally capable of making you a happy and successful person, able to achieve whatever you want. So here's the big question: What will you be carrying around between your ears for the rest of your life – a beautiful mind or a self-defeating Monster?

Our Neurotic World

Controlling your mind's awesome power and making it work for you is a learned skill, just like driving a car. It seems ironic indeed that we require young people to take a driver's training course before they can get a license to drive on public streets, roads and highways, yet when it comes to learning how to master their mind – something potentially much more dangerous and destructive than a motor vehicle – we offer nothing, and require nothing, before turning them loose into life.

The whole idea behind this book is to do something about that. You cannot learn how to drive by just reading a book, and this book will not teach you all there is to know about mastering your mind and keeping the Monster under control. That is a life-long task, of course. But I hope to get you started by convincing you –

- that you have a choice between a mind that usually works rationally, and one that is almost always neurotic,
- that learning to think and behave more rationally is easy and well worth the time and effort, and
- that the world would be a much better place if everyone were to learn how to use their mind more effectively, rather than permitting their mind to destructively use them.

In the rest of this book, you will learn a little bit more about how minds work, why they do not always come up with the right answers, how to recognize the bogus information and ideas they sometimes generate, how to keep that from happening, and what you can do about it when it does.

The conversation will sometimes be about you, but more often about people in general. That is because happiness and success in life is not just a matter of coping with your own potential "Monster," but also with everyone else's. As Albert Ellis quipped, most people are neurotic. If that is true, and has been true for a long time, then the logical conclusion is that the world you find yourself living in is one that has been prepared for you largely by neurotics. You might therefore reasonably expect to discover a lot of things that reflect the neurotic thinking of those who, over the generations, made up the beliefs, customs and rules that you have inherited.

When conflicts arise – and they surely will – it is very helpful to be able to answer the question, "Is it everyone else, or is it just me?" It is often difficult to decide it is "everyone else" – that everyone else is wrong, and you are right. That unpopular position often pressures people to make the bad mistake of conforming their thinking to neurotic conventions. By the same token, it is no good going through life fighting against everything that is flawed and possibly unjust. Life is so full of such things that there would be no end to your struggles.

The well-known *Serenity Prayer* (Reinhold Niebuhr – 1934) asks, "God, give us grace to accept with serenity the things that cannot be changed, courage to change the things that should be changed, and the wisdom to distinguish the one from the other."

That is the general idea, but I suggest that rather than rely on God to bestow this gift upon you – which might, or might not happen – you take to heart the seventeenth century advice of the English politician cum American founding father Algernon Sidney – "God helps them who help themselves."

Find a comfortable chair in a well-lighted place, and read on.

Chapter 3
Your Beautiful Mind

What if I were to say to you, "Some people are a lot smarter than others."

Would you think I meant that some people have bigger, better or more powerful brains than others? It is often said that, on average, people use only about ten percent of their brain's capacity. Nobody knows who came up with that encouraging fact, or how it was determined. It obviously does not mean that ninety percent of the brain is wasted, since a lot more than that lights up when researchers do brain scans.

Some suspect the idea originally came from William James, a well-known 19th century psychologist and writer, who actually only suggested that most people function well below their mental potential.

All Minds Are Created Equal

My statement, as framed above, is incorrect. A correct observation would be, "Some people learn how to use their minds more effectively than others." But that probably isn't saying much. When one takes the time to have a good look at the system each one of us is endowed with, it is very easy to agree with James' assertion – that we all operate well below that system's natural capability and potential.

It is also easy to see why that is. Has anyone, up to this point, taught you anything about how that system works, and what its capabilities are? The answer to that, of course, is almost always, "No."

This seems strange indeed, given the fact that happiness and success in life depends a lot upon how well you learn to use this system. On the other hand, not much was known about the mind until my generation, so the general attitude has been, "What's to teach – some people are just brighter than others. If you're among the more well-endowed, you're blessed; otherwise just suck it up and do the best you can with your limited mental ability."

I suspect that healthy brains are more or less equal in terms of potential. One person's brain probably is not much different than another's. How smart a person is probably depends only upon how well they learn to use it.

Before going any further, let's think about what your mind is, how it works, and what it is capable of doing. It is true; given what there is to know, very little is understood at this point in time. However, the little that is known is certainly enough to impress, and even leave you in awe of your neurological machinery.

So let's have a look.

How the Machine Works

The "machinery" is called your *nervous system*. Your nervous system consists of billions of specialized cells called *neurons*, which are distributed all over your body. Two central and highly compact components of your nervous system are your brain and your spinal column, which are referred to as your *central nervous system*.

There are three types of neurons. Some are sensors (sensory neurons), which pick up information about your environment and what is going on, while others (motor neurons) carry signals to muscles. Some (called *interneurons*) function merely as intermediate wiring. In any case, a primary function of nerve cells is communication; to transmit sensor and control information.

If you have ever used a microscope to look at cells, you probably envision cells as somewhat like an egg – blobs of stuff with a yoke in the middle (cytoplasm surrounding a nucleus, all neatly packaged within a membrane.) Neurons are different. Nerve cells consist of a nucleus having root-like extensions that act like wiring. These tiny "roots," about one-hundredth the size of a human hair, make connections from one cell to another in a highly organized manner to form specialized networks. Some of these "wires," called *dendrites*, receive signals from other neurons. Others, called *axons*, carry signals out of the cell. Axons can be very lengthy, sometimes as much as a couple of feet.

The signals transmitted through a nerve cell are electrical pulses, which have a well-defined shape and amplitude. The neurons that make up a particular network, or signal path, are not physically connected. They communicate with each other across tiny gaps, called *synapses*, between the transmitting cell's axon and the receiving cell's dendrite. Signals are exchanged across these gaps chemically, rather than electrically. When an electrical signal arrives at the end of one cell's axon, it causes molecules to be released which migrate across the synapse to the next cell's dendrite. When this chemical signal is received by that cell's dendrite, another electrical pulse is generated, which then travels through that cell, from dendrite, through the nucleus, and to the end of its axon. This is how signals pass through specialized networks, from sensors to the brain, and from the brain to muscles.

For a broader view of how this works, consider the sense of touch.

Were someone to touch your back very lightly, a sensory neuron would detect that and generate a single electrical pulse. That signal would travel through a particular network of nerve cells, in the manner described above, through your spinal cord to a particular area of your brain. That area of your brain, called the *somatosensory cortex*, contains a complete map of your body, and the signal would arrive at a neuron in that body map which represents the precise spot on your back that was touched.

As the pressure of the touch was increased, the nerve signal would change from a single pulse to a series of pulses. A poke to that spot on your back would generate a burst of pulses, the number of pulses indicating the pressure of the poke. Thus, so far the brain knows exactly where you are being touched, and how hard.

The sense of touch is actually a system of several senses, called the *somatosensory system*. The sensor neurons that make up this system can detect pressure with a degree of sensitivity that provides information about shape, softness, texture, vibration, and so on. They also provide signals that are analogs of temperature and pain (which includes sensations like itching and ticklishness). The brain receives and evaluates all these signals, and is able to come up with a lot of information about what's going on – where you are being touched, and by what.

Using an alternate route, the same signals are transmitted to another part of the brain which interprets them for danger and, if needed, produces and instant, involuntary response. For example, if instead of being touched you are pinched, touched with something hot or cold, or pricked with a pin, you will very likely lurch, arching your back to draw quickly away from the offending source without any conscious forethought. While that's happening, providing instant protection if needed, the regular channel still operates as usual to figure out what is going on.

The somatosensory system (sense of touch) is distributed over your entire body, from head to toe. It is not uniform; some parts are more heavily equipped with sensory neurons than others, and the types of sensory neurons are not always present in the same proportions. For example, if you bite your tongue it instantly hurts badly, because your tongue has many pain-sensing neurons. On the other hand, it has relatively fewer temperature-sensing neurons, so burning your tongue happens often unless you are careful to avoid it. Finger tips are very sensitive; a good thing for blind brail readers and safe crackers. The middle of the back is the body's least sensitive area.

Mind Boggling Performance

The purpose of this discussion is not to provide a lesson in neurology, but to engender an appreciation for how awesome your neurological system really is. This single aspect, your sense of touch, involves billions of neurons and miles of network wiring. Your brain very comfortably works in the background, constantly monitoring and interpreting all these inputs, plus those from the other four senses (sight, hearing, smell and taste) to keep itself constantly aware of what is going on around you. Meanwhile, it is also busy doing other things in the background, such as regulating your breathing rate and heart rate, managing appetite, digestion and the elimination of wastes, overseeing your immune system, and more.

And it ordinarily all works flawlessly!

Imagine a perfect day at Atlanta International, the world's busiest airport. Hundreds of thousands of people – passengers, visitors, flight crews, ground support personal, maintenance people – coming and going, all happily doing their thing without any accidents, mistakes, or nuisances. All sorts of mechanical, electrical and electronic equipment works just fine, without any glitches or failures. The flights all arrive and depart on time, and there are no traffic or parking problems, making it easy to come and go at the airport.

This, of course, could never happen at "ATL," or any other airport. On the other hand, your autonomic nervous system, which is far more complex and much busier than any airport, normally works just this way – performing an almost infinite variety of functions perfectly, day in and day out.

If you ever begin to think that your brain is lame, or does not work as good or is not as powerful as someone else's, remind yourself of this. Even on its worst day, your nervous system is more capable and reliable that anything man ever has, or probably ever will, devise.

The Thinking Machine

Autonomic refers to functions your nervous system carries out without any conscious effort on your part – mostly sensory and motor functions. These include your heart rate, digestion, your respiration rate, salivation, perspiration, the diameter of your pupils, urination, and sexual arousal. While most are involuntary, some autonomic functions, such as breathing, can also be regulated by your conscious mind.

Wait just a minute! "Conscious mind?" What's up with that?

The stuff you just read about is a product of science – *neurology* and *neurobiology*. Thanks to our amazing advances in technology, scientists have been able to physically look into neurons and synapses to see what is going on – to actually measure electrical signals and observe chemical activity. Researchers are often able to reduce autonomic functions to simplified models, which they can then study in terms of inputs vs. outputs, watching what is physically going on in neural networks and the brain. Therefore, scientists have learned some facts about how the system works.

But the system does something much more interesting than just regulating body processes. Ironically, very little is known about how it does it – so little, in fact, that there isn't even a good name for the function.

We talk about this function using words and expressions like *thinking, the mind,* mental, *consciousness, awareness,* and even *spirit,* and *soul.* But there is no name for this function equivalent to the commonly used and generally understood term we use for the system's *autonomic* functions.

So before going any further, let's decide upon a single name for this function.

Brain, Mind, Soul, or Spirit?

Scientists have begun referring to this function as *mind*. That actually makes a lot of sense from a technical point of view, but the use of that term seems a little risky, since most people already have an idea of what it means, and those ideas often differ quite broadly.

For example, scientists now suspect that this function is biological, and that it will eventually be explained as electro-chemical activity like, but much more complex than, the autonomic functions. They often refer to their research as *the New Science of Mind*. Up to this point, however, people have not thought of the mind in that way. Instead, the general idea has been that the mind and the brain are two different things, the mind being partly physical, receiving inputs from the brain, and partly spiritual, receiving thoughts and feelings from metaphysical realms, such as God and ghosts.

Confusion with religious ideas can also come into play because of the fact that the title "Science of Mind" was invented in 1926 by author Earnest Holmes, who published a religious book by that title and went on to establish a self-help religious movement in the Christian Science tradition, which was also popularly known as the "Science of Mind."

Until science decides to call this function something else, we should probably stick with their term; *mind*. We can then think about our neurological apparatus as having two general functions – its autonomic functions, and its *mind functions*. The mind functions involve knowing, which includes perceiving, recognizing, conceiving, judging, reasoning, imagining and memory.

Whether or not these mind functions are purely a matter of neurobiology is a very controversial issue. We will think about that later on.

Cognition and Memory

At this point, the New Science of Mind has little to show for itself other than that title. Nobody really knows exactly how the system accomplishes any of the cognitive processes we refer to as mind functions.

Scientists, notably Nobel Prize winner Eric Kandel and his colleagues, have observed that learning modifies neurons. In experiments with a simple animal, the California sea slug, they found that short-term memory somehow results from temporarily enhanced chemical activity within the synapses between particular neurons. In attempting to discover how that was converted to stable long-term memory (which is the essence of learning) they found that the process involved enhanced chemical activity within the whole of the nerve cells, including the nucleus, which resulted in the development of new synapses connecting the neurons in that particular network. These physical changes would obviously facilitate communication within the network, but that does not explain how long term storage – learning, in other words – is achieved.

Eric Kandel told about the above findings in his book, *In Search of Memory*, published in 2006. This was as much as was understood about memory at that time, so you can see how little we really know, compared to what there is to know.

Let's think about how powerful and complex some of these mind functions are.

Consider, for example, your bedroom. When you think about your room, a virtual picture develops in your mind's eye. It will be three-dimensional, accurately scaled, and very detailed. This kind of information is, researchers think, stored in a matrix of neurons which form a virtual map of the physical space you call your room. When you think about your room, you are actually retrieving images and information previously stored at different points within that matrix during your actual experiences in your room. You might have stuck some of this information into your memory through conscious effort – for example, the location of something you had carefully hidden. But most of the information will have gone into your long-term storage without any conscious effort, simply as a result of repetitive observations and experiences.

To consider the complexity of this cognitive function, think about your bedspread – its pattern and colors, the material it is made of and its weave, its weight, its smell, and whether you left it on a neatly made-up bed or lying in a heap. How is all this detail about that single item recorded by neurons in your bedroom map, and how many neurons does it take to store this much detail about this single, rather irrelevant, item?

Now think about all the other details contained in your bedroom map. Think about thinking about your room. How does the mind find specific bits of information in that matrix, retrieve it and assemble it into what appears as a very realistic virtual picture?

With age and experience, the extent of this mapping function becomes truly astounding. I can visualize every room in our house, the back yard, and the front yard. Beyond that, I can readily conjure up an image of our neighborhood. I can do the same for every home I've lived in since somewhere around the age of four.

I can also easily find my way around town, so I evidently have a very detailed map of the whole town in my memory. In fact, I could drive from my town in Michigan to New Orleans, San Francisco and many other places without a road map. How? Evidently I have done that often enough to have created another rather extensive map in my memory; one containing lots of information about our nation and its highway system.

If called upon to do so, I could even draw a fairly accurate map of the United States purely from memory. When I think about doing that, I "see" in my mind's eye a large, colorful map of the United States. It is probably the map Miss Ringleberg pulled down like a window shade when teaching us to name the states and their capital cities. More than that, I can remember that third grade room, and where it was located in Central School, which burned down years ago. I remember the building's red brick, sandstone, black iron pipe railings, squeaky hardwood floors and narrow staircases. I can remember the geography program the class presented for our parents, singing the song, "Faraway places, with strange sounding names. Far away over the sea. Those faraway places with the strange sounding names, are calling, calling, me." I can remember the loud, rasping clang of the manually operated fire alarm bell. These images have been in my long-term memory for almost sixty years. For the most part, these particular memories are the result of experience and repetition, not of any conscious learning effort.

A conscious learning effort, a deliberate and organized attempt to acquire and make sense of information, and stick it into long-term memory, is the objective of education. By this time in your life, you will have done a lot of that too. In school you have learned how to speak, read and write at least one language, and at least a little something about literature, art, mathematics, science, history, geography and probably more. Elsewhere you have been taught other things, such as how to play a musical instrument, a sport such as skiing, soccer or golf, activities such as camping, climbing or sailing, and so on.

How much do you know? Were you to write down everything you know, how thick would your book be? How in the world is your mind function able to store all this information and manage it in a way that makes it so easily retrievable? Nobody has a clue.

Furthermore, there is no evidence to suggest that there is any limit to memory, or what your mind is capable of learning. Any suggestion to the contrary that you might read or hear anywhere else will be pure theory or speculation – or, worse yet, poppycock made up to pitch some philosophy or product.

Strange as it might seem at a time when man can send a spacecraft to Mars and land it with precision under remote control, at this point in human history, very little is known about how your mind works.

Imagination and Fallibility

Whether conscious or sub-conscious, learning involves cognition and memory - acquiring, interpreting, and storing information.

Eric Kandel spent a lifetime just trying to figure out how memory works. What is much more interesting and mysterious at this point, is how the mind interprets new information, and uses information it has already learned.

In imagination, your mind uses what it knows to solve problems. This is a kind of creative process where your mind is free to use whatever information it already has, to create information it wants, but does not have. The problem might be a need to figure out how to accomplish a mundane physical task, or could involve a more highly creative activity, such as drawing a picture on paper or writing a story. The imagination process usually involves borrowing bits and pieces of existing knowledge and assembling them into concepts that are new and different, as you work towards a complete solution by filling in blanks.

Since the result of imagination is the product of existing knowledge, different people with differing knowledge banks are likely to come up with quite different approaches to solving a particular problem. *Brainstorming* is a technique for taking advantage of that, to obtain the best ideas that the available minds are able to come up with. "Two heads are better than one."

This also often leads to misunderstandings.

As your senses, in one way or another, acquire new information, your mind evaluates it for meaning and significance according to what it already knows. Different minds, having different sets of background knowledge to work with, are likely to come up with differing views regarding the meaning and significance of new information.

For example, eyewitnesses often provide widely differing accounts of the same observed event. None of them is incorrect or untruthful. Each person is simply reporting what they saw – *in their mind's eye* – which is, for them, the facts of the matter or "truth." These differences in perception often lead to disputes when those involved insist on having it their way. People often dismiss these disputes grudgingly saying, "Well, you have a right to your opinion." – but not really believing that. Inside they are really thinking that the other person is either too dumb to see that they are wrong, else too stubborn to admit it.

Minds also seem to abhor voids. When understandings are incomplete because of missing information, the mind tends to fill in the blanks using the same imagining process. Sometimes we call this "jumping to a conclusion," but it often happens without our even being aware of it, and we come to accept it as part of the actual observed evidence.

Minds also are capable of coming up with their own tricks to simplify and streamline their work; shortcuts which we are often never aware of. For example:

Yuo'll poralby be azamed taht you can aulaclty uesdnatnrd waht you are rdanieg. Tankhs to the phaonmneal pweor of the hmuan mnid, aoccdrnig to a rscheearch at Cmabrigde Uinervtisy, it deosn't mttaer in waht oredr the ltteers in a wrod are, the olny iprmoatnt tihng is taht the frist and lsat ltteer be in the rghit pclae. The rset can be a toatl mses and you can sitll raed it wouthit msuh of a porbelm. Tihs is bcuseae the huamn mnid deos not raed ervey lteter by istlef, but the wrod as a wlohe. Amzanig huh? Yaeh, and you awlyas tghuhot slpeling was ipmorantt!

Closely related to this is what is sometimes called *the paradigm principle*, where "the mind modifies the data to confirm the reality it knows to be true." From the above example, you can easily understand why it is always essential to have someone skilled in the art proofread the final draft of your own writing. But another reason you cannot do this for yourself, is because your mind already knows what it means, and what is supposed to be on the page, and will cut to the chase, autocorrecting misspelled words, ignoring grammatical and punctuation errors, and even inserting missing words and phrases.

But it gets worse than this. Minds struggle to make sense of things using the information they have, and a mind that believes something very strongly, usually because it has hosted that belief for a long time, will often refuse to "see" facts or truths that challenge what it believes, even when that reality is plainly evident. Quite to the contrary, it will modify the new data to confirm the reality it already knows to be true.

As a simple example, by the time I was nine-years old and in the fourth grade, my mind had somehow decided that the name "Acme" was pronounced "A-ceem," and I had a rather heated argument with my best friend, who claimed it was pronounced "Ack-me." We finally took the matter to our teacher, whom I was certain would quickly straighten him out on that. When she took his side, I was even more adamant. They were both wrong! Meanwhile, in the back of my mind I vaguely realized that he was right the first moment I heard him pronounce the word correctly. It made sense, given the spelling, and I had probably heard it pronounced that way before.

Nevertheless, another part of my mind insisted on clinging to what it had, for a long time, believed was true.

It is very important that you realize that the human mind – your mind – although marvelously complex and wondrously capable, is also inherently *fallible*.

As your mind evaluates new data for meaning and significance, it will frequently come up with cognitions that differ from those of others, and are sometimes seriously flawed or wholly incorrect.

This is fact you will probably find difficult to accept. Children often equate being grown up with no longer ever being wrong. After having spent ten or more years growing up under the influence of parents and other adult authority figures, whose assertions and opinions you have always accepted without question, you were probably looking forward to the day when you would finally be grown up, and would be just as wise as them.

Ironically, the more rigid you are in that respect – the more you insist on always being right – the more fallible your thinking is apt to be. Conversely, learning to be more accepting of your humanity produces a mind more open to possibilities and thereby capable of doing better work.

It also results in a personality that interacts much more easily and productively with others.

Chapter 4
Personality

You are two in one. *Personality* is the person most people see. *Character* is who you really are inside.

Character is the real deal – the core features and traits that make up who you really are. Very few people know this side of you. Those few might include a couple of family members, and one or two of your very best friends – people you trust enough to open up to. Personality is made up of all your visible physical, behavioral, temperamental, and emotional attributes. This is the *you* that everyone else knows.

Because most people know you only by your personality, and since relationships with other people have a lot to do with a person's success and happiness in life, you had better take charge of this "other you," and not just let it be whatever it will otherwise become. In order to do that, you need to know at least a little bit about how personality develops, why it often differs from who we really are, and how that causes problems.

The Time Line

The core of your personality was formed very early in your life, from sometime before you were born, and during your early childhood.

Not everyone agrees that newborns have any cognitive ability. Those who do not therefore do not believe that babies are able to sense anything and process information while still in the womb. They are apt to think that any personality development at that stage is strictly a matter of genetics and inheritance. Your mother would likely tell you otherwise. Unborn babies often seem to react to things going on outside the womb, like sudden noises, music, and to the mother's emotional states. While it is easy to agree that a person's physical aspects, such as their body type and looks, are inherited, so far nobody is able to explain how nonphysical aspects of personality are genetically passed from parents to child, if indeed any are. Whatever the case, nature or nurture, by the time you were born, some rudiments of your personality had probably already begun to develop.

It is true, of course, that your sensing and thinking abilities were very limited at birth. In the womb, nature was concentrating on what needed to be done. That meant seeing to it that your brain was developed sufficiently to take over your body's processes at the moment of birth. But after that, the brain's development activity quickly changes and is greatly expanded.

After your birth, your brain's sensing and thinking capabilities began to develop rapidly and massively. While still in your infancy, the foundation of your temperament was established. That included such things as:

- *Openness* (sometimes also called Intellect) – appreciation for art, emotion, adventure, unusual ideas, imagination, curiosity, and variety of experience.
- *Conscientiousness* – a tendency to show self-discipline, act dutifully, and aim for achievement; planned rather than spontaneous behavior.
- *Extraversion* – energy, positive emotions, dominance, and the tendency to seek stimulation and the company of others.
- *Agreeableness* – a tendency to be compassionate and cooperative rather than suspicious and antagonistic towards others.

- *Neuroticism* (sometimes called Emotional Stability) – a tendency to experience unpleasant emotions easily, such as anger, anxiety, depression, or vulnerability.

Next came childhood. As a child, you built upon this foundation by developing habits that reinforced its various aspects. For example, if you are the sociable type, you developed play habits that involved doing things with other kids – team sports, scouting, youth groups, sleep-overs, and camping. If you are more of a loner, you were probably more into reading books, playing video games, hiking, and other activities that did not depend upon your being able to get along well with others. Practice makes perfect. The more you thought the way you thought and did the things you did, the easier it became. Eventually, it all became second nature. All in all, it was just the way you were, as far as others were concerned, and perhaps even in your own mind.

By the time you reached adolescence, your personality was already quite firmly established. And it all happened on its own, with some prompting by your parents and other authority figures, of course, but otherwise not as a result of any conscious reasoning and decision-making on your part.

But now comes the difficult time in life when you begin to think about who and what you are, and how you fit in. This is often called the *identity crisis*.

When you begin to think about these things, you might discover that deep inside, you are not very happy with the way you are. But at this point you will find it very difficult to change anything. The reasons are simple. First, your personality has become well entrenched by virtue of the habits you have perfected during your early and late childhood. Old habits are hard to break. You might also believe that you are the way you are because of genetics or inheritance – because it runs in your family. Or you might think you are so flawed and unworthy that change would no longer make any difference; that you have already ruined your life and cannot undo what has already been done. Or you might vaguely suspect that change is needed and possible, but you do not know how, or where to find out how.

You will struggle with these issues for a few years, and might even change some things as a result of your conscious thinking about them. But gradually you will become tired of always having to think about how everything you say and do defines who and what you are, and what others think of you. The seeming futility of it all will eventually lead you to conclude that, for better or for worse, you are what you are. At that point, you will decide to accept yourself as you are, whether others like it or not (even though a little voice inside keeps whispering that you are letting yourself down).

Beyond that point, you enter the rest of your life – the teen years, through early, middle and late adult life. You will bring with you the personality you accepted as an early teen, and over all your remaining years, significant change is unlikely.

How You Learned Personality

Most of what constitutes your personality is learned. You will probably agree that you can control your behavior, temperament, and emotions. Your physical appearance, which includes looks, body type, and stature, is also an important part of your personality. It has a lot to do with first impressions. Are you as willing to believe you have any control over that? If you think not, you would be mistaken.

Your attitudes, the way you behave, your emotional responses and your physical appearance are controlled by your mind. Your mind performs these executive functions unconsciously, as a matter of habit or routine. Nevertheless, it regulates these things in ways it deems appropriate, according to what it has learned. A lot of that learning was not voluntary. Your mind picked things up in a wide variety of ways. Here's how that happened.

First, there is the natural process of becoming familiar with and understanding your environment as a result of day to day experiences. This is how your learning began as an infant. Before you had any language to work with, you learned a lot about your little world by watching, listening, feeling and tasting things – in other words, by vision, hearing, touch and smell. Experience was also a good teacher. When you toppled over, you discovered (by the lump on your head) that the carpeted living room was a better place to try your legs than the ceramic tiled kitchen. When you grunted so hard your contorted face turned red you probably noticed how entertaining that was for your parents and anyone else watching. When they were then called upon to deal with your soiled diaper, you probably noticed they were not as pleased with you.

Babies have very poor vision at birth. It took eight months for your vision to improve to the point where you could see things at a distance clearly. Because of this, you lived in your own little world, where a lot of common things probably produced emotions that were not friendly. For example, a sudden sound that does not normally disturb anyone who is able to see its source, such as the friendly family dog barking happily when Dad comes home, might frighten the dickens out of a baby, to whom everything beyond its fingers is a blur. For the same reason, you might have felt abandoned and alone when your mother was not intimately near, even though she was perfectly visible to everyone else in the room. If she was not speaking, you were apt to think that she had suddenly and mysteriously disappeared.

Things improved rapidly between ages one and two when your language skills began to develop. Not only could you communicate better, which led to a lot less frustration, but people took more interest in you. Each new word was a source of amazement and delight to your parents, and perhaps an entertaining event to others. That produced lots of much needed positive stroking. Between ages two and three, you probably had a vocabulary of fifty words or more, and were able to put two or three words together to create short but meaningful sentences, such as "Want Popsicle!" And you were probably able to understand sentences that were much more complex.

With the advent of language, social learning begins. This is when parents begin to "parent," telling you what is acceptable and good, and what is considered inappropriate and bad, and how to do, or why not to do, this or that. It is also the time when you began to learn by observing and emulating your parents, older siblings, or others whom you looked up to. But this was strictly a matter of accepting information and instructions, obeying orders and directions, and monkey-see; monkey-do. It was not a time when you gave any rational consideration to the merits of what you were being told, or the behaviors that you were copycatting. Elders, especially parents, were gods who knew a whole lot more than you, and were never to be questioned.

You also learned unconsciously. While awake, and to some extent while sleeping, the senses are continuously receiving inputs. A part of your mind monitors all this activity for inputs that need to be brought to your conscious attention, but that does not mean that all the rest are ignored. Much, if not all, of that probably also goes into memory, and may remain there forever.

Consider, for example, the English autistic savant, Stephen Wiltshire. Upon just casually viewing a scene, he is capable of reproducing the whole thing by quickly sketching it in great detail. He has, for example, drawn complete and accurate panoramic views of Tokyo, Madrid, Rome and other cities after having a single helicopter sight-seeing ride over the area. This is sometimes called the *sponge concept* of learning. Nobody has a clue as to how this works; how much is committed to memory, how it is filed, or how it is retrieved. But it is certain that a lot of information is processed sub-consciously, and what goes into the mind constitutes learning.

Sometime during your late childhood, you begin to develop intellectual learning skills. This involved learning by voluntarily receiving information, for example by seeking advice, reading books, or receiving formal instruction. It involved evaluating and making judgments about what went into your mind. Now you began to have some control over your cognitive function and, by virtue of that, the development of your personality from that point forward.

However, what was already in your mind got there mainly by happenstance. You can now understand that whatever your personality was like at that point in your life, it was not something you could take much credit for, one way or the other. If others typically found you to be engaging, that was certainly your good fortune. If not, that was regrettable, but not your fault. At that point, most of us are a mixed bag, sometimes pleasing and sometimes not, and on average falling somewhere between these two extremes.

Outcomes

The extremes are called *balance* and *neuroticism*. This sounds wrong, since balance would suggest the middle of something. In this case, however, balance is the positive situation; the best outcome you can hope for. Neuroticism lies on the opposite side of the curve, where most of us, you probably included, unhappily find ourselves as childhood fades away, and we embark upon adolescence.

As mentioned in Chapter 2, neuroticism is actually a misnomer, a term coined over 200-years ago, before there was much understanding of the mind/body relationship. When a disorder could not be explained as a physical ailment of some kind, it was assumed to be caused by a general affliction of the nervous system; a "neurotic condition". A century later, people began to use the term differently: an enduring tendency to experience negative emotional states – such as a general apprehension about life, anxiety, self-doubt, lack of self-confidence, insecurity, pessimism, guilt, depression, and anger – was diagnosed as neuroticism, and such people were called neurotics.

Fifty-five years ago, the American Psychiatric Association published the first edition of its "Manual of Mental Disorders," which more narrowly defined such conditions as a variety of "disorders." These included ten "personality disorders" which were sorted into three classes:

- odd or eccentric disorders,
- dramatic, emotional, or erratic disorders, and
- anxious or fearful disorders.

In our time and place, neuroticism seems to be the typical human condition. About one in every half-dozen people are seriously neurotic, struggling with the disorders described in the DSM; usually depression, anxiety or phobias. When Albert Ellis inferred that almost everyone was neurotic, he was no doubt including situations such as those described by the famous psychiatrist Carl Jung. He was especially interested in cases where although a person was adjusted well enough to everyday life, they had lost a fulfilling sense of meaning and purpose, no longer found credible answers in religion, and so could see no readily apparent way to make life better. That, of course, describes a lot of people, and these are people who would not describe their condition as a "disorder," or seek treatment.

To lessen the stigma of being diagnosed with a disorder, the word is now often replaced with "organization." That makes sense. If neuroticism is typical, then that is the normal condition and, as such, it can hardly be defined as a disorder, even if it is a highly undesirable condition.

Neuroticism begins in childhood and, once established, is likely to continue though one's life. Intense personality issues are almost certain to result from hard knocks in childhood, such as physical or emotional abuse, neglect, poverty, sickness, a parent's sicknesses, death, or psychological problems, divorce, immigration, accidents, and deformities. It is easy to see how these hurtful and traumatic things would seriously frazzle a young person's confidence and sense of worth.

But the same thing happens to almost every child, even in the absence of such seriously unfortunate circumstances. While reading the previous section about the learning process, you were probably struck by how often you were bombarded with negative comments, observations and experiences while you were growing up. From infancy on, you were constantly being corrected and directed. Your first word was probably "No!"

The parent who is able to minimize the negative impacts, and offset those which cannot be avoided with positive inputs, is rare indeed. That requires a godlike level of understanding, patience and sensitivity. I have never met anyone, or ever heard of anyone, who had such parents.

But even under the best of circumstances, you would still have been adversely affected. Every person's childhood is a unique experience, and emotional pain is deeply personal – not something you evaluate on a comparative scale. I have also never met anyone who felt that growing up was anything better than a very trying and painful experience. Almost everyone believes that their experience was unique, and worse than everyone else's. That is almost always blamed on parents, and neurotic adolescents often feel that their parents were the worst ever.

The usual outcome of childhood upbringing is that as you approach adolescence, you come with a nagging and inescapable feeling that you are flawed and unworthy. You keep these bad personal feelings about yourself secret, for fear that if others were to know what you were really like, they would no longer love you, or wish to be your friend. In fact, you might not actually understand exactly why you feel the way you do – why you feel that others are better than you, or why you feel phony – like you are not really the person others think you are.

To keep these feelings from bugging you all the time, and to keep anyone from discovering your secrets, your mind devises sneaky strategies and creates fictions. These are usually invented in a moment of need as an immediate solution to a potentially embarrassing or painful situation. They are not the product of any careful thought, intentional scheming or villainous conniving on your part. Your mind just quickly conjures them up on its own and foists them upon the situation at hand, often surprising even you. Over time, what seems to work becomes a habit.

For example, you might have become quite good at blocking thoughts about things that produce bad feelings. That's called *denial*. Or you might have become adroit at changing the subject whenever your thoughts or conversations begin to get too close to a sensitive issue. That's *escapism*. You probably came up with ways of excusing your faults or mistakes by pointing the finger at other people or extenuating circumstances, eventually getting into the habit of playing "ain't it awful" – being quick to point out everyone else's faults and how bad everything is. The term for that is *rationalization*. People do that all the time.

You probably also created an artificial version of yourself that is no more real than a character in a movie. People do this all the time too. The usual choices are these:

- the *dependent* type – weak and inferior, passive and subservient – a manipulative way to avoid physical, intellectual or emotional competition by letting others win by default – a good way to get attention from, or be protected by, aggressive types.
- the *aggressive* type – intimidating, controlling, and combative – exploitive of others' weaknesses – "The best defense is a good offense."

- the *perfectionist* – distant and difficult, dislikes having to co-operate or depend on others – "When I want it done right, I have to do it myself."
- the *avoidant* type – the loner – avoids others because of previous bad experiences that confirmed feelings of inferiority and worthlessness.
- the *Peter Pan* type – superficial and self-centered – obsessed with youth, having fun and seeking adventure – prolongs childhood by avoiding adult responsibilities – *"I am Peter Pan ... I am Peter Pan in my heart."* (Michael Jackson at Neverland - age 44)

These descriptions no doubt bring to mind some people you know. In the psychological vernacular, these schemes and fictions are called *ego defenses*, and there are lots of them. Sigmund Freud's daughter Anna, the baby of his family, published a book in the 1930's explaining ten major ego defense mechanisms. Since then the list has been expanded to twenty-two, with an additional twenty-six minor *mental mechanisms*.

This is certainly a testament to how crafty and powerful the Monster can be when it comes to self-defense. It also exposes how widespread the problem of neuroticism actually is. Ego defense mechanisms are to neuroticism as coughs are to the common cold. A personality that is defined by these defensive habits is one that obviously suffers from an enduring tendency to experience negative emotional states – the definition of neuroticism.

The cause of neuroticism is always the same – feelings of inferiority. The original source of these feelings is always negative childhood messages and experiences. Unfortunately, neuroticism is the usual outcome of one's first ten or twelve years in life.

Balance

These bad feelings are often called "low self-esteem" or even "self-hatred." A better term is *inferiority complex*, because your bad feelings usually come only from certain personal aspects, rather than a belief that you are all bad, or totally worthless. This is a good thing. Realizing that your bad feelings arise from a complex of certain things that you think you do not like about yourself, raises a possibility of honoring what you think is good about yourself, while dealing with the issues that make you feel bad.

The bad feelings almost always come from a sense that you are not meeting the standards of others in some particular ways. The "others" are originally parents and older siblings. After that, it is other authority figures, close friends and peers.

Everyone needs to feel a little love, approval, respect, and attention, and this need is life-long. Unfortunately, others often make this conditional upon our meeting their standards, or upon *reciprocity*. If you do not do what they want, or as they want you to do it, you get the cold shoulder. If they do not get what they want, they pay you back by withholding their love, affection, respect and support. This tactic works because you believe the opinions of people who mean something to you, especially your parents. It is a mighty strong motivator; especially when employed against a child by a parent, the one person in the world a kid loves the most, and depends upon as their sole source of support, safety and security.

Since most people are neurotic, they are preoccupied with their own feelings. They are therefore much more apt to act out when they do not get what they want, than to lavish praise and affection on you when they do. When you miss the mark in their opinion, you hear about it. When you do good, the best you will probably get will be a perfunctory thank-you, and often not even that. The net result is that during your childhood you take hits more often than you score points. You get many more "cold pricklies" than "warm fuzzies." The negatives far outweigh the positives, so you wind up emotionally out of balance.

In other places in this book, I talk about fallibility. Human beings are imperfect. Everyone thinks, says and does things that prove displeasing to someone else, are just plain wrong, and often turn out to be regrettable. There is no way to avoid this. Neurotics already feel bad about themselves, and when these situations arise, they are likely to be interpreted as verification of those terrible feelings. That is what gives rise to ego defense mechanisms. But those never work. People can almost always see through them. Deep inside, you know they are a lie, so that strategy is like trying to put out a fire with gasoline. They only add to your already bad feelings, so are no defense at all. In the long term, they are actually self-destructive.

What does work is to strive for balance. The way to achieve that is mostly a matter of common sense and practice.

Here's how:

1. Decide to accept the reality of your own humanity, and learn from your experiences. When you find that you have gotten yourself into a tight situation, forget trying to somehow escape from blame. Defuse the situation by apologizing for having given rise to what proved to be an unpleasant or difficult situation, see what you can do to fix it, and value whatever lessons you can take from the experience. Then also excuse yourself, rather than beating yourself up emotionally. If you can learn to accept yourself as an imperfect human being, an unfinished work-in-process, no better and no worse than everyone else, and sure to screw up again in the future – you will have no need to resort to silly, ineffective, and self-destructive ego defenses.
2. Quit doing to others the kinds of things that lead to your own bad feelings. Other people are just as vulnerable to verbal and

emotional abuse as you are. When things do not go just exactly as you would like, you gain nothing by becoming angry, critical or cold-shouldered. Don't wait for an apology. Just be a friend, pitch in and help resolve the situation. This is not about being a goodie-two-shoes or brown-nosing. Do it for your own sake. You cannot feel good about yourself after treating others badly.

3. You cannot change your personal history. All the bad stuff that has happened up to now went into your memory, and will remain there forever. You cannot erase it. The best you can do is to keep from dwelling on it, and in time, it will be re-filed further and further back. In the meantime, these old memories will cause bad feelings to come bubbling up every now and then, often without warning or any obvious relation to what's going on at the moment, but causing you to feel apprehensive, anxious, fearful, insecure, pessimistic, depressed, guilty, ashamed or angry. When that happens, see it for what it is – a relic of some obsolete information, which probably was not valid in the first place. Or you can see it as the Monster in action again, and just say, "Oh, stop it!"

4. Everyone's life has good times and bad. There were times when you experienced nice doses of positive regard – a little love, glowing approval, genuine respect, and devoted attention. When the bad feelings resurface, they always eventually go away on their own, but you can help chase them back by fetching some moments out of the archives that are more worth remembering. Remember how your memory works: the more frequently you access a block of data, the closer it is filed to the top of the stack. What is used less gets pushed down further and further back into the archives. Refusing to spend a lot of time wringing your hands over unhappy memories will result in their being re-filed further and further

back as your mind receives and processes new information and re-sorts the old, making it more and more difficult for them to percolate through all the more current and more useful stuff.

As long as you are a living, breathing human being, there will never be a time when you will never have to cope with bad feelings. The best you can do is *balance*, which is also sometimes called "self-acceptance." That means honoring your humanity by accepting all your shortcomings, and believing that (in the words of Al Franken's Stuart Smalley), "You're good enough. You're smart enough. And, doggone it, people like you!"

In a larger sense, keep in mind that everyone struggles with balance, and very few succeed until they are well beyond middle age, if at all. Neuroticism affects people in high places, as well as everyone else, and is therefore responsible for most of the world's problems, from petty squabbles between friends to wicked genocides. As you adjust your personality, moving towards balance and away from neuroticism, the positive consequences will accrue not just to you, but to all whose lives you touch. Your example will show others that balance works better and feels better than neuroticism, and that the Monster can be subdued. That will encourage them to give it a try. So by helping yourself, you will be doing a big favor for all those people, and as the movement grows, for humanity itself.

Albert Einstein once made an interesting observation that seems to fit here. This is what he said:

"Man is, at one and the same time, a solitary being and a social being. As a solitary being, he attempts to protect his own existence and that of those who are closest to him, to satisfy his personal desires, and to develop his innate abilities. As a social being, he seeks to gain the recognition and affection of his fellow human beings, to share in their pleasures, to comfort them in their sorrows,

and to improve their conditions of life. Only the existence of these varied, frequently conflicting strivings accounts for the special character of a man, and their specific combination determines the extent to which an individual can achieve an inner equilibrium and can contribute to the well-being of society." (Einstein, *Why Socialism?* – Monthly Review, NY, May 1949)

Chapter 5
The Three A's

Social Reality

In our culture, people are valued according to looks, money and power, in that order. Some call this code "the three A's" – *attractiveness*, *affluence*, and *achievement*. Whether you think this is superficial and unfair does not matter. What matters is that this *is* the way it is.

You do not have to comply as far as your treatment of others is concerned, and I hope you will not, because that would definitely be self-defeating. It is right for you to believe that we all receive the breath of life as a gift; that each human life – yours included – is precious, and valued according to standards not of this world. However, you do have to be realistic in what to expect from everyone else.

First Impressions

Some say that first impressions are created within seven seconds. That is a good indication of how superficial and unfair these impressions are – others having passed judgment on you that quickly and with so little input. Unfortunately, first impressions are also sticky. Once formed, they're difficult to change.

If your grooming and dress is grungy or bazaar, if you are always broke, and if you can always be relied upon to finish last, or not at all, you can depend on the low opinion of others – even others who are just as careless or rebellious about these things as you are. In your heart, you might know you deserve better than that, but they will not know. Very few others will have any way of knowing what is in your heart. All they know is what they can see, and if the image you project is not favorable, their opinion of you will not be favorable.

Suppose you defiantly assert, "I don't care what others think!" The only people who say that are those who are not well accepted and respected by others. It is a childishly defensive outburst – about the same as saying, "I don't care to have a richly joyful and rewarding life!" You *must care* about what others think of you. The following few pages will tell you why.

If you can get this through your head, you will eventually come to accept the fact that others will usually be sizing you up according to the 3-A's, and you can then decide to make the most of it. You can easily enhance your stature in all three areas – attractiveness, affluence, and achievement – and without being pretentious or manipulative. You can also learn how to do this in ways that make people feel good about themselves, and good about you, without being phony or condescending.

It is important that you do this. In fact, this might be the most valuable of all the things you ever learn, and all the skills you ever develop in life.

Here is why the good opinion of others is important for you to cultivate ...

The "Self-Made Man" Myth

Getting along well with other people is essential for success and happiness. When I was younger, I used to boast about being a "self-made man." The fact is, however, that most of what I have achieved in life came from opportunities made available to me by others because, for whatever reasons, they wanted to do something nice for me.

When I resigned from my last job before going into business for myself, my boss asked me who else would be leaving his company to join me. When I told him there would be no others, his response was advice; he said I would not be able to achieve much on my own and should think about bringing others into my plans. He was right, of course. In fact, that had been his key to success – his ability to bring people like me into his business. He often repeated a favorite play on words: "Companies are only as good as the people they keep."

Later on, I learned that networking is an essential business skill, and the ability to do that successfully is an extremely valuable business and personal asset. People will give you great ideas and wonderful opportunities, simply because they like you – and you will do the same for others, for the same reason.

There are those whose lack of *people skills* make them difficult to like, and cooperation is therefore much more difficult for them. Difficult persons sometimes succeed anyway because someone loves them enough, and is insightful enough, to look beyond their coarse exterior and see the innate goodness within that each of us brings into this life.

In other cases, a troubled person's abilities are sometimes valuable or important enough to engender success and recognition in spite of their personality. And sometimes it is just a matter of being in the right place at the right time – moments of glory occasionally elevate special people to an honored place in history. However, beyond their special moment, such lives usually remain troubled and end in failure. Think about people like Abraham Lincoln, or Generals Ulysses S Grant or George S Patton.

Abraham Lincoln is credited with preserving the union. However his neuroticism resulted in frequent bouts of debilitating depression, and his feelings of inferiority resulted in a lack of assertiveness which extended the length of the Civil War, resulting in thousands of unnecessary causalities.

General Grant, credited with finally turning the tide in the Civil War, gained hero status and was ultimately elected President. However, his election was a sham, he not being savvy enough to realize that he was being exploited and manipulated by powerful political interests. Being a poor judge of character, he became involved in some bad deals and business failures. He died a debtor.

General Patton is universally recognized as one of the greatest military genius' this country has ever produced. He was well aware of his genius, but was also afflicted with "foot-in-mouth disease" – not caring much about what other people thought or how they felt about things he said and did. He believed that his performance as a great soldier showed what kind of a man he was, and everything else was just "a lot of crap." That proved his undoing. After several stunning achievements on World War II battlefields, he wound up being very unhappily sidelined after having repeatedly embarrassed his superiors and even the President.

Consider also the many poets, authors and artists who insolated themselves to the extent that the greatness of their work was never appreciated by others until after their death – Vincent van Gogh, Edgar Allen Poe, and many, many more.

Could these lives be considered happy and successful? Does the quality of what they bequeathed to humanity justify the misery of their existence? Even if you answer yes to these questions, the fact remains that their ultimate fame arises from the good opinion of others, even if arising only after their death. How much more effective, creative and happy might these lives have been had these people not been handicapped by their lack of people skills?

There are plenty of examples on the opposite end of the spectrum. One of the best-selling self-help books of all time is Dale Carnegie's *How to Win Friends & Influence People*. Written in 1936, with over fifty-million copies having been sold, it is still in print with the current edition in its forty-fifth printing. That's a lot of interest in networking skills. Ronald Regan was known as "the Great Communicator." He became a very successful President of the United States by virtue of his ability to win friends and influence people. A very successful local religious leader, on accepting a retirement award, commented simply, "I appreciate everyone's kind and generous comments, but I'm not sure I deserve all this praise. I just always thought it was my job to make everyone else look good."

There is no such thing as a self-made man – unless you are referring to a person who is manifestly unsuccessful and unpopular. You need other people, and other people need you.

Your Influence On Others

You will probably be somewhat skeptical when I tell you this: people want you to be happy and successful.

People will admire you for the efforts you put forth towards success and happiness, and will value your achievements. That does not come as a noble or altruistic gesture on their part.

Those who saddle themselves with a negative attitude are usually not very attractive, find it difficult to achieve much, and are therefore not usually very affluent unless they inherited, or are being supported by someone else's wealth. Such people never find much to be happy about. What good are they to anyone else? Trouble is not a scarce commodity. Nobody will ever be eager to share your bad news and dark outlooks. Happy and successful people, on the other hand, bring high spirits and encouragement to others, and are therefore really nice to have around.

If you have ever done much fishing, you have probably noticed how others tend to gravitate towards someone who happens to be catching more than they are. In the same way, if you appear to be happy and successful, others will unconsciously be moved to "throw their line into your pond," so to speak. The happy fisherman might be more successful because of his better bait or superior skill, but others usually do not think about that. They simply assume he is fishing in a better spot. By the same token, others are likely to envy your "luck" or "natural gifts." A few will understand that you did not become what you are by accident.

Whichever the case, you will most likely experience others expressing their admiration by what they do, not necessarily by what they say. Their wishing to associate with you and be your friend is your evidence of their admiration and respect. The simple fact that others tend to gravitate towards people who are happy and successful proves, by simple logic, that there is a healthy demand for such people.

In other words, others want you to be happy and successful.

The Purpose of Life

What does "happy and successful" actually mean? In the simplest perspective, it means attractive, affluent and achieving. This is where the three A's come from. If this is beginning to sound superficial and self-serving to you, reconsider the very purpose of life itself.

You come into this life alone and with nothing, and you will leave it the same way – alone and with nothing. It therefore does not seem logical that the attainment of wealth, popularity and power is your life's intended purpose.

Having realized that, some believe that there is a special scrip for them in a nebulous "book of life" – that they were born to carry out a mission of some sort. This is sometimes a belief in *predestination* or *reincarnation*, and sometimes just a subconscious strategy for coping with the inevitability of death, by hoping to live on forever in legend or history books. Yet, heroes and martyrs are seldom remembered beyond their own generations. So, it would seem that nobody is special or essential to life as we know it. We are here briefly, and then we are gone. And life simply goes on.

Still others believe that they were born to carry on as partners in creation; that their duty is to leave behind a world that is better in some way than the one they were born into. Indeed, we marvel at our own intelligence and ingenuity, in awe of our present-day intellectual, scientific and technological achievements. But these tend to introduce as many problems as they solve. They contribute a lot to change, but not so much to making the world a better place for everyone. The reality is that history is largely a never-ending story about how various peoples gave rise to great civilizations, all of which eventually ended ignominiously, collapsing into chaos and poverty. In our own time, we produced thermo-nuclear devices capable of destroying creation, as we know it. Having become afraid to the point of backing down from that prospect, our wanton consumption now poses an even more sinister threat to our existence; yet another mass extinction caused by global warming (yes, there have been others), and perhaps caused this time by man himself, through over-population and unrestrained consumption. Hence, the continuation of creation would not seem to be the real purpose of life either.

In the end, life seems to be a gift to be enjoyed, not a purpose to be fulfilled. You are born into abundance, with everything you need for a joyful life. Our purpose in life is to honor that by living richly joyful and rewarding lives. This we can do by realistically accepting life for what it is, and by helping each other make the most of it.

Gooses and Ganders

"What's good for the goose is good for the gander."

You are probably not familiar with that expression, since you are the product of the *X-Generation*; the "what's in it for me right now" generation. Nevertheless, everything you do to enhance your own happiness and success works to the benefit of everyone else.

I am not suggesting that self-ishness is an appropriate strategy. Quite to the contrary. That never works because deep down inside you will always feel bad about yourself for having taken advantage of someone else for your own personal gain. You will ultimately feel that any success achieved was undeserved, and you will therefore wind up unhappy.

When you pass up opportunities to gain at someone else's expense, you will have gained, rather than lost. You will have added to the content of your character, rather than accumulated more guilt. As others come to appreciate that you are a person of character who can be trusted implicitly, win-win opportunities will present themselves with increasing frequency.

My last boss is a perfect example. After a previous business failure, he started over, with only $1,500 invested in his new company. Twenty years later, he sold it for $8.5-million. As mentioned above, he became a success by virtue of his ability to attract people who were an asset to his company. He was imaginative and gutsy, but otherwise had no formal business skills. He wasn't a manager, marketer, salesman, accountant or engineer. In fact, the day I first met him, he was sweeping the floor in the plant's dinky lobby. I assumed he was the janitor and I was a little bewildered when he put the broom aside saying he would like to see me for a few minutes in his office.

As his fortune grew, gossip would occasionally accuse him of getting rich by using others. But that was certainly not true. He hired people whom he recognized as having potential – not so much according to knowledge and skills they could bring to the job, but according to his perception of what they were capable of. That quite often meant that he had more confidence in a person's potential then they did themselves. Everyone whom he hired found wide open opportunities to improve their job knowledge and skills, and thereby enhance their personal earning power. The rapidly growing company also provided opportunities for people who wanted to try new career paths. A young man who came in as a maintenance helper wound up as President of one of the company's divisions. I came in as a field service technician, and was given the opportunity to create and manage a whole new division, earning a seat on the company's executive committee. Like me, several others took what they learned there to form companies of their own.

So while the boss ultimately walked away with much more money than anyone else, his leadership improved the fortunes of his several hundred employees and their families. All in all, that seems like a fair exchange.

I never thought the boss, "Mr. C" as we usually referred to him, was in it for the money anyway. In fact, it appears that he spent a good portion of his millions on philanthropic projects, mostly aimed at improving the quality of life for residents of the company town and his little hometown. He was a private person, who rarely talked about his personal cares and feelings, but I eventually came to understand that he was driven simply by a desire to be liked and appreciated. He certainly accomplished that in my case and, I suspect, in hundreds of others. He was a perfect example of what I am trying to tell you.

Everything he did to enhance his own happiness and success worked to the benefit of everyone else.

Attractiveness

When you look into the mirror, what do you see? Most people do not see themselves as good looking at any age. That's because most people have an unrealistically low opinion of themselves.

But even beyond that, it is impossible to evaluate your own looks because the conclusion depends upon a set of criteria which are totally subjective, and ordinarily apply only to others.

Nobody understands exactly where the mind gets its ideas about features it finds visually appealing or physically attractive. There is, of course, wide agreement on what constitutes good looks, yet not everyone is equally attracted to individuals who are generally accepted as being good looking. Eventually you will come to realize that you personally find certain people visually interesting, but you will probably have no idea why, or what it is they have in common that triggers an emotional response in you. You will probably not realize that your particular set of criteria will somehow generally exclude individuals who look like you, or someone closely related to you, such as a parent, brother or sister. You are apt to see these people as plain or common – just as you probably see yourself when looking in the bathroom mirror.

Neuroticism also heavily influences your opinion of your looks. If your level of self-acceptance is very low, you will believe that you are not very attractive to others, regardless of how good looking you might actually be.

Having a video or series of candid photographs taken of yourself would solve part of the problem of trying to evaluate your own looks. Then you could come close to seeing yourself physically as others see you – something like listening to your own tape-recorded voice. But you would still not be able to evaluate your appearance in the same subjective way as others. Although in the photographs you can see views of yourself as others see you physically, you cannot evaluate your appearance as they might, since your criteria set is not exactly the same as theirs.

Emotion also affects these judgments in a highly significant way. Good looks are not much of an asset when accompanied by bad behavior. A person who is snotty, narcissistic or dishonest will not be perceived as good looking; the good looks will be dismissed as a mask that person hides behind. Emotion works the other way around also. For example, when I look at my wife, I still "see" the slim, athletic and beautiful nineteen year old girl I married thirty years ago. This is typical; people who love you will always see you at your best, and those who do not, will not. There's an old saying: "People you love can do no wrong; people you hate can do no right."

Looks always becomes a big deal as boys approach adolescence. When it comes to good looks, there are many shades – cute, nice-looking, pretty, beautiful, attractive, handsome, hot, and so on. Young boys usually fall into the "cute" category. Then nature often intrudes in a way that seems rudely perverse as boys go through puberty, changing cute young boys into homely adolescents. Hormone changes and growth spurts result in features that are out of proportion, unsightly body hair, acne, and ruddy skin complexions. Happily, this stage does not last very long. By age sixteen, most adolescents will have begun to blossom into handsome young men. Unfortunately, that does not last forever either.

A personality based upon good looks is like a house built on sand, since physical beauty quickly fades as you enter the adult years. For the average young man, the trim, angular body features begin to disappear in the mid-twenties as muscle begins to turn to fat. The stress of career struggles and family responsibilities begin to show up as permanent facial features. The scalp begins to thin, then disappear, seeming to show up elsewhere as unwanted body hair – on the back, chest and stomach.

Rather than wasting your time pouting about things you have no control over, there is much you can do to make yourself very attractive to others. Short of cosmetic surgery, there is nothing you can do about your basic facial features. You are also stuck with your physical body type – tall, or short – slim, muscular or rounded. Nevertheless, you can control every other aspect of your appearance.

Here's how ...

Smile

By the time I was twelve, I had stopped smiling. I hated my life and did not feel like I had that much to smile about. But it was not just that – my teeth were in really bad shape. If smiling could not be avoided, I smiled only with tightly parsed lips. I suppose that made me look like the village idiot, but anything more would have exposed my nasty upper front teeth, which were badly decayed along the gum line. Joining the Air Force at age eighteen was a good move for me, because they fixed all the damage the "tooth-worms" had done. When the job was finished, every tooth in my mouth had a filling, and I could smile again when I wanted to – which was not often. I had lost the habit.

People sometimes put on a sober, annoyed or sad look as a strategy for getting attention. Looking serious all the time is a ploy for gaining respect by leading others to think you are a very intelligent person with deep thoughts or important responsibilities. Looking angry or sad is an attempt to get attention in the form of sympathy. To all but the most naïve, these strategies never work. These facial expressions send negative messages that turn people off. Everyone has plenty of problems of their own. They do not want to know about yours.

Smiling is easy and does not cost anything, so you can begin using this idea right now. Naturally, you will not want to go around smiling like a fool all the time. However, you do want to look like you are interested in life and having fun. That means getting out of the habit of looking stressed, angry or unhappy. The look you want to project is one of peacefulness and self-confidence, keeping your smile ready to shine at a moment's notice. Practice relaxing your facial muscles until that becomes a habit.

In time, you will find that the effort you have put into lightening up pays off in more ways than one. Not only will others find you more approachable, you will become more relaxed and buoyant, and life will become much more enjoyable.

Personal Hygiene

As you now know, people you meet size you up within seconds of first laying eyes on you, and those first impressions are never easy to change. Keep that in mind before rushing out the door in the morning without shaving or brushing your teeth.

It is not easy to be delicate when discussing this subject. People who are unkempt, dirty, and stinky are repulsive to everyone else, even other unkempt, dirty and stinky people. Unless you are homeless, good personal hygiene is easy. It is mostly just a matter of getting into the habit.

When I joined the Air Force, I was put into a "flight" of seventy-two young guys, ages eighteen to twenty-one. That made for a neat marching unit composed of four *elements* of eighteen men each. The first thing the Air Force did in basic training was to clean everyone up, and I was surprised at how many needed cleaning up. There were several "scumbags" in our flight – guys who were strangers to showers or bath tubs, and had apparently never been taught anything about how to take care of themselves. They usually were not eager to learn, until being treated to a "G.I. Shower" – being taken into the shower room by other guys, stripped naked and cleaned up using a scrub brush and brown *Fels-Naptha* laundry soap. In one case, that was prompted by almost everyone in our barracks getting the crabs. All that miserable itching and burning in our crotches made it real clear why the Air Force was so hot on personal hygiene.

Crabs are usually transmitted by sexual contact. If you are wondering how that could happen in a military barracks: evening showers were mandatory in basic, with each element, eighteen young guys, showering together in turn. The small shower room only had six showerheads, so that meant three guys rubbing butts under each one, and brushing past each other's naked bodies on the way in and out of the latrine. The crabs had a field day jumping from one guy's pubs to another's, and it wasn't long before we all had itchy red blotches on balls and crotches.

There was a joke about the G.I. treatment for crabs, using a knife, razor and lighter fluid. You shaved just one side, doused the remaining hairy side with the lighter fluid, lit it afire, and as the crabs fled into the clearing on the shaved side, you stabbed them with the knife.

Once well infested, crabs are a bitch to get rid of. I finally got rid of mine by scrubbing the red blotches with the Fels-Naptha soap and a standard government-issue scrub brush, then dousing those raw and bleeding areas with rubbing alcohol. That smarted – I came close to being the first man on the moon. The "G.I. treatment" might have been less painful.

But I digress.

A generation after my tour of duty, our oldest son also chose to enlist in the Air Force, and the rest of our family made the trip to Lackland Air Force Base at San Antonio, Texas to attend the impressive and touching graduation ceremony that is now put on as the finale of basic training. As we strolled around the base, I was struck by how squeaky clean and well-groomed all the young airmen were. Only a few weeks earlier these same guys were the ones you would commonly encounter on the street in civilian life, looking somewhat less than slovenly, perhaps, but otherwise casually unkempt, which seems to be the *in thing* now. When I was a part of that scene at Lackland fifty-some years before, I had not realized what a good job the Air Force was doing in cleaning us up, probably because it happened over a period of weeks while our T.I.'s were terrorizing us in other ways. The point is this: young guys clean up really well, and it does not take very long to learn how.

Establish a routine for yourself, and make it a habit. Get up on time in the morning, and before doing anything else, lock yourself in the bathroom and do this:

1. splash cold water in your eyes
2. wash your face, leaving it wet
3. wash your armpits using a washcloth
4. wash your crotch the same way (all of it)
5. apply deodorant or antiperspirant
6. brush your teeth – and your tongue
7. shave (carefully)
8. comb or brush your hair
9. put on clean underwear and socks
10. put everything away, clean the sink and wipe the counter dry

This will take you fifteen minutes or less. Never skip it. Once it becomes habit, it will never seem like a burden or nuisance – just something you do every morning, no more of a bother than putting on your trousers, shirt and shoes.

When you are young, an electric shaver will probably do. If you use one, use it as instructed, which usually means your face must be dry. However, wash your face first to soften up the hair. Eventually you will probably need to use a regular razor. A wet face and a light touch are the keys to a close, comfortable shave. Cuts and razor burn will otherwise result, and that will discourage regular shaving. Never skip a day or two. That allows the hair to grow and toughen up, making things much more uncomfortable when you do eventually shave it off. Cuts will happen. When they do the bleeding is inconvenient and the scabbing is unsightly. Dabbing a *styptic pencil* on the cut will stop the blood flow by constricting the capillaries in the skin. Keep one on hand; get it at the drug store or where you buy your shaving supplies. Otherwise *alum* also works – a common spice found in the grocery store.

Brush your tongue? What's with that?

Have you ever encountered someone whose breath smells like a barnyard? That comes from bacteria that develops on the tongue, usually towards to the back. Brushing teeth will not help much, nor will mouthwash or breath mints. The bacteria must be physically removed. Tongue scrapers are available for that, but your toothbrush will work just as well, and you can do the job as part of your tooth brushing routine.

If you smoke cigarettes, it will be much more difficult for you to keep from being objectionably stinky to others. Since smoking is now becoming increasingly less common, you will certainly be noticed, and especially if you smoke in enclosed areas, such as a car. It is not just a matter of smoker's breath. Cigarette smoke, like any other gas, conforms to the law of partial pressures, meaning that it always disperses from a greater to a lesser concentration until equally distributed with all the gasses in the space around you. In other words, it gets all over everything. Air is ordinarily odorless. Smoke is not. Therefore everything in a smoky area becomes stinky – including you, your hair, and your clothing.

I was a smoker for about sixteen years, before stopping thirty years ago. Stopping might have been easy for me, since I did not begin smoking until I was twenty-one. I took up smoking only because they took lots of smoke breaks in the Air Force, and I always felt uppity and left out. A pack of cigarettes cost a quarter then, or only 9-cents overseas where there was no tobacco tax. Smoking was common then. Now it is more common to encounter people who have quit the habit, and it seems that the odor is much more offensive to ex-smokers than to those who have never smoked at all. That is also working to your disadvantage if you are a smoker.

If you smoke cigarettes, or live with others who smoke, you will need to be a lot more careful about keeping yourself and your clothing clean.

Dress

"Clothes make the man. Naked people have little or no influence on society." Mark Twain is credited as having said that a little over 100-years ago. However, he might have lifted that line from another writer and humorist, a Roman called Quintilian, who said "Vestis virum reddit" (means the same thing) about 2,000-years ago.

Here's a folk tale from India, *The Brahman's Clothes* ...

There was once a holy man who had two wives. Like many Brahmans he lived by begging and was very clever at wheedling money out of people. One day he decided to go to the marketplace dressed only in a small loincloth like the one the poorest laborers wore, to see if sympathy would move people to give more generously. But, on the road, in the marketplace, and in the village, no one greeted him or made way for him, and when he begged no one gave him alms.

He quickly tired of this, hastened home, and putting on his best turban, coat, and waistcloth, went back to the marketplace. This time everyone who met him on the road respectfully bowed low and made way for him. Every shopkeeper to whom he went gave him alms, and the people in the village who had refused before, now gladly made offerings to him.

The Brahman went home prosperous and happy. Smiling to himself, he took off his clothes, laid them out neatly, and prostrating himself before them three times, sung praises: "O source of wealth! O source of wealth! It is clothes that are honored in this world and nothing else."

This little story reflects the facts of life about dress more accurately than Samuel Langhorne Clemens or Marcus Fabius Quintilianus. The reality is that dress is a negative motivator, meaning you get little or no credit for doing it right; just denigration when you do not.

"Doing it right" means dressing appropriately and tastefully.

"Appropriately" means wearing the right thing for the occasion. You would not wear your best dress-up ensemble to dig in the dirt and pull weeds; by the same token, you should not show up at your graduation ceremony wearing your regular school or work clothes.

Over-dressing is just as inappropriate as missing the mark in the opposite direction. Forget about the "I don't care what people think" rationalization – that is just an excuse for being too lazy to learn how to dress right and to manage your wardrobe. Of course you care. Forget also about making a statement. Circus clowns stand out from the rest of the troop because they dress funny. People do not marvel at their creativity or individuality; they laugh at them because of their unconventional appearance. The objective is that you do not want to stand out because of your dress, one way or the other.

It is easy to know what to wear: dress by example. Think about what everyone else will be wearing, and dress accordingly. If the situation is unfamiliar to you, ask someone who would know for advice on how to dress for the occasion.

"Tastefully" means wearing things that match, are stylish and in good condition.

Good taste is not something that is inherited. Some seem to come by it naturally and never have to think much about what looks good together and what does not. Others have to put a little more effort into the choices they make. When shopping for clothing, lay things out in the store to see how they look together. Select things according to how well they match up with each other, or with things already in your wardrobe. Never buy individual items because you think they look kewl or sweet, even if they do not go well with anything else.

If you have problems coming up with ideas, notice the store displays and manikins. When you see a combination you like, take those items to a dressing room and try them on to see how they look on you. Fashion magazines and other publications are also useful. When you see something that impresses you, take the picture along when you go shopping. But, keep in mind that what looks good on a fashion model, might not look the same on you. Models are chosen to show off the clothes, not the other way around. If your height, body type, complexion, hair color and so on are not the same, the outfit might not suit you as well as it does the model.

Men are usually not very comfortable shopping for apparel, so tend to be impatient and undiscriminating. Do not go shopping until you are in the mood and have the time to do it right. Always try everything on for size, fit, comfort and looks.

Style is important. Fad is not. Style is about good taste. Fad is purely about marketing. Good taste is always in style; fads seldom last beyond one season. Clothing is expensive. Do not spend a lot of money on things that will be out of style well before they have worn out.

Speaking of expense, a limited budget is not an excuse for inappropriate dress. You can shop for kewl in upscale stores like Abercrombie & Fitch or Aeropostale, or be more practical, shopping in places like Steve & Barry's. At the moment (summer 2008), Steve & Barry's are selling "everything for $8.98, or less," and that includes jeans, shirts, jackets, and shoes. Go across the hall to another shop in the mall, and you will find the same merchandise offered with a different label, and at a much higher price. It all comes from China.

Better yet, swallow your pride and visit your local *Goodwill* store, or other second-hand shops. We live in a very affluent, throw-away culture, and good quality, lightly used stuff often winds up on the racks in these shops. Formerly the butt of some tasteless jokes, this kind of bargain hunting has become sort of a cult thing. The people you find shopping these stores will probably surprise you. You will have to sort through lots of items, and visit the store frequently since the stock changes daily, but every now and then you will discover a really neat piece of merchandise, and it will only cost two or three bucks!

Charm

Charm is a basic component of attractiveness. It incorporates the above physical aspects of how you present yourself to others, but also includes other facets of behavior or personal decorum. A charming person observes the norms of polite society in a way that others find interesting, pleasing or stimulating, and thereby attractive.

Successful people are usually also charming people. Charming people are always successful people. They always seem to be in a good mood, and genuinely interested in what you are doing and what you have to say. They come off as confident, yet humble and caring; serious, yet with a quick wit and delightful sense of humor.

As with taste, charm is something that develops with learning and practice. Nobody inherits a charming persona. A generation ago, that was an essential skill for any girl who wished to marry well. Charm schools use to be common, especially charm schools for girls. Unfortunately, the 1960 – 1970 era belittled charm as an *establishment* hang-up, rallying around slogans such as "Do your own thing!" and "Let it all hang out!" We forgot the value of charm, and it has remained largely forgotten ever since.

Charm has been replaced with a mode of permissiveness that condones its opposite: coarseness – behavior that is conspicuously tasteless and impolite, vulgar language including revoltingly gross expletives, crude jokes, an earthy sense of humor, and obscene gestures.

In 1993, Massachusetts Institute of Technology dean of undergraduate affairs Travis R. Merritt, became fed up with this appalling situation and decided to do something about it. His thinking was that MIT fell short in preparing young adults for successful careers when it bestowed degrees upon geeks and nerds lacking even a minimum of essential social skills. Now in its 15th year, "MIT Charm School" is an annual event, where faculty and staff help students learn better etiquette. The experience is very brief, but at least gets the message across that crude behavior is not conducive to success in professional careers.

Harvard also participates, but otherwise few other colleges and universities have seen fit to follow MIT's example. To the contrary, many seem to be manufacturing *education snobs*, instilling conceit instead of charm.

How many people do you know whom you consider to be classy or charming? Little wonder! Private charm schools and summer charm camps have become extinct.

So, here is a great chance to capture the admiration of others. If you are typical, you can easily make big changes by simply cleaning up your act:

- Stop trying to bring attention to yourself through behavior that is tasteless, inconsiderate, and impolite.
- Quit with the vulgar language, profane expletives and obscene gestures.
- Base your sense of humor upon things more mature and sophisticated than body functions and the ethnicity or social status of others.

Goodie-Two-Shoes!

So, now you are apt to be thinking, "Wow – what a tight-ass!" Not the case at all. There are two good reasons to do all this, and neither one of them has anything to do with being righteous or a goody-goody.

Let us review.

In the beginning I said that in our culture, the social reality is that you will generally be valued according to the three A's — attractiveness, affluence, and achievement. So far, I have been talking only about attractiveness. The components of attractiveness are your smile (or, in other words, your *demeanor*), personal hygiene, dress and charm. The obvious reason you would want to improve in these areas is to enhance your attractiveness because you wish to more favorably impress others.

That probably sounds a bit superficial and manipulative, however it is anything but. Here is why.

First, nobody will respect you when you look bad and your behavior is rude and crude, nor will they think you are kewl. The reason is simple. That kind of presence disses them, and they know it. What does it say to others when you obviously do not care enough to give them your very best? The answer is that you are obviously attempting to meet them at what you think is their level, and in your estimation, their level is not very high. Here is another way to think about this; how do you feel about yourself when someone treats you respectfully and thoughtfully — as if you are somebody in their estimation?

Second, virtue is indeed its own reward. The feeling that you are not very attractive to others is a cancer that eats away at your self-respect. Learning to show a little class and charm is great therapy for low self-esteem. The positive feedback you will get from others as you do this will make you feel increasingly better about yourself, just as it makes them feel better about themselves.

That's the whole point of this book. Neuroticism produces different sorts of problems and unhappiness for different people, but neuroticism always comes from feelings of inferiority. As those feelings begin to be offset by the positive feedback that is sure to come your way, your problems and sorrows will begin to turn into achievements and joys.

Affluence

Affluence means wealth – the amount of money and how much *stuff* you have. If you are less than eighteen, you are probably thinking there is not much you can do about that – if your family is rich, you have it made; otherwise you are just screwed. If that is what you are thinking, there is good news for you!

The affluence issue is really something you do to yourself. Nobody has ever told you they are better because they have more money and more stuff. When struggling with feelings of inferiority, you habitually compare yourself to others. Thinking about friends and acquaintances who are blessed with more money, property, and other material goods than you confirms the feelings your already have about yourself – you are not as good as they are. You try to compensate for your bad feelings by getting as much or more than others have. But that never works, because your comparative level of affluence is not really the cause of your bad feelings, and even if it was, no matter how successful you are in moving up, there will always be someone with more. This futile game is called *Keeping Up With the Jones'*.

Affluence is relative. If you are living in the United States or another developed country, you are blessed with an abundance way beyond anything your grandparents ever dreamed of. It is also an abundance that is available only to a privileged few in the world, even today. By our standards, the majority of the human race is very poor. However, if you were to go back in time, or to places you would consider backward and impoverished, you would find the people there about as content with what they have as we are – until you showed up.

Paradise Lost

While working as a field service engineer and living in Los Angeles, California, some friends and I frequently spent summer weekends in Mexico's Baja peninsula at an out-of-the-way place called Santo Tomas. Totally lacking in amenities, the place was avoided by American tourists. The little village was home only to a handful of Mexican fishermen.

These dream weekends were filled with beauty and adventure. Santo Tomas offered fresh air, lovely blue skies by day and awesomely starry canopies at night; beautiful vistas in any direction – the sparkling Pacific Ocean on one side and rugged hills on the other. It also provided exciting wildlife experiences – flying fish, dolphins, whales, seal and bird colonies. Its volcanic earth hosted extraordinarily delicate, colorful, and sometimes treacherous, growing things; plus assorted small creatures like quick-tempered scorpions, and the large fearsome-looking, but cowardly, black beetles we called "dumb bugs", because when discovered they would bury their heads in the earth and stick their butts in the air.

It also offered peace and quiet, solitude, space and freedom – things highly valued by young guys coming out of L.A.'s cacophony, constraint and coercion. Santo Tomas gave us the opportunity to experience life as it seemed life was meant to be. Like our Mexican fishermen friends, our days ended just after sundown, and we slept peacefully until awakening just before sunrise. And we awoke like children – fully refreshed and eager to meet whatever adventures the new day might provide.

We came to Santo Tomas in a brand new unmarked company panel truck, a flashy, white, stretched Dodge Ram, loaded with food and supplies just bought at Ralph's, a L.A. grocery chain, our lavish, but haphazardly assembled larder including vanilla wafers for the Mexicans' three resident dogs. We came fully outfitted with all sorts of sporting goods and camping equipment, and dressed in our newly purchased Montgomery-Wards sportswear. In varying degrees, we were the envy of our Mexican hosts, and especially of their young boys who sometimes came from their permanent homes in

Ensenada to work alongside their fathers and learn how to make a living from the sea.

Their eyes saw only our apparent affluence. They could not know its true cost, and in their wishing, they devalued what they already had. For us, Santo Tomas was *paradise lost* – a life and a time we could sadly long for, but could never return to. Most of our lives were spent grubbing for the money that allowed us to experience, now and then, and for just a few hours, what they were privileged to enjoy every day of their lives for free.

Affluence has nothing to do with happiness, or your value as a human being. More money and more stuff will not make you a better person, or guarantee the good life. Our Mexican friends had food, clothing and shelter, and with these basic needs met, certainly enjoyed life as much as we did, and maybe even more. It goes without saying that we Americans were certainly not better in any way than our Mexican hosts. To the contrary, the only times we ever felt it wise to secure our belongings inside our truck and lock it up were those few times when other Americans were around. The little Mexican community was close knit, family oriented, openly friendly and entirely trustworthy – very unlike the American places we came from.

Nine-to-Five

Getting rich might, in fact, increase your enjoyment of life – depending upon what you have to do to get the money. If you come by it easily, such as by buying a lucky lottery ticket or inheriting from a rich uncle, and are smart enough to manage it wisely, a windfall could buy you the good life – meaning freedom from financial concerns and being able to do as you please.

The odds of that ever happening to you, or anyone else, are somewhere between extremely unlikely and zero!

For all but a lucky few, money must be earned by working. There are many different flavors of work, from lowly ditch-digging to serving as chief executive officer. But it all boils down to the same thing – making your time and talent available to someone else in exchange for money.

How much you are worth to someone else is usually determined by how much responsibility you take off their shoulders. Menial work without much responsibility provides meager paychecks, but you only have to work eight hours a day, and outside of that your time is you own. Big wheels make big bucks and only have to work half the time each day – whichever twelve hours they want. Then they get to take their work home when leaving the office.

I used to scratch my head while watching the "factory rats" line up at the time clock at three-thirty, then rush out to the parking lot, jump into their car or truck, and squeal its wheels as they dug out and went speeding away. Why were they in such a hurry? I wondered why, if they hated their work so much, did they not find something else to do.

I was fortunate. I liked doing what I was doing. In fact, had I been independently wealthy, I would have willingly done my job for free.

I finally realized that some people have a life.

I was still single at the time. My apartment was upscale and comfortable, but Spartan. I did not party or date anyone. I was not interesting in fishing, bowling or golfing. I was actually *avoidant*, but did not realize it at the time. I was just most comfortable at work and enjoyed its challenges and rewards, so that is what I preferred to do all the time. Happily, I was being well paid for doing what I liked to do.

I eventually figured out that for most others work was a necessity rather than a pastime. It was a means of financing the kind of life they wanted – such as being married with children, having a nice home, driving a late model car, spending time with friends, fishing, golfing, boating, vacationing, and so on. When they rushed away from the plant, it wasn't because they hated the place, it was because they were excited about whatever plans they had for the rest of the day.

So there are two lessons in this.

First, it is a lot easier to get up in the morning to go to a job you like. Your enjoyment of your work will also show in your performance, guaranteeing success in your career, and in how well you get along with others – including those you love the most: your family.

Second, your job provides the income that supports the cost of your lifestyle. You must find a job you like, and preferably one that pays enough to support your spending, else you will have to adjust your lifestyle to what your earnings can support.

The "Bad Life"

You are probably thinking, "Well, that's big news – who doesn't already know that!"

Of course, everybody knows these things. Nevertheless, people very commonly find themselves stuck in a job they hate, and up to their neck in debt. There are a variety of reasons why.

The most common reason is that people are not willing to deprive themselves of things they do not really need, and loose credit makes it possible for them to live, for a while at least, well beyond their means. After sinking well into debt, they are forced to take any job they can find that will allow them to meet their payment obligations.

Others might think that they fell into this predicament through no fault of their own, after having lost their dream job and the lucrative income it was providing.

An affluent person who spends up to the limit of his income is no different than the grunt who spends more than he earns.

Whether you spend money you do not have, or spend money just because you have it, the reason is usually the same – you are trying to buy things that are not for sale. In other words, you are responding to a gut feeling that if you could just do, or have, a certain thing, doing or having that particular thing would make others think better of you, or would make you happy in some other way.

It is the Monster at work again!

From the time you were born, you began learning that growing up was a matter of advancement. You were not taught that you were okay as you were, or that you should relish each stage of your life as a precious one-time gift. Instead, you were constantly reminded that you were small (or young), ignorant and incapable, and that you needed to overcome these limitations if you were ever going to amount to anything – which generally meant becoming equal to or better than the adults who were telling you all these things.

Growing up began to look like a series of milestones you needed to get past, the earliest of which included learning to walk, getting potty trained, then learning how to dress yourself. You were led to believe that things would get much better when you got to be five, and could go to school. Then it was ten, because that two-digit number looked a lot bigger than nine. Then 12 (the end of grade school) - 14 (working permit) - 15 (high school) - 16 (driver's license) - 18 (graduation; age of majority) - 21 (vote and drink).

As you grow up, your parents and other authority figures will begin to fade from the picture. But they will have succeeded in making you easy prey for an even more sinister force. Popular marketing and advertising will take over, appealing to your hang-ups to create feelings of need and desire. Credit cards will promise to empower you, coaxing you to buy things you do not need and can not afford, quietly cutting themselves in on every deal.

By the time you reach your adult years, the mindset will have been well-established. You will always feel that what you are and where you are at is never okay. You will think that you must continually strive and connive to improve your situation. You will also feel obligated to prove to yourself and to everyone else that you are becoming a smarter and more important person. The easiest way to show that is to produce some tangible evidence of it, and for that purpose, money is a very handy yardstick. If you have cash, you flaunt it. Otherwise, in lieu of cash, you can show that you have lots of the stuff that money can buy, using your "plastic money" to get it. Thus you continue down the path to *the bad life*, led hand-in-hand by agents who further cultivate and take advantage of your childish attitudes about affluence.

This is how your subconscious drive to accumulate more and more money and things originally develops, and grows until it begins to ruin your fun. Most people eventually get over it, but it is not usually because they finally see the fallacy and futility of this kind of thinking. Recurring episodes of being mired in debt prove to be no fun at all, as the mailbox fills up with unpaid bills and most phone calls are from collection agents. The lesson is finally learned, but it is usually the wrong lesson. They finally just give up, having become tired of the struggle, or incapable of going any further with it, and resigning themselves to finally face what they decide is "reality" – that they will never be able to amount to anything after all.

The lesson that should be learned is the one I have just laid out for you. The affluence rat race is childish and self-defeating behavior. The race never has any winners, since there is no such thing as enough. No matter how much you have, you will always feel you need more.

A person who is usually flat broke and cannot pay what they owe is called a *deadbeat*. During your adult life, there will be few situations more damaging to your self-respect than falling into that category. Once you are tagged a deadbeat, it is very difficult to overcome that stereotype. No matter how truly affluent you might become thereafter, people who knew you before will still consider you untrustworthy and dishonest.

Living within your means is simple. Once you begin to use rational thinking to manage the Monster, you will discover that you no longer tend to value yourself on the basis of affluence. At that point, you will also discover that you no longer need to prove anything to anybody. You will then begin to accumulate unspent earnings, and will enjoy the feelings of security and respectability that come with a growing bank balance.

A person who pays his bills on time and has money in the bank is called *creditworthy* – a title that suggests maturity, intelligence, responsibility and trust. That is the image of affluence you must learn to project.

Achievement

Achievement, in the usual sense, refers to the ultimate accomplishment of something out of the ordinary, usually as the result of a lot of effort, and often in spite of obstacles and discouragements. Unlike affluence, achievement never comes easy.

The 3-A's suggest that people value *achievement* and therefore admire achievers. That is usually not the case. If it were, people would be more appreciative of all the effort that preceded the ultimate achievement. In fact, others are almost always inclined to overlook that reality.

I once heard a great pianist, I have forgotten who, complaining disgustedly about people who thoughtlessly depreciated his accomplishments by saying they admired his "gift" – suggesting that his ability was God-given, rather than the product of thousands of hours of learning and practice.

In the same vein, all-time American super-achiever Thomas Alva Edison once said "Genius is one percent inspiration and ninety-nine percent perspiration – I never did anything worth doing by accident, nor did any of my inventions come by accident. They came by work."

Achievement, in the 3-A's context is not about accomplishments, or the dedication and work that precedes them. It refers to something much shallower – celebrity or popularity.

Achievers get a lot of attention, and that attention is what elicits the interest of others. Being the center of attention – a person that others are keenly interested in – is called *celebrity* or, in the school age vernacular, *popularity*. People envy celebrity, and are attracted to it like moths to the flame.

Various theories attempt to explain this phenomenon. Most claim that it arises from the fact that people are social beings by nature – asserting that this is a relic of our survival of the fittest evolution which has been passed up genetically through the generations. I suspect the real explanation is not that complex or mysterious.

When you were born, you were totally helpless and dependent. The cognitive function of your mind then began to develop very rapidly. In your infancy, feelings of helplessness and dependency became the root of your earliest sense of who and what you were. You quickly became aware of the presence of a nurturing person, sensing that she appeared whenever you were in need. A sense of dependency developed as you began to believe that she could be trusted to assure your survival. While lying on her breast, the warmth of her body and the touch of her bare skin were comforting, and the familiar cadence of her heartbeats, reassuring – the earliest manifestation of feelings you would later come to know as "love."

As your brain's cognitive function continued to develop and your senses became more acute, you began to become aware of the presence of others – your father and other family members. Their frequent attention to you helped accelerate the development of your mind, and their affection for you deepened your sense of security and love.

So, during your first year or two of life, your security and survival needs were met by your having become the center of attention in your family. Your rapidly developing mind became aware of the connection between all this attention and your security and survival. You felt comfortable and safe when receiving the attentions of others, but fearful when abandoned or deliberately neglected. Thus, the sense that celebrity guarantees security and survival became ingrained among the very earliest of your cognitions.

Without really understanding why, you now feel driven towards centers of attention, and fear being left on the outside, looking in. As you grow up, you encounter competition and learn that you cannot be the center of attention all the time. In lieu of that, you settle for being near the center of attention. If you cannot do that physically, you adjust your thinking to make an emotional or attitudinal connection with whomever or whatever is, for the moment, capturing everyone's attention.

The results of this kind of thinking are all around you. Popularity is envied way above academic achievement in the halls of middle schools and high schools. Young people are usually very reluctant to excuse themselves from bandwagons, for fear they will be thought of as oddballs or "tools," and get pushed away from the mainstream. The entertainment business, which receives most its revenue from youthful fans, trades on popularity much more than talent. The key to a star's success is a great publicist, a person whose full-time job is to get them attention. At the other end of the spectrum, within our penal system the worst punishment, short of death, is solitary confinement – being forcibly and permanently excluded from where the action is.

If you allow yourself to be subconsciously driven to achieve things by your need for recognition, you will be a very busy, overworked person. Celebrity is very short-lived because the competition for attention is so keen. Today's hero quickly becomes tomorrow's old news. The classic entertainment industry question, "Yeah, but what have you done lately?" has driven many performers to exhaustion in the quest to maintain their star status – the obsession often ending in suicide or an otherwise untimely death.

When I was in middle school and high school, I was not popular. The popular ones were kids who seemed to have an entitlement by virtue of their good looks and their family's status in our small town. As a matter of fact, that was true to a large extent. But the popular kids were mostly trading on their family's achievements, not their own. As you might expect, that lasted only until the end of high school. Looking back from this point in my life, I can tell you that very few of the popular kids amounted to anything as adults, and many of them evidently have had a very troubled life. Meanwhile, many of the ones who would have never been tagged "most likely to succeed" in the high school yearbooks, grew up to have very happy and successful lives. This makes sense, when you think about it: the popular kids' continuing struggle to maintain their status might very well have been motivated by a childish obsession with the need to remain at the center of attention, revealing a degree of emotional immaturity that probably persisted well into their adult lives.

Does it now occur to you that this is not a healthy emotional situation, that such obsessions are a relic of your infancy rather than a manifestation of any real need?

The remedy for this obviously lies in increased self-acceptance and self-confidence. That should accrue automatically as a person grows up but, as you can see for yourself as you observe others from your age on up, emotional maturity is often very late in coming.

You have already read about how you can easily enhance your stature by understanding the role of attractiveness and affluence. That was mostly all just a matter of common sense. But what about achievement — celebrity or popularity, in other words? How can you accommodate this 3-A's reality in ways that make people feel good about themselves, and good about you?

The answer is much simpler than you might have guessed. It is, "What goes around, comes around."

When you were busy being the center of attention as a baby and toddler, someone else was your center of attention. That made them feel good, so the situation was not as all one-sided as previously suggested.

Paying attention to others always works in your favor. When you give others your full attention, you become their center of attention — the most important person in the world to them at that particular moment. When others are speaking to you, give them your full attention. That means listening attentively to what they are saying, watching their facial expressions and paying attention to their body language. Try your best to understand what they are trying to tell you, which is not always communicated clearly with words only.

Good listeners —

- never allow themselves to become distracted by thinking about how they will respond to what someone else is saying
- never assume they know where another person is going without having to listen any further
- never interrupt to interject their own comments or questions before others have finished saying what they wish to say
- never gaze off in another direction or stare at the floor while listening to someone else talk

Interacting with others is not always a matter of one-on-one conversation. You will often find yourself involved in meetings, casual social situations and recreational activities involving more than just one other person.

"Two's company; three's a crowd." By human nature, odd numbers can be awkward. If there are three, for example, you will probably find it easier to interact with one of the other two, and will therefore naturally be inclined to pay more attention to that person, to the exclusion of the third party.

Whenever you are involved in an activity with three or more people, be keenly sensitive about how it feels to be left out or marginalized, and do whatever it takes to make sure that does not happen to anyone. Most people are neurotic, so such gatherings are always likely to include someone who insists upon being the center of attention and, at the opposite extreme, wall flowers. Dealing effectively with either type means giving them what they want – recognition.

The person who seems to insist on being the center of attention is likely to be an *extrovert*. There is nothing you can do to change that, and confronting them head-on – for example by telling them to simply butt out or shut up for a while – is bound to lead to embarrassment and hard feelings. Instead, give them what they want. For example, in a meeting situation, seat them at the head of the table, ask them to handle routine activities such as invocations and benedictions (or opening and closing comments), the reading of the minutes, announcements, or other documents. Refer to them often by mention and make frequent eye contact. Use similar tactics in other situations. When these types begin to feel that they are accepted and valued, their behavior usually becomes more reasonable and cooperative.

Dealing with introverts – the wall flowers – also requires sensitivity. Nothing is more painful to this type of person than mentioning their quiet and withdrawn behavior in front of others. For example, never attempt to be inclusive by saying something like, "Well, John, we haven't heard anything out of you yet – now everyone is going to shut up while you tell us what you think?" John already knows that he has lacked the confidence to speak up, and will feel that you have exposed him in front of the group. A better strategy for helping John get what he wants is to speak privately with him, then when the opportunity arises, you can ease him gently into the conversation by saying something like, "John and I were discussing this before, and he suggested ... well, perhaps I should let him explain." Beyond this, most of the tactics you come up with for dealing with extroverts will work just as well for introverts – placing them physically at or near a place that will ordinarily be the focus of others' attention, mentioning their name and making eye contact, asking them to help out with some routine or easy tasks, and so on. The result will be the same; as they begin to feel comfortable in the situation they will begin to come out of their shell.

Dealing with people in this way will work to your personal advantage because you will become a center of their attention. They will see you as one who is truly decent and a really nice guy, and they will be eager to tell everyone else about their close association with such a wonderful person – just as people feel prompted to mention their connection with a celebrity.

Why Bother?

At the beginning of this chapter, I told you that people will ordinarily size you up quickly according to superficial judgments of your appearance, affluence and achievements – the "Three A's."

I told you not to waste your time in philosophical rants about whether or not valuing and labeling people is appropriate, and the superficiality and unfairness of the 3-A paradigm – that you must simply accept the reality, rather than futilely flail away at something you can never change. Your duty is to yourself. You have a life to live, and you have choices. You can make it a life of struggle, disappointment, bitterness and grief. Or you can choose success and happiness.

If you choose the latter, you will only be able to achieve that with the help of others. They will not play that part because you are obviously needy and are pleading for help, but rather because they like you and want to be a part of your life – and because their association with you pays off for them by somehow making them feel better about themselves and life in general.

You make that possible for them by being the kind of person people think highly of and are proud to be associated with. You do that by paying attention to the 3-A's, and leveraging that paradigm to create the kind of image that leads people to positive conclusions about you. In the process, you will discover that you are actually turning into the person they think you are.

You do have to make an effort. Happiness and success do not come for free; if that were true, there would be no need for you to be reading this. The whole idea behind this book is that minds which are not understood and managed by their owners usually turn into monsters that eventually destroy their hosts. Of course, there are no absolutes when talking about people – sometimes that does not happen. But look around at the world. You can see that the percentages are not in your favor.

For the most part, we are not taught anything about the mind, and how to manage it. We are led to assume its proper development is something that simply happens automatically as we grow up. When the inevitable emotional issues eventually become a big problem, only then are we advised to do something about what is going on upstairs. By that time, the Monster is well entrenched as a very capable enemy.

If all of what you are now reading seems to suggest new ideas that look like they will involve a lot of work, get this: the short term misery involved now in learning how to be happy and successful is nothing compared to the travail of the life that is almost certain to follow if your do not take control now.

Chapter 6
Straight A's

Dropping Out

One of the best ways to get a head start on a crappy life is to quit school. Oh, yeah – you have heard it all before. "Drop-outs have a hard time finding a job and never get paid much."

If you decide to drop out of school, you will be in good company. This year in the U.S., there will be over 1.2-million drop-outs. Right now, someone makes that move every twenty-six seconds. Someone dropped out just during the time it took you to read these two opening paragraphs.

At the moment, the drop-out rate in urban areas averages about 50%. In big cities like Detroit it is as high as 75%. If you live in the burbs, a small town, or out in the country, your chances of staying in school are a little better; the situation there is just the opposite – about 75% graduate from high school.

Education or Initiative?

Drop-outs often argue that education does not guarantee success – that it is things like initiative, imagination and ambition that make people rich and famous. To prove their point, they cite other famous quitters who did well for themselves – Henry Ford, the Wright brothers, Thomas Edison, Will Rogers, Mark Twain, and maybe their grandpa.

But these men all lived in a different time.

I was recently involved in the restoration of an old, one-room schoolhouse on Michigan's South Manitou Island. My father received his education there, and graduated from that little school. He graduated after the eighth grade, and that was the end of his formal education. He was 13-years old. That was common then. An eighth-grade education was considered quite adequate for any practical person. High school was thought of as higher education. A person usually continued on to high school for the same reasons they go on to college today. After my mother died, I eventually inherited a couple of old composition books, which she and my grandmother had lovingly saved for 75-years; from back when Dad was a schoolboy. At twelve or thirteen years old, his handwriting was careful and impressively legible. The subject matter reflected by his completed assignments seemed more like today's high school fare than eighth grade work, so I suspect that he had actually received an education equivalent to today's high school graduate. He went on to a successful career in the U.S. Coast Guard, eventually retiring at the top enlisted rank.

My Dad was born in 1910, a grandson of settlers' children who could remember the Civil War and Abraham Lincoln. Those were different times. Waves of European immigrants had swelled the population. They came by government invitation to claim homesteads that could be had for free. The country was rapidly expanding westward. As the economy began to change from agrarian to industrial, that hopeful and energetic population began to move off the farms and into growing cities. Opportunity abounded. There was money to be made by any man who was willing to roll up his sleeves and put out a good day's work. Industry promoted technology. Those who were imaginative and creative were rewarded with fame and fortune, and everyone else with even more opportunity - opportunities to become proficient in doing new and exciting things, which resulted in the robust development of an affluent middle class.

That was then.

This is now. Who can you point to in the past generation or two who came out smelling like a rose in spite of having dropped out of school in their mid-teens?

Today's economy is a mature economy, meaning that it is not booming with lots of new things happening. When today's new things do produce new opportunities, they are usually professional or high-tech positions, not jobs that you can easily get into just by cleaning up and showing up. Otherwise, the employment situation is stagnant – too few of the same old jobs chased by too many applicants. It is a buyer's market, and those with jobs to offer can afford to be picky. It is not uncommon for those seeking even menial factory jobs to be subjected to hours of written tests as part of the interview process. The surplus of job-seekers means that employers do not need to offer big pay to attract top notch help, and those with jobs are frequently being forced to accept significant cuts in pay and benefits. Sadly, the affluent middle class – the world your grandparents grew up in, and maybe even your parents – is rapidly shrinking.

College degrees used to be a big deal, but are now common. A bachelor's degree is no longer impressive, and gives one an advantage only because most jobs that pay anything more than the minimum wage now require it. A high school diploma is even less impressive. So you can see what your employment prospects are going to be if you do not have even that. Unless you are uniquely talented or extremely lucky, you will be stuck at the bottom.

The Simple Life

My grandparents, on both sides of the family, lived off the land as subsistence farmers. Odd jobs generated some extra income to pay for things they could not provide for themselves. Neighbors helped neighbors as needed. There were no insurance premiums, utility bills, or car payments. Out on South Manitou Island, where my father grew up, the islanders usually mysteriously disappeared whenever the county sent out a tax collector, else got him drunk and sent him back to the mainland wearing a happy grin, but with empty pockets.

Again, that was then; this is now.

You cannot live that way, at least not in America. You cannot homestead; all the land is owned by somebody. There is not much you can provide for yourself. Most of what you need will have to be purchased with money, which means you will need to have some way to obtain money. That usually means you have to get a job, else turn to crime.

The simple life is no longer available in America. It is only a fond memory – or a daydream.

Hanging in There

Without trying to sound pessimistic and discouraging, I have to tell you I am glad I am not you, because things, right now, are not very easy for a young man who is just starting out on his own. It is much tougher for your generation than it was for mine or the two or three generations that came before. Unless you are planning a career in one of the professions, your best bet for easing into the workaday world of adult life is probably the military. That will at least provide some training and experience which will help open up better civilian opportunities to you. Meanwhile you will be able to coast for four years, enjoying a fairly easy life, absolute security regarding your personal needs, and travel. This very suggestion is quite revealing – the military used to be any sensible young man's last choice.

Indeed, at this particular point in time, things are not easy for boys navigating the passage into a man's world. With all this in mind, I ask you: Why would you be in a hurry to jump into this situation? Why would you not choose to enjoy the easy life for a couple of more years by staying in school?

Boredom

The answers to that vary widely. People quit school for a lot of reasons. When boys throw in the towel, however, it is usually because of boredom.

If that is your problem, that indeed is *your problem*. School is not naturally boring. Boredom usually happens for two or three reasons.

The first one might be because you are actually too smart. Every class includes people with a variety of learning styles and abilities, and curriculums are designed with the hope of striking a happy medium – not too hard or moving too fast for the slowest learners, nor too easy and moving along too slowly for the more capable students. If you happen to be among the more capable – and drop-outs often are – learning under these circumstances can become drudgery.

The second possibility is that you have fallen behind and your graduation prospects seem dim. You feel the situation is probably hopeless, and that you are therefore just wasting time by continuing on.

A third possibility is that you have more pressing things on your mind – emotional problems of your own, problems at home, trouble with the law, a love affair, a pregnant girlfriend, drugs, or what have you. These kinds of concerns make it nearly impossible for you to concentrate on your studies. They feel so dire and pressing that classroom activities seem like a distraction, homework assignments take last priority and the whole school thing just seems totally irrelevant.

Another reason you might quit is childish rebelliousness. You feel like you are getting big enough to make important decisions about your life, but your parents or other adult authority figures insist on making them for you, or strongly advising you about what you should do. It is not that they are wrong. It is just that you are sick of them always telling you what to do. You would like to tell them to go to hell, but do not dare to risk a pay-back – like coming home and finding your clothes and all your stuff on the front porch. So you take a less in-your-face approach – getting as many F's as you can while pretending to be trying, and sobbing about how the teachers are all jerks who treat you unfairly because they do not like you. After a few semesters you are too far behind to be able to catch up and graduate with your class. Since you cannot graduate anyway, you might as well drop out. Good for you! You showed them! After all the fights over the preceding six or eight years, you finally won.

These situations, and any others that might be causing you discouragement, can be fixed. No matter what your record has been up to this point, if you are of normal intelligence, *you can easily become an honor student*. Yes, that's right; you will need a B+ average to get on the honor roll. But that is not a big deal. Middle school and high school is not that difficult. Even if, up to this point, your grade point average is near zero, 3.5 is easily within your capabilities, and you can get there within one semester.

It is not about being "a brain." Honor students are not necessarily smarter than anyone else. They have just learned how to be good at being a student. Being good at "student" is a skill that you can learn too, and quickly. It is actually quite easy. If you have taken this book seriously up to this point, you are already on your way to a better experience at school.

Now consider these secrets.

Teachers' Pet

Somewhere in the school's office, there is a folder with your name on it. It is your dossier. Inside that folder are pictures of you at various points during your school career, some personal information, and a record of your performance. Your performance will be indicated by *grades*, from A through F. Educators who have not met you will not value you according to the 3-A's (attractiveness, affluence and achievement). Instead, they will judge you according to the grades they see in your record, as will anyone else who has any reason to see your file between now and the rest of your life.

Once entered into this record, these marks will never change. During your life, they might become extremely important in determining whether or not you will be able to continue your education and if so, where and at what cost. They might influence whether or not the military will be willing to induct you, at what rank and in what career field. They might even have some bearing on your civilian employment opportunities. From this point of view, your record might seem almost like a book of life, your grades permanently engraved in it by tongues of flame wielded by the hand of God.

In reality, it is your teachers, using a No. 2 pencil.

People in their early teens usually go through a *smart ass* stage, competing with their peers for attention as they struggle to figure out who they are and how they fit in. It is tempting, during this time, to show off by being rebellious and impudent with respect to parents and other authority figures. That usually gets a snicker out of other smart asses.

In the best of all worlds, you would pass through this idiotic stage quickly, or bypass it altogether. But this is the real world. It is more likely that you will get stuck in the habit of criticizing and disrespecting your teachers, because you think that is what your friends expect you to do. Or, to put it the other way around, you fear that if you interact with your teachers in a friendly and respectful manner, your friends will call you a suck-up or teacher's pet.

That might very well be, but after school is over, all those friends will be long gone, and whether they thought you were kewl or a tool will not make any difference, one way or the other. What will always remain is that folder, with the marks your teachers wrote into it.

This might be news to you: *adults are just older children*. Your teachers are people, just like you, but a little older and a little more experienced. Like you, they have feelings, moods, emotions, and most of them are, like almost everyone else, neurotic.

No, this isn't about your being Mr. Nice Guy just for the sake of being decent. It is about your grades. Letting your teachers feel that you like them, appreciate what they are trying to do, and are interested in their class will, all by itself, absolutely guarantee against your ever receiving and F, and will otherwise raise your grades by a half to one full point. If you are getting D's, this will probably win you C's, or C's will probably become C+'s or B-'s.

How can this be?

It will happen simply because your teachers are ordinary human beings, who naturally respond in a positive way to being treated right. Is this a trick, or a sneaky strategy? Of course not. It is inappropriate only if you are not sincere, and try buttering teachers up in a phony way. Don't bother; you are probably not that slick, and not many of them will be that gullible.

In life you will certainly encounter people who are hard to get to know and like. That is usually the result of personalities which are not naturally compatible. However, when that happens, you will remember that it is half your fault – part of the problem is that your personality is not compatible with theirs. This never means you will never be able to get along with these particular people, it simply means that the relationship is going to be a little more difficult to develop. With patience and sensitivity, it will eventually work out. When the great cowboy-humorist Will Rogers was once asked what he thought of the then controversial Russian Communist Leon Trotsky, his reply was, "I bet you if I had met him and had a chat with him, I would have found him a very interesting and human fellow, for I never yet met a man that I didn't like."

While some may not warm up to you as easily as others, there is no reason why you should not honestly like and appreciate all your teachers. So there is no reason for you to ever feel guilty about receiving better marks because of your positive relationships with those doing the grading.

In what follows we will also talk about how you can learn to develop an interest in your studies, whatever they are. Meanwhile, exhibiting that interest by participating in class is one of the best ways to make teachers feel respected, and good about what they are doing. Young students are often reluctant to ask questions and volunteer responses because they feel inferior to everyone else, and fear that speaking up will confirm that they really are. But sitting in class like a bump on a log is sure to showcase your neuroticism much more vividly than speaking up and demonstrating that you are earnest about learning and earning better grades.

So this is the first secret – make it easy for your teachers to favor you with better grades because their feelings toward you are warm and fuzzy, rather than vacant or, worse yet, cold and prickly. This, all by itself, is a valuable lesson in life. Your school experience provides a great opportunity for you to learn how to naturally and honestly respect and appreciate those who are in a position to do good things for you.

Paying Attention

The second most important secret is to develop an ability to pay attention. Paying attention in class is another sure way to respectfully demonstrate interest in your teachers' efforts, and in middle school and high school that is often enough; paying attention and participating actively in class will sometimes eliminate the need for you to do any outside study. Otherwise it will enable you to easily zip though the assignments you do have to bring home.

However, the further you go in your educational career, the more you will be expected to learn on your own outside of the classroom. That generally means reading, studying, and writing papers, so you will need to learn how to focus on such activities, avoiding all the attention thieves that try to intercede and disrupt your concentration.

Your wonderful, highly powerful mind is easily capable of multi-tasking. While you are concentrating on one thing, which usually involves receiving and deciphering visual and audible inputs – complex functions, in themselves – your mind busily scans and sorts, making relational connections between whatever you are concentrating on and information already in your memory. Meanwhile, your system is busy doing lots of other things in the background – performing all the autonomic bodily control functions, while also monitoring, in a quiet and subconscious way, what is going on all around you.

Your primary level of consciousness is able to pay attention to only one thing at a time. Your background monitoring system interrupts that train of thought whenever it thinks your primary attention needs to be focused on something else. These interrupts bubble up according to a subconscious priority system that evaluates the apparent importance of whatever is going on in the background to whatever you are concentrating on at that particular moment.

For example, if at this very moment the odor of smoke was detected, an interrupt request would be generated with a priority high enough to instantly divert your attention from this page, and redirect it to investigating the source of that odor. On the other hand, the routine sound of passing cars on the street outside would ordinarily not capture your attention.

What controls attention? What mediates these interrupt requests? At the moment, nobody really knows. Nevertheless, this is an important issue. If you learn to pay careful attention and concentrate upon the matter at hand, you will enjoy the advantage of always understanding more readily and accurately, and learning much more easily.

This is simple common sense. Divided attention is always likely to result in misunderstandings. In conversations, for example, you might be listening, but might not be hearing if your mind is switching back and forth between what someone is trying to tell you, and other distractions – such as what's going on elsewhere in the room, or thinking up a response to what the other person is saying to you. Reading is another example; you have probably experienced the frustration of having read a whole paragraph without having the slightest idea what you have just read, because your mind drifted away from the page to other things.

Your inherent ability to understand and learn is just as good as anyone else's. The only difference between you and anyone else is your ability to manage the priority system that controls your attention. Although so called "attention deficit disorder" has become a fad condition among young people, and therefore the focus of much research, whatever it is that prioritizes distractions has yet to be discovered. Other than hypnosis, there is no magical way to control your attention.

Learning the skill of paying attention is mainly a matter of replacing bad habits with simple management skills and a little self-discipline.

The bad habits that produce attention deficit problems originate in the same old place – neuroticism. That causes you to feel constantly dissatisfied and restless, rather than happy and contented. As neurotics always do, you assume that everyone else is having a great time in life. That leads to feelings of being left out, or of missing out, which drive you to get more involved with people and things. You habitually choose entertainment over enrichment. Your hunger for acceptance drives you to obligate yourself to others and their agendas. By the time you enter the adult world, you will have overwhelmed yourself with distractions, and will have developed the very bad habit of always having too many irons in the fire.

Blogger Roger Ehrenberg paints this picture: "If there is one thing I am, it's over-stimulated. Too many activities. Too many obligations. Too many e-mail. Too many social networks. Huge emphasis on my wife and two boys; coaching, playing, living, loving. Which leaves time for ... recovery, maybe. Something has got to give. I love to read; I don't read enough. I love to write; I don't write enough. I love art; I don't see enough of that, either. I love meeting interesting people; I do some of that but would enjoy spending more time with really cool people I can learn from. Bottom line: my attention is very broadly scattered and I hold it all together (most of the time), but I feel like I should be happier and more satisfied given my tremendous effort in all areas."

As suggested by these last few words, all this fun and busyness is wasteful of your time, talent and money, because it does nothing to solve your real problem – your neurotic way of thinking. Meanwhile, it leaves you with a lot on your mind. The constantly nagging feelings of restlessness continue, and whatever you are doing at any given moment is never able to capture your undivided attention.

From this you can see that replacing your childishly neurotic approach to life with thinking and behavior that is more rational will also improve your performance in school, because you will be much less impatient and much less easily distracted. That will surely come with time. Meanwhile, here are some ideas you will find useful:

- Minimize the number and diversity of your interests and activities by eliminating those which are not really necessary, or truly enriching. This will reduce the background noise in your mind.

- Give yourself a break from all your fun and busyness with a regularly scheduled time of seclusion and quiet.
- When it is time to concentrate, turn off attention thieves such as email, Facebook, IM, the radio or television, your iPod and your cell phone, and isolate yourself so as to minimize the possibility of distractions. You can learn to ignore distractions, or your mind can become accustomed to those which are constant and predictable, but that requires effort on the part of your mind, and the mental resources being used for that purpose will then not be available to your studying.
- Sleep is directly related to learning. During sleep, a unique cycle of brain activity lasting about 20-minutes occurs about every 90-minutes. The purpose of this activity is thought to be the consolidation of the day's learning, refreshing the brain's cognitive capability for the next day. The mind also has an internal clock of its own, and expects these cycles to occur at about the same time each day. Interfering with these cycles significantly impairs your mind's ability to function efficiently. The average person requires five such cycles per day for optimum mental acuity. 5 x 90 = 450 minutes, or about 7½ hours of sleep per day. Like it or not, this is how your body and mind works. You will not miss out on anything by getting to bed on time and getting a good night's sleep. On the other hand, you can be sure that trying to pack a few more hours into your day by depriving yourself of sleep will prove costly in terms of performance and happiness. Prior to today's research-intensive culture, people used to apply common sense to matters such as this. Benjamin Franklin wrote, "Early to bed, and early to rise, makes a man healthy, wealthy and wise." Assuming that he practiced what he preached, this advice evidently worked out well for him

since he was successful as an author, diplomat, inventor, physicist, politician, and printer, while also being an enthusiastic ladies' man.

- Develop a professional attitude towards your role as a student. "Student" is your main job. Other things, such as play and a part time job, are important, but come second.

- If there is any secret to success for learning, it is good reading and vocabulary skills. The ability to read rapidly with good comprehension makes short work of homework assignments. Reading more slowly than your mind is capable of, or stalling when you encounter unfamiliar words, gives your mind too much dead time to fill between words, phrases and sentences. Minds abhor voids and quickly find something to fill them. Read as rapidly as you can. Continue on past words that you are unsure of to see if the context makes their meaning evident.

- Minds also love novelty, and always tend towards the easiest route to whatever seems more interesting and fun – much as a hound dog loves hunting and will strain at the leash. The upstart of this is that a keen interest in what you have to learn will guarantee sharp focus – which guarantees that you will learn more about the subject – which will further build your interest.

- Learning is an exponential process; the more you do it, the easier it becomes. Knowledge that was learned with difficulty earlier is available to facilitate later learning.

What Learning Is and How to Do It

Leaning is simply a process of receiving information, making sense of it, and moving it from your short-term memory to your long term memory.

As you have already read, nobody understands how your memory works. When somebody finally figures that out, learning will probably be easier, and the education process will be much more efficient and effective. For example, there are people who are strangely blessed (or cursed) with total recall, also sometimes called "photographic memory." English autistic savant, Stephen Wiltshire, the sketch artist mentioned in Chapter 4, is an example. Others can do similarly amazing things, like quickly read through any book, and then recite any single page, or the whole book, word-for-word from memory. These are rare exceptions, but they prove that the human brain is capable of performing at this level, and in most cases, researchers cannot point to any profound difference between the brains of these highly exceptional people and any others. You might very well be capable of amazing memory feats, but at this point nobody can tell you how to unleash that capability.

For now, therefore, you will have to settle for what we have found out so far, and that is that the mind's storage decisions are evidently based upon *interest, emotion* and *repetition*.

Repetition

You learned about repetition in your first years of school. That's how you learned your numbers and A-B-C's. You can probably still sing the little alphabet song, or say the simple little rhyme you used to recite while counting on your fingers ...

> "One, Two – buckle my shoe.
> Three, Four – shut the door.
> Five, Six – pick up sticks.
> Seven, Eight – lay them straight.
> Nine, Ten – a big fat hen!"

I started school while I was still only four years old. That was a mistake, because most of my classmates were five, and there is a lot of difference between a four-year-old and kids who are five. I quickly became "the dumb one," and remained "slow" until my last two years in high school. However, in grade four or five, I figured out how to ace spelling tests. The reason I figured that out was that I had always done so poorly on that highly visible activity. It was highly visible, because spelling tests were usually corrected and graded by passing our papers forward to the kid sitting in front; then the teacher would give the correct spelling of each item. The kids merrily crossed out those which were misspelled, and then tallied up the result. Anyone who got "100" got to stand up and be highly praised. At that point, I would quietly shrink down in my seat, trying to be as inconspicuous as possible. I usually got more words wrong than right, and everybody always knew it. I was, after all, the dumb kid. Then I learned how good repetition works. I went through the list of spelling words each day, (1) looking at the word, (2) saying the word, (3) writing the word, and (4) saying the word once more – and repeated that sequence at least five times in a row. When the day of the spelling test came, I knew them all. From then on, I almost always got "100." Finally, there was at least one thing that I was good at!

The same thing applies to whatever you are studying, although as your studies become more and more advanced, the repetition process becomes more sophisticated. Simply repeating things over and over again quickly becomes boring, and thereby self-defeating. Instead, you can approach the same material with different objectives, and from differing perspectives, and you can study different material with the same objectives and perspectives.

For example, when learning from texts, a quick once-over will never do. You browse, *read, study* and *review*. The first time through, just look things over to see what it is all about, and how the information is presented. Then read the material rapidly in order to get a more comprehensive idea of what it is about, and to catch aspects that pique your interest, raise questions or cover things you already know. On the third pass, study the material by reading more carefully and thoughtfully, marking key words, and phrases, sentences or paragraphs that summarize important ideas which seem likely to show up on exams. If questions arise that are not answered in the text, add appropriate notations in the margins, so you can look elsewhere for those answers. In your reviews, you look at your mark-ups. During the first review, you will probably need to revisit various sections of the text to remind yourself why you marked certain words or passages. Then, looking at your mark-ups in the days that follow should bring their meaning immediately to mind, indicating that you have succeeded in getting the information transferred to your long-term memory.

Another route to repetition is to check out other sources of the same material. Other sources often include other textbooks, encyclopedias, biographies, fiction and non-fiction novels, scientific papers, special reports, personal interviews with experts, and so on. You're lucky; with the Internet now at your disposal, the possibilities are very broad, and the search itself is often challenging and fun. Also, no two people are ever alike; every alternate source you consult will have at least a slightly different take on whatever it is you are trying to learn.

Cultivating Interest

That brings up the connection between interest and ease of learning. As your interest increases, you naturally become more deeply engaged and thoughtful about whatever it is you are studying. Without being aware of it, your thoughts will also be highly repetitive, because you have these matters more constantly on your mind.

When your interest becomes sufficiently high, the learning process seems a lot more like fun than like work. Happily, the more you know about something, the more interesting it becomes and the easier it is to learn new related material. Unhappily, the reverse is just as true. When starting from scratch in an area you know little or nothing about, especially when the subject is not one of your own choosing, learning often seems like a lot of work, and entirely pointless. This is when you need to roll up your sleeves and cultivate interest.

There is nothing that cannot become interesting. After all, even if you personally have zero interest in a particular subject, there are millions of others who do.

Knowledge breeds interest; interest breeds knowledge – it is as simple as that. If your starting knowledge is near zero, you will have to make an effort to begin building interest. Begin with light material that is easy to stay with – movies, biographies, audio books, archived television programs – and move up to more advanced resources as new possibilities and recommendations are presented through the material you are presently enjoying. Get to know someone who is more advanced and obviously interested in the subject and get together now and then for conversations. If there are businesses or institutions that are somehow exploiting the knowledge area you are dealing with, find out what the deal is there; people, especially important people, are almost always eager to talk about themselves and what they do.

Story time again; I will tell you about a personal example of how powerfully interest influences your ability to learn.

When I was in high school, I made the mistake of taking Physics. I quickly learned that physics was all about science and math, so dropped out just as soon as I figured that out. After all, I was the dumb kid, and had just passed the required Algebra I class with a mercy grade of D-, and that only with after-school tutoring by the teacher. From then on, I took classes like Dramatics and Practical English.

After graduation, I decided to join the U.S. Air Force, and the recruiter guaranteed that I would go into electronics. That seemed right, since I had always enjoyed tinkering with old radios.

Wrong!!! It turned out that electronics school was all about science and math!

The school involved six hours of intensive classroom instruction every day, beginning at 6 o'clock in the morning. By noon, I was always "snowed," as we called it then, meaning mind-boggled. The first 18-weeks covered the fundamentals of electronics. The second 18-weeks was called "Sets," – actual hands on training with real electronic navigation equipment – radio systems, radars, and so on.

Between the first phase and the second phase, students were sent home on leave for two weeks. I was not happy during those two weeks. I had just barely avoided flunking out in First Phase, and the word was that that was nothing compared to what Second Phase was going to bring. Flunking out meant that I would wind up either in Air Police or Food Service – in other words, directing traffic or washing pots and pans for the duration of my enlistment. My prospects seemed glum indeed, and as my leave time dwindled away day by day, my anxiety level ratcheted up click by click. I did not want to go back, but knew that if I did not, they would come after me. The day finally came when I very reluctantly began the trip back to Biloxi, Mississippi and the Air Force. I tried to be brave about it as I boarded the train here at our little C&O depot, but the tears came in a rush as I took a final look out the window at my family on the platform waving goodbye, and I wept almost all the way to Chicago.

The young conductor was sympathetic, assuming that this young man was being torn between love and duty. I was happy to let him think that. I was really feeling quite ashamed of myself. There I was, an eighteen-year old soldier in uniform, sitting there looking out the window at the Michigan countryside speed by, awfulizing over what might be coming when I got back to school, and sobbing like a two-year old. I was also angry that I had let myself be so dumb during the first half of the school; I knew I was better than that.

Perhaps it was resignation, or maybe I grew up a little during those two weeks away from the school, but Second Phase went a little easier than expected. I always did well enough on the written tests to offset my lousy performance in the "practicals," which involved hands-on problem-solving attempts on the equipment itself. When it came to that part of the exams, I was usually in a quandary, permitting myself to be mind-boggled, rather than approaching the task in a rational, logically methodical way, as I had been taught. The instructors would artificially induce a failure of some kind, which the student would then be required to diagnose and fix. My problem usually was that I could not actually see that anything was wrong with the system, sometimes even foolishly thinking they were trying to catch me up. I managed to pass and graduate from the tech school, although one instructor told me that I would never amount to anything as a repairman, because my hands were too shaky.

When transferred to my first permanent duty assignment after finally finishing with school, I quickly discovered how useless I was in my new job. The group I was assigned to was responsible for all the electronic navigation equipment on twelve B-52F bombers and a dozen KC-135 tankers. I was frankly floored that they would let a dummy like me anywhere near those airplanes, and hardly dared touch anything. I was just a helper, of course, always working with a more senior airman who did know his stuff, but in the beginning, I wasn't much help. The school had never mentioned the most basic things, like what the black box covers were actually called, how to put them back on, or how to safety-wire things, and so on. I had to be taught even those stupid little tasks. It was called "OJT" – On the Job Training.

I slowly began to learn, however. As my mind began to relate the stuff I had learned in school to the real world, things began to click more and more frequently and easily. It occurred to me that the

Air Force might do much better by assigning young airmen as helpers in the real-world job first, then putting them through the formal schooling. Knowing where and how the equipment was actually used, the people who were actually using it, how the lives of an aircrew might someday depend upon properly functioning navigation equipment to bring them safely back home, how the lives of innocents in enemy territory might someday depend upon the precision bombing that our equipment helped to assure – all those considerations made it much easier to develop a serious interest in the work I was doing, and engendered a desire to learn how to do the job as good as I could.

Indeed, one of the systems we had in the real world that had never been mentioned at all in school was a Doppler radar system. Its purpose was to provide ground speed and drift information to the IBM bombing and navigation computer in the B-52's and the tankers' little analog navigation computer. In our shop, only two guys knew anything at all about the mysterious Doppler system, and although they were considered the gurus, that was very little. As a result, the system rarely worked right, if at all, and the air crews were used to coping without it, manually entering occasional guesstimates for such important parameters, rather than having precision inputs provided automatically in real time.

Then one day I was ordered back to Biloxi for Doppler school. Again, I was reluctant. Doppler was a loser. It was a classic government SNAFU, a con job, smoke and mirrors – the Air Force had been sold a bill of goods; it never worked, probably never did or never could. I had become fairly proficient in dealing with our other systems – search radar, beacon radar, VOR (omni-range navigation radio), radio beacons, and TACAN (Tactical Air Navigation) systems. I did not want to get dumped into the Doppler quagmire – never a good day there – constant bitching about the system's piss poor performance and reliability. Let the gurus keep it.

The gurus suddenly became my very good friends, patting me on the back in encouragement as I headed out (secretly eager for me to succeed and return quickly to take the monkey off their backs.)

Doppler school was like "déjà vu all over again" – but unlike my previous experience, this time it was interesting and fun. Getting up at 4 o'clock in the morning to get to school by six was easy. I was eager to get there, and noon usually came too soon – just when things were getting really intriguing. Then, after six weeks, it was suddenly all over, and I was on my way back to my home base.

The gurus were happy to see me, presenting the Doppler bench to me with their blessings and best wishes, then picking up their tool boxes and kissing it goodbye forever. It was as if their war was finally over.

My confidence and excitement soon ebbed as the tide of troubles began to flow. My experiences with the mock-ups in the school lab were not very representative of real-life in the field. Doppler was indeed a bitch! What made it so difficult was that it operated as a loop system. Troubleshooting any other equipment was a logical process of working through it from inputs to outputs, to discover exactly where malfunctions occurred and why. In the Doppler system, the output became part of the input, so any disturbance in any part of the loop affected conditions in every other part. That happened in a black box called the "frequency tracker," which had been thoroughly explained in school, but glossed over as far as troubleshooting was concerned with an assertion that it rarely caused any trouble. The reality was that it was often just other way around – the frequency tracker was often the problem. I wound up spending lots of time scratching my head and guessing, and my guesses were almost always wrong. Crap! The monkey was now on my back – I had been sucked into becoming the next guru (the next "sucker").

Then came a Tech Rep from General Precision, the vendor who had designed and manufactured the APN-89 Doppler Radar

System for the Air Force. He was a tall, slim, and rather eccentric elderly fellow who arrived in a huge, yellow Mercury convertible, the trunk of which carried a full size VM (Voice of Music) stereo console. The stereo got unloaded at his motel room, so he could listen to LP recordings of classical music in high fidelity in the evenings. He endeared himself to me immediately by listening briefly to my doubts and pouts, then offering his analysis of the situation; "Well I can see you don't know your ass from a hole in the ground. But don't worry; I'll have you straightened out in a week." I do not remember my actual response, except that it was equally forthcoming; probably something like, "Ha! I'm sure it'll take a lot more than a week. If we ever get one of these fouled up pieces of crap working as advertised, that'll be a first!" And so, with the communications protocols thus having been clearly established, he and I went about the work of getting me straightened out.

Looking around near the Doppler bench, he asked, "Where's your APM-89?"

We had a seven-foot high thing with all sorts of lights, dials and gadgets setting in a corner of the shop. It had been uncrated, but never used. We called it "the Doppler console," but nobody knew what it was supposed to do, or how to use it. The Doppler school neither had one of these, nor ever mentioned that such a thing existed. I assumed it was just another "piece of crap" GPL had foisted on the Air Force. That made my new mentor angry as all hell. Almost in a fit as he squatted down and poked his index finger repeatedly on the floor at the end of the Doppler bench, he barked, "Warner, you get that damned thing over here right now, and put it right here!"

The main purpose of the Doppler console was to open the loop, enabling one to troubleshoot the system in a logical and successful way, an otherwise impossible task. After he had taught me how to use that important piece of equipment, things very rapidly improved at the Doppler bench. He was indeed an expert on the

APN-89 system, and taught me lots of little tricks of the trade that only a highly experienced expert would know about. By the time he left, I was probably as much of a Doppler expert as any other "rat G.I." in the Air Force. In short order, our Doppler reliability was way up – to 89%, which was unheard of among SAC's Strategic Wings. I became sort of a "boy genius," and was eventually honored as *Outstanding Airman* of the 4228th Strategic Wing, then *Airman of the Month* of the 4th Air Division.

So, "What's the point of that long story?" you ask.

It is this: I began as a dummy, and ended up as a genius and hero, and it had nothing to do with growing more brains. It was simply the result of my developing an interest in what I had to do. That process began in tech school, probably motivated mostly by a fear of what would happen if I flunked out. After school was over, getting into the field where I could see what the real deal was really all about, and how I fit into that picture, easily sparked increasing interest. Finally, a mentoring relationship with a man over three times my age who was, without doubt, an expert, put the frosting on the cake. In other words, nothing succeeds like success. Interest promotes knowledge, which promotes more interest, which promotes more knowledge – and before long, you will become an expert!

Another important point: it does not take very long to grow from dummy to expert. This story happened over less than eighteen months.

In my case, all this happened by chance. I lucked out. I did not know any better at the time, so was entirely dependent upon luck. Luck is not very dependable. You can achieve the same results by intention. Cultivate an avid interest in whatever it is that you have to learn, and that task will become much easier and a lot more enjoyable. Once you become engaged, it will not take very long for you to get from the bottom to the top.

Learning the Hard Way

There is an old story, told in various versions, about a father who persuades his young son to climb high into a tree, then encourages him to jump. The boy is naturally afraid, but his father lovingly promises to catch him. After a few successful trial runs, the boy climbs high into the tree for the real deal. The boy jumps. The father then steps aside, letting him crash to the ground. As the boy lay there crying, bruised and broken, the father bends over and quietly says, "Let that be a lesson to you boy. Never trust anybody!"

That is called "learning the hard way," an expression you have probably used yourself. It refers to learning which is motivated by traumatic, frightening or embarrassing circumstances.

Highly exciting or emotional experiences easily burn things permanently into your memory, as in the above example. But trauma, fear and embarrassment are poor motivators for learning. In the Air Force story above, much of my learning was originally motivated by fear and embarrassment – fear of becoming an Air Policeman or mess steward. Worried about the embarrassment of failure – about what my classmates, friends and family would think of me if I flunked out.

Trauma is a great teacher, as far as retention is concerned. Lessons learned that hard way are never forgotten. Trauma is also a *mean* teacher. Whatever the unforgettable lesson is, it is also usually accompanied by "Post-Traumatic Stress Disorder" (PTSD), which is likely to prove much more debilitating than an unlearned lesson. War is an attempt to teach people lessons using trauma. Our so-called "criminal justice system" sometimes resorts to the same foolish strategy in subjecting people to penalties such as solitary confinement or capital punishment.

It will probably seem to you that this particular discussion is hardly generic to the task of learning how to improve your performance in middle school or high school. That is as it should be. Nobody should be trying to motivate you by beating you over the head. Unfortunately, that does happen. Somewhere, as you read this paragraph, a kid is being punished by being slapped around or beaten because of another bad report card. That is inappropriate and dumb, because it never works and almost always produces consequences that work to everyone's disadvantage. If you are that kid, you need to know that sort of treatment must stop immediately. Chapter 9 will tell you how.

Fear and embarrassment are the more common emotional motivators in middle school and high school. You fear exams, fear the embarrassment of failure, fear losing college opportunities because of an unimpressive grade point average, fear being kicked off the team if your grades are not up to par, fear losing privileges at home if your performance does not suit your parents, and so on.

These feelings might very well get you to spend more time on your school work, and that might actually produce some small improvement. However, they are not conducive to providing a good learning environment, because most of the time you will be preoccupied with these negative feelings. You will rarely be able to become fully engaged in a positive way with the things you are trying to study and learn, so anything better than mediocre performance will be difficult to achieve.

You might recall my poor performance in the Second Phase of the Air Force's electronics school in the hands-on activities. Although I knew the equipment well enough to pass written exams with high marks, when it came to actually working on the radio and radar black boxes, *aphonia paralytica* (performance anxiety or "stage fright") would quickly turn my brain into mush.

I could feel my face and ears turning red. Soon the beads of sweat were soaking my armpits and drizzling down the small of my back into my butt-crack. Then the background noise in the room seemed to disappear as I became totally preoccupied with worry. "Gotta think ... gotta think! ... Calm down. ... What to do ... what to do??? They're watching me ... I'm just stupidly standing here with my finger up my ... Oh, I hate this! Look; my hands are shaking again. What time is it? ... my time is almost up ... gotta think ... can't think ... Concentrate, goddammit!!! You dumbass, you're blowing it again!"

Each time this happened, it set me up for an even worse experience the next time. As you know from having read the rest of my Air Force story, this had nothing to do with brains or capabilities, since in the end I turned into an outstanding maintenance technician. Instructors who were more capable would have realized what was going on, and should have done something to stop it. If I could have only had just one success, it might have made all the difference. Or someone might have shocked me into snapping out of my neurotic stupor and thinking more rationally – into worrying about things that counted.

> "As you ramble on through life,
> whatever be your goal,
> keep your eye upon the doughnut,
> and not on the hole."

My job was to see to it that the navigation systems on some Air Force airplanes worked right. When I arrived at my first permanent duty assignment, the bomb wing was participating in a SAC (Strategic Air Command) cold war mission called "Steel Trap." Two bombers took off every day at 10 o'clock in the morning. They would be in the air for 24-hours, landing at the same time the next morning right after another pair took off. Each one therefore had two full crews aboard – twelve men – and often an instructor pilot and a maintenance man or two. During that twenty-four hours, they flew three east-west loops, the first taking them out over the mid-Atlantic, the second out over Europe, and the third right up to the Iron Curtain – the borders of the Soviet Union. Each bomber carried two hydrogen bombs, and in his attaché case the Aircraft Commander had a sealed envelope containing his emergency war orders, which identified the two places in the U.S.S.R. that those weapons would erase from the face of the earth, were it ever to come to that. Other SAC bases also flew two or more Steel Trap missions every day, so radars in the Soviet Union saw a steady stream of American nuclear-armed bombers coming at them all day long, every day. The Soviets, of course, had their own version of this game, which was jointly called "MAD" – meaning "Mutually Assured Destruction." It was insanity, for sure, but were all hell ever to break loose, the accuracy of our bombing – and the lives of hundreds of thousands of "enemy" innocents – would depend upon the electronic equipment in the B-52's that was being cared for by young men like me – barely more than boys. So would the likelihood that the twelve or more souls in each one of those bombers would be able to get safely back home to their loved ones.

I never gave any of that a thought while standing there stupidly worrying about my petty, neurotic self-conscious issues to the point of becoming mind-boggled and useless.

My problem was what is now called "Avoidant Personality Disorder." As a part of that, I hated opportunities to confirm the negative feelings I had about myself – that I was slow, and not very bright. As you can see from my bad example, permitting yourself to be driven by neurotic emotional issues is self-defeating. Your constant preoccupation with fear and embarrassment is likely to produce just what you are trying to avoid – the failure you fear, and the embarrassment that will come with it.

If you have somehow developed this bad habit, use my example to understand it for what it is – just a bad habit that has arisen from your neurotic and irrational ways of thinking. This whole book aims at getting you over that, so if you take it seriously, you might find this particular hang-up fading away with little other effort being necessary.

Otherwise, familiarity is the key to success. Confront whatever it is that you fear so much, until you get used to it, as you surely will. Your mind will eventually figure out that the consequences of a poor performance are not terrible or catastrophic, and that will open the way to big improvements.

Higher Education

The higher you go in education, the more you will be expected to do on your own. Students often have problems making the adjustment between high school and college, because the college paradigm is often much different than what they have become used to.

Institutions and professors vary widely in style, of course, but as a general rule you can expect a whole lot less handholding after high school. In the classic approach, professors present you with a syllabus for their class, then expect you to study within that framework, mostly on your own, using the required texts and other recommended references. Lectures are provided to augment that information, and are presented in a theater setting, where you may participate only by listening and taking notes. There might be an opportunity to ask questions following the presentation, but lectures are otherwise not usually intended as interactive learning sessions.

Since courses are, for all practical purposes, canned by the syllabus, which defines everything from schedule details to final grading criteria, much of the classroom activity is routine, and can handled by teaching assistants, You might therefore rarely see the professor. Since the learning process is not highly interactive, you will probably not usually have many opportunities to become personally acquainted with your professors or their teaching assistants. Since the grading criteria are usually highly defined and impersonal, you should not expect such relationships to have much bearing on your grades anyway. You might feel somewhat put out, since it will often be quite obvious that these people have no desire to get to know you, or to take any personal interest in you. Those kinds of relationships are considered appropriate only among people who have been around for a while, such as colleagues and graduate students.

The classic study paradigm is "1-2-C", meaning that if you follow the syllabus, for every hour you spend in the classroom, you will need to spend two hours studying on your own to earn at least a "C" in the class. An overall "C" average is also usually the minimum requirement for graduation. Therefore it makes no sense for you to continue on when your academic performance is below this level. Taking all your classes into account, you will have to maintain overall grade point average no lower than a stated minimum – usually between 1.6 and 2.0 – for the semester and overall, else you will be dismissed. Poor performance during a single semester may result in *academic probation*, rather than dismissal. However, to avoid *academic dismissal* following the next semester, you will have to earn grades high enough to bring your overall average up to the "C" level. Once you fall behind, making up the numbers can be very difficult, so dismissals are the usual outcome. Once dismissed, you will not be permitted to reapply for admission for a period of time, or until you can demonstrate greater proficiency as a learner.

As you can see, what goes on in high schools will not prepare you for life at regular colleges and universities. Academic dismissals in the freshman year are very common. Whatever the stated reasons may be, the underlying cause is almost always a lack of maturity, which shows up as a failure to understand and accept that success in college requires a high level of self-discipline, and work. Regardless of the hype you might hear when visiting such schools prior to submitting your application for enrollment, nobody there will care if you wind up dismissed. They have your money, and a big stack of applications from people eager to fill the vacancy.

If your intention is to continue your education after high school, you should begin practicing self-discipline and work by taking responsibility for your own education in high school, as you will have to do in college. But there is another reason for doing this, which will give you an immediate benefit.

The word *collegial* refers to college and college students, of course, but it also suggests a feeling of equality among colleagues. Whether or not you intend to continue your studies beyond high school, getting into this paradigm will pay off. Your teachers are all college graduates, so will have become comfortable with and proficient in this way of learning. If you become *collegiate*, your teachers and other school staff members will feel that you are much closer to them temperamentally and philosophically. This will set you apart, in their estimation, from the rest of the student body. Your more professional approach to academics will fit the paradigm they were taught to respect while in college, and that will automatically translate to favored treatment for you, and better grades.

This, of course, gets back to the "teachers' pet" ideas. Teachers and school personnel are only human, and all human thinking is fallibly tainted with each person's emotions and unique perceptions – some valid; some not. Everyone, even those who prefer to be thought of as professionals, wants to be liked and appreciated. As the eccentric Englishman Charles Caleb Colton wrote almost 200-years ago in his famous book *Lacon*, "Imitation is the sincerest of flattery."

Bored, Behind or Befuddled?

George Santayana, the Spanish philosopher, essayist, poet, and novelist, is best known for his oft-quoted remark, "Those who cannot remember the past, are condemned to repeat it."

Education is the means by which we pass on what we have learned to our future generations. You probably never think of your schooling as a gift of great value, because you have never seen or experienced the alternative. You started school around age five, and you are stuck there until you are sixteen (in most places) because that is the law. School is compulsory. You are not there by choice, and after the hair begins to grow under your nose and elsewhere, you will feel newly capable of making decisions for yourself, and resent having to do what someone else thinks is best.

While education is compulsory, it is also a gift. It is free in every state of the United States. This has been the situation only for about 100 to 150-years; depending upon what state you happen to live in. Before that, only the children of those wealthy enough to afford private schools were privileged with any formal education. The rest usually learned whatever trade their parents happened to be in, which was usually farming.

Free compulsory education did not come about easily. Benjamin Franklin, Thomas Jefferson and Benjamin Rush are credited with first promoting this "outlandish" idea in the late 1700's, arguing that a democratic republic required an enlightened and educated citizenry, and that the government therefore had a duty to assist in the education of the people. Many of the upper crust thought that educating lower class urchins was a bad idea – one that would cause them to become restless and forget their proper place. The wealthy saw no reason why they should be forced to pay for schooling other people's children. Among the poor, people resented the idea of the government interfering in family matters, and complained that forcing their young'uns to fritter away their time on useless book-learnin' would not get the chores done or put meat and 'taters on the table. In city factories and rural forests and mines, operators fought this stupid idea, arguing that it would eliminate a plentiful source of cheap labor and ruin the country economically.

The idea eventually began to win support on a state by state basis, but it took over two-hundred years for free compulsory education to become fully implemented throughout the whole country. My grandparents were among the first to benefit from it in Michigan – only two generations back from me. Before that, countless of generations on both sides of my family were probably stuck in the roles of illiterate peasant farmers, simple tradesmen or soldiers, having no desire to better themselves since there was no opportunity to do so.

In Covington, Kentucky, there is a new statue of Abraham Lincoln as a boy, with an ax in one hand and a book in the other. The base of the statue has this inscription: "I shall study and prepare myself, and some day my chance will come." If there was ever a boy who started out in life at zero, it was Abraham Lincoln. His mother died when he was only nine, after which Abe, his older sister, and ne'er-do-well father existed in abject poverty, living like barn animals in an open-sided hut. In another famous statue, Lincoln the man sits looking out over the Reflecting Pond on the National Mall in Washington D.C. – our nation's most revered and beloved President.

Education bestows upon you the gift of opportunity.

If you have an idea of what you want to do with the rest of your life, or no idea, school sometimes seems pointless. But education broadens your knowledge of what life has to offer, and exposes you to possibilities you will not ever have previously considered. Somewhere among them you might find the kind of career described in the previous chapter – the work you would happily do even without pay. This in itself is reason enough to persevere.

But there is also another reason. If you decide to drop out, you will not only be choosing for yourself. You will also be choosing for the family you are likely to have – your future wife, and whatever children you might be privileged to father. I never knew lover who did not wish to give his sweetheart the moon, a father who did not want the best for his children, or a man who ever thought he had done his best by way of his family. During my life, I have never known anyone who, in later life, was happy about having dropped out.

Deciding to quit is always an immediate solution to a short-range problem. Expediencies often have unanticipated long-range consequences which dwarf the problems they solve. Give it some long, hard thought.

If you are bored with your studies, you can create interest.

If you are behind, but you can demonstrate that you are sincerely interested in improving your academic proficiency, you will discover that school personnel will be eager to make whatever allowances are needed so you can catch up and graduate.

If you are befuddled, you can learn how to control your invalid negative feelings and thoughts and concentrate on what is really important – your opportunity to learn about the world, and thereby make a more abundant and joyful life for yourself, and your children.

Chapter 7
Bad Habits

There is a myth about Benjamin Franklin, at age twenty, coming up with a list of *Thirteen Virtues*, which he adhered to closely for the rest of his life.

1. Temperance: Eat not to dullness and drink not to elevation.
2. Silence: Speak not but what may benefit others or yourself. Avoid trifling conversation.
3. Order: Let all your things have their places. Let each part of your business have its time.
4. Resolution: Resolve to perform what you ought. Perform without fail what you resolve.
5. Frugality: Make no expense but to do good to others or yourself: i.e. Waste nothing.
6. Industry: Lose no time. Be always employed in something useful. Cut off all unnecessary actions.
7. Sincerity: Use no hurtful deceit. Think innocently and justly; and, if you speak, speak accordingly.
8. Justice: Wrong none by doing injuries or by omitting the benefits that are your duty.
9. Moderation: Avoid extremes. Forebear resenting injuries so much as you think they deserve.
10. Cleanliness: Tolerate no uncleanness in body, clothes or habitation.

11. Chastity: Rarely use venery but for health or offspring; never to dullness, weakness, or the injury of your own or another's peace or reputation.
12. Tranquility: Be not disturbed at trifles, or at accidents common or unavoidable.
13. Humility: Imitate Jesus and Socrates.

One writer says, "Benjamin Franklin's 13 virtues are unique, and obviously served him well since he is one of the most respected and most accomplished men in the history of the United States."

Poppycock.

It is true that Franklin was highly accomplished and respected, but it is also true that he fell far short of the glory of his list of virtues. He was only human.

Franklin created the list as an experiment while sailing back to America after a visit to England, quite possibly out of boredom, although he was, in fact, an avid researcher. In this case, his intention was to experimentally determine whether or not it was possible for humans to be perfectly virtuous. After a couple of weeks, he determined it was not.

In fact, Ben Franklin was known as an enthusiastic diner, an incorrigible womanizer, and an ostentatious dresser. Some of his lesser known sayings:

- "Beer is living proof that God loves us and wants us to be happy."
- "There are more old drunkards than old doctors."
- "Old boys have their playthings as well as young ones – the difference is only in the price."
- "After three days men grow weary of rainy weather, a guest, and a wench."

That sounds like the kind of talk that came from a man who knew how to have a good time. He paid for those good times – his eating and drinking habits caused him to suffer with the gout for much of his life.

Around 700 BCE, the Greek poet Hesiod wrote, "Observe due measure, moderation is best in all things." There are lots of sayings like that. Why is moderation in all things so highly recommended in classic literature and folk sayings? The answer is, because anything done to excess is often harmful in some way to one's self, or to others.

Vice or Victimization?

The great vices of our time are sex, drugs and alcohol. You are probably already sick and tired of hearing about it. Much of the advice, such as "Just say no!" and "Total abstinence is the only safe sex." is indeed senseless – the same old supercilious proposition: "Don't let me think. Just tell me what to think."

There is nothing intrinsically wrong or dangerous about sex, drugs, or alcohol. In fact, these each have properties that are quite beneficial. When problems arise in these areas, they are the result of *habit*.

A habit is a learned behavior. A habit results from behavior that is so regularly followed that it becomes almost involuntary. Habits can be good or bad. Looking both ways before crossing a street is a good habit. So is making your bed every morning. The one automatically keeps you safe, and the other takes the pain out of having to make the bed by letting it just happen without your having to be nagged about it.

A bad habit is a persistent compulsive behavior which you know to be physically, psychologically, or socially harmful. (Do you smell the Monster creeping into this conversation?) There is bad, and BAD, however. Constantly biting your nails or scratching your package is unsightly, but not harmful to your physical health. These habits might be a bit detrimental to your emotional health and social standing if you happen to be caught in the act. But, what the heck; nobody is perfect, and there are lots of more serious sins, such as being a drunkard or a stoner.

I do not like the word "addiction." It encourages scapegoating, which is not helpful.

Demonizing substances or activities for being habit forming, points the finger away from the fault. Rather than taking responsibility for what is in your head, you lay the blame on whoever made the substance available or the activity possible. How does it help, to assert that booze, pot, nicotine, copulation, pornography, or anything else, is highly addicting? Anything can be highly addicting; even golf or stamp collecting. Blaming something or someone else is a kind of magical thinking: the fault is theirs, not yours, so your situation is in their hands, not yours, and will improve just as soon as they change their behavior. That gives you a free pass, doing nothing to encourage you to deal with *your* learned behavior that is causing problems for *you*, and perhaps others.

When people begin to blame the substance or activity involved in their bad habits, the question logically arises, "If a thing is so highly addicting, then why doesn't everybody get hooked?" That usually leads to hypotheses which are even more unhelpful – the ideas that some people are genetically predisposed to habituation by whatever the substance or activity happens to be. That absolutely takes the monkey off your back – it is not really your fault after all; it is your parent's fault! You are the unfortunate victim of a bad ancestry. This works, because victimization has been in the vogue in our culture for a long time now. The most damning aspect of this is its hopelessness – the idea that you are stuck with this liability forever.

I bristle whenever I hear someone say, "Hello; my name is so-and-so. I am an alcoholic."

My father, during most of my childhood, was a drunk. He mostly drank beer, which would relax his inhibitions, permitting him to become revoltingly vulgar and heartlessly mean. Occasionally he would get plastered on the hard stuff, which was always a good thing, because he could not tolerate booze, and would pass out before becoming abusive. Unfortunately, he would usually pass out embracing the toilet bowl. That was not good, since our house only had one toilet. Having to wait until after dark to pee out of my upstairs bedroom window because I was afraid of waking the unconscious bear in the bathroom was not good for my kidneys, or my self-esteem.

Dad took up serious drinking during World War II. He spent the war sailing all over the world aboard the "DE-386," a sleek Coast Guard destroyer escort, otherwise known as the *U.S.S. Savage*. When sailors went ashore after months at sea, it was not usually to see the sights or study the local culture. It was to get drunk and get laid. Dad went to war as a generally sober and responsible young man. He came back six years later as a drinker, although still responsible. He never drank on duty, and never missed any duty because of drinking, but was rarely sober while off duty.

He came by the drinking habit honestly. He grew up on northern Lake Michigan's South Manitou Island, where drinking was just a way of life. Everyone made their own supply of hard apple cider, so they would have something on hand in case the beer ran out while weathered in and unable to get to the mainland. His Great-Uncle Bill was the premier island bootlegger, operating a still that produced a decent grade of white lightening, which a few Juniper berries could turn into an acceptable gin. His Uncle Harry, a Coast Guard Lifesaving Station Chief, was court marshaled and dishonorably discharged, allegedly for being drunk on duty during a drowning crisis. (The family called it politics.) All of my male ancestors from the island were serious drinkers. One of my great-greats was supposedly killed by a case of beer. He had gone over to the mainland to stock up, returning to his boat with a case of beer on his shoulder. He slipped as he stepped from the dock onto his boat's gunwales, and as he fell into the water, the heavy wooden case with twenty-four full bottles of beer came down on his head. He drowned right there by the dock. The beer was successfully rescued.

Nobody thought anything of all this drinking, except for the occasional irritated or battered wife. "All in the family," we always thought, but it was not a genetic thing. It was just what "real men" did at the time; a cultural thing, really. Any man who would not have a beer with you was either an uppity bastard or a candy ass.

So Dad was a drunk from WW-II until about 1965 – about twenty-five years. Then, because his five children all hated and disrespected him, he suddenly decided, "Well, you sonsabitches can all kiss my ass! I'll show you; I'm gonna have something too!" He then abruptly went out with Ma and bought a brand-new home, creating new lawns that looked like pictures in *Better Homes and Gardens*. After that sudden moment of decision, he never touched another drop of anything except water, coffee, and *7-Up*.

My mother always excused his drinking as an addiction, claiming that he was an alcoholic – that he was sick. This was his way to showing us all that she, and we, were all just plain full of crap.

The *Diagnostic and Statistical Manual of Mental Disorders* refers to most of what we would call "bad habits" as Substance Abuse Disorders, Sexual Disorders, and Impulse Control Disorders.

The substances are usually alcohol, cocaine, marijuana, heroin, ecstasy, special-K, crack, and also caffeine and nicotine. Sexual disorders include exhibitionism, fetishism, frotteurism, pedophilia, masochism, sadism, transvestitism and voyeurism. Impulse control disorders include anything not defined as some other disorder, such as explosiveness, kleptomania, gambling, pyromania, and so on. The most recent edition of the manual refers to genetic predispositions as a *theory*, not a proven fact, while offering other possibilities – most of which amount to self-defeating habits arising from neurotic personalities.

Sensible Avoidance

Recalling that habits gradually form from repetitive behaviors, a way to avoid picking up a bad habit is to never engage in the behavior to begin with. But in the real world, life is messy and full of choices and, as Franklin proved scientifically, that is a lot to ask of mere human beings. Total abstinence in anything is highly unlikely. This is where moderation comes into the picture. There is a little jingle that goes:

> "All the water in the world, however hard it tried, could never sink the smallest ship unless it got inside, and all the evil in the world, the blackest kind of sin, can never hurt you in the least, unless you let it in."

The sensible person avoids letting bad habits get established by figuring out how much it is going to take to sink their ship, and then remaining well within prudent limits. Notice those words – *sensible* and *prudent*. Neurotics tend to be weak in these areas, and therein lay the problem.

But therein also lays the solution. If your boat is foundering in troubled waters, so to speak, trying to calm the seas will be a waste of time. You need to plug the hole in your boat. In other words, prospective bad habits are all around you, and always will be. Neurotics have a penchant for adopting self-defeating behaviors, so have little resistance to these pressures. The answer is clear; you need to deal with the nutty ideas that are causing your neurotic behavior, before trying to break your bad habits. Otherwise, they will just keep coming back, "like a bad habit," as the expression goes; else will be replaced by some other unwanted behavior.

Here is a good example. Nicotine is supposedly highly addicting. I began smoking when I was about twenty-one. By the time I finally got married, at age thirty-seven, I had a three-packs-a-day habit. I had tried to quit a few times using various schemes, but none of them worked. Then my new wife announced that she was pregnant. She also smoked but, of course, she stopped immediately for the sake of the new baby's health. So I did too. I did not have to quit; I just stopped. It was effortless. I never started again. Was I addicted or genetic predisposed? Nah, it was just a habit.

Your mind is not weak and vulnerable. Your mind is strong and powerful! If you do not take control of the Monster, it will exploit that strength and power to take control of you. You will have all sorts of bad, self-defeating, habits, and the Monster will try to convince you, one way or another, that it is not your fault. The Monster will also try to make you believe that you are weak, and do not have what it takes to beat your bad habits.

Poppycock!

Coercion vs. Persuasion

I assume you have already been preached at enough about alcohol and drugs. I do not intend to parrot what you are probably already tired of hearing.

The most commonly used chemical substances are caffeine and nicotine. These are also deemed the most benign. However the evidence implicating smoking as a factor in heart and lung problems is now solid. It is not necessarily the nicotine that is involved, but rather other irritants associated with cigarette smoke. It would appear that this is a problem that is solving itself, as smoking is rapidly becoming a thing of the past, in the United States, at least. Smoking, once promoted as a sign of sophistication, is no longer seen as classy. Now it is just a messy, foul smelling habit that an increasing majority of the population are finding objectionable. Smoking is being banned ever more extensively in work places, stores, restaurants and bars. Health insurance premiums are being upwardly adjusted for smokers, and taxes on tobacco products are increasing to the point where the habit is hardly affordable to anyone other than the rich, few of whom have the habit anyway. Smoking will soon be a thing of the past.

When I was a young boy, tobacco chewing was still in the vogue. Every public building – banks, the Post Office, the courthouse – had brightly polished brass cuspidors, or "spittoons," placed on the floor in every convenient location. Old farts would gargle up goobers, and then bend over and spit them out into these receptacles. That is hard to believe by today's standards, even for me. How nasty! How nasty?

Us kids passed around an old joke about a guy who was so thirsty he thought he would take a little sip out of a nearby cuspidor. He ended up drinking its entire contents and when someone remarked, "Boy oh boy, you must have been really thirsty!" his reply was, "I just couldn't stop – it all came out in one long string!"

Cultural bad habits come and go. They often begin as something invented by an eccentric few, gradually catching on as a fad, and practiced by people who wish to be among the trendy. If they become sufficiently widespread, they eventually lose their hep or kewl image, becoming common. Then interest begins to wane. How fast that happens depends upon the nature of the practice. The visibility of unattractive or unhealthful qualities, if any, tends to increase rapidly with the decline in faddishness. In that case, what was once considered groovy may become gross. In any case – sometimes sooner; sometimes later – most people move on to something else.

Attempting to break people of their bad habits by outlawing them is puerile, if not simply idiotic. That never works.

There is an old truism that teaches, "You cannot legislate morality." That is a simply way of saying that morality informs law, but law does not inform morality. When an overwhelming majority in a culture has very strong feelings about the benefits of a certain standard of behavior, or the dangers of its disregard, that standard is usually codified as a law. A minority has the right to very strong opinions, but attempting to force others into compliance with their minority opinions by enacting laws is never successful.

Another old truism is, "An unenforceable law is a bad law." The purpose of law is to serve the best interests of the majority. Law and order only works when supported by the majority it is intended to serve. When that is not the case, laws will be regularly disregarded, even by reasonable and prudent people. A no-win situation then arises. Rigorous enforcement breeds contempt for the enforcers, but if not enforced, respect for the legal system in general is impaired.

Bad law often brings the law of unintended consequences into play. Examples are prohibition and the so-called "war on drugs." Prohibition has never discouraged drinking, nor has the war on drugs done anything to curtail drug use and trafficking. Meanwhile, both create black markets that make things even worse by artificially inflating prices, engendering the production of inferior quality and even dangerously flawed products, and giving rise to powerful, well-funded and vicious criminal elements. Moreover, because the black market is so profitable, sellers become very aggressive and capable marketers, bringing increasing numbers of buyers into the trade. In that way, such laws actually promote the very thing they were intended to prevent. Although national prohibition has long since been repealed, a more sensible approach to the control of other chemical substances is still strongly resisted by those who never permit facts to get in the way of their opinions, and by factions that are profiting from the commerce such laws create, on both sides - enforcement and the black market.

Elsewhere I mentioned that some friends and I regularly enjoyed weekend outings in Mexico's wild and beautiful Baja peninsula.

We were very conscientious about how we left the place, carefully policing up the area before departing. At the end of one of our earliest trips, after having collected a couple of large black trash bags with cans, bottles and assorted junk and refuse that others had left behind, we asked our Mexican host how to dispose of them. With body language that said, "Oh, no problem!" he took them to the edge of the cliff overlooking the beautiful Pacific Ocean and threw them in. After that, we took the trash home with us.

When I was young, it was just as common for everyone to roll down a window in the car and throw their trash to the wind. By the mid-1950's, almost every family had finally become affluent enough to own a car, and it was common to go out for Sunday afternoon rides. With everyone throwing trash out the window, the scenic quality of the highways and byways quickly began to suffer. Most people thought it was a shame, but still threw *their* trash out the window while merrily rolling along. Then signs began to appear in some places – "Littering punishable by ten years in prison or $10,000 fine or both." Not only did that not do much good, the threats gave rise to fear and resentment, making things seem just that much more unpleasant. Then the National Council of State Garden Clubs borrowed the Pennsylvania Resources Council's "Don't be a Litterbug" slogan and caricature, and launched a national campaign to clean things up. That was soon followed by a "Keep America Beautiful" campaign organized by a national trade association of bottlers in hopes of avoiding the necessity for bottle deposit legislation. Then the Ad Council began creating public service spots for radio and television broadcasters. Within a few years the problem of careless and indiscriminate trash disposal was over.

This was a typical case where an accepted practice began to acquire an increasingly negative image as it became more and more common. By showcasing those negative images, the campaigns merely accelerated the paradigm change that would have otherwise developed naturally over a longer period of time. People are inherently proud and individualistic, and will always resist being intimidated into compliance with standards arbitrarily dictated by others. But people are also naturally sensible and caring about their environment. When encouraged to sacrifice the convenience of throwing their trash out of the window in favor of preserving the beauty of their roads and highways, the general public responded favorably to something that was clearly in its own self-interest.

When it comes to changing habitual behavior that is culturally common, coercion and punishment never work. Persuasion is usually much cheaper and much more effective in the long run.

The Lure of Forbidden Fruits

I just mentioned "people are inherently proud and individualistic, and will always resist being intimidated into compliance with standards arbitrarily dictated by others." That resistance often takes the form of rebelliously doing just the opposite of what you are told. Adam and Eve were told not to eat the apples, but they were persuaded to partake of the forbidden fruit anyway – so here we all are, in the resulting world of crap!

The evidence from research, and from common experience, indicates that the use of cannabis is no more harmful to one's heath or dangerous to the public than the use of alcohol. In my personal experience, I would prefer to have pot-smokers as neighbors rather than beer drinkers, because druggies are typically reclusive and quiet, while drunks tend to be boisterous and obnoxious. It is common knowledge that long term heavy drinking inevitably produces all sorts of medical problems, whereas problems resulting from marijuana use arise more from the smoking than the chemical substance itself. Costly and fatal accidents resulting from alcohol impairment are common, whereas similar casualties owing to the use of marijuana are hardly ever heard of. Nevertheless, the use of alcohol is legal;

the use of cannabis is not. We laugh off drunkenness; ganja users go to jail. This does not make good sense. Given the evidence, it would seem like this should be exactly the other way around.

Being young, you are apt to be in your individualistic prime, a time when nonsensical rules prompt a strongly rebellious spirit, leading you to set aside your rational way of thinking about your best interest. This is sometimes called the "forbidden fruits syndrome" – a desire that arises for things that you cannot or should not have. "Candymen" love this, of course, and know how to leverage it to win new customers.

The fact that the law is dumb does not justify self-defeating choices. That you can flaunt the law and get away with it does not make you special in any way. In this case, it makes you as dumb as the dumb law – suckered in by drug producers and marketers who are smart enough to make the decision you should have made, since they are usually not users of their own products.

I do not pretend to be an expert, but suspect that most drugs are probably no more addicting or medically harmful than alcohol. Since both alcohol and other drugs are a fact of life in your culture, you need to use rational thinking about their use. It is probably true that these substances can be safely enjoyed when used responsibly. However, illegal drugs present some special problems.

The first is cost. The bad law creates an artificial shortage, driving prices sky high in the resulting black market. Unless you are independently wealthy, a drug habit will almost certainly ruin you financially. I have never seen a stoner who did not wind up skinny and stone broke. Smart dealers groom recreational users by passing out freebies, but once they develop the habit, its increasing cost forces them into borrowing, begging, or worse – thievery.

The second special problem is the law. Getting busted is expensive – financially, emotionally and socially. Users are likely to get off without much more than a legal slap on the hand (suspended sentence, public service, and so on). However, lawyers' fees and court costs make getting off easy very costly. After that, the arrest and successful prosecution produces a record that is sure to cause subsequent employment and admission problems, so the expense of that episode continues to escalate indefinitely. Worse yet, habituated users are likely to become dealers, either simply because they have the stuff and make it available to others, or because the expense of their habit forces them into some sort of cooperative arrangement with their source of supply. The enforcers are much more earnest about prosecuting dealers. If you become involved in that, they will do their level best to ruin you.

When the forbidden fruits syndrome entices you to form bad habits, it is the Monster at work again – just another one of its dirty little tricks, and one that you can easily derail with a little rational thinking.

Eating Disorders

More common than any of the above bad habits are eating disorders – from anorexia and bulimia to obesity.

Self-Inflicted Malnutrition

Anorexia and bulimia are, more or less, the same thing. Anorexics and bulimics are both obsessed with an aversion to getting fat. Anorexics try to avoid eating, while bulimics cannot avoid ingurgitating. Both deal with the unwanted intake with devious strategies for puking it up or crapping it out. Taken to the extreme, the nutty fear of fat results in death, either by starvation or as a result of conditions that arise from purging practices and other bad habits associated with these behaviors.

Nobody really knows how many young people are involved in these hang-ups. Estimates range from four to ten percent – four to ten in every hundred. Most are girls. Boys account for only about a tenth of those so affected. So that is a lucky thing for you. You probably will not be affected – until you discover that your hot, Barbie Doll girlfriend is exchanging your Whitman's Samplers for boxes of ex-lax.

Since anorexia and bulimia are mostly a girl thing, it is sufficient for our purposes to simply point out that these reveal, yet again, the Monster at play, and the fact that the Monster's play can become fatal.

These are not diseases, but merely another form of neuroticism. It is not remarkable that, for the most part, only girls and young women are affected. The imagery presented to females by marketing and advertising, especially by the glamour industry, is that slim is youthfully feminine and sexually attractive. The implied message is that fat is repulsive. Meanwhile, the imagery presented to males is just the opposite – that skinny is wimpish.

It is true, of course, that slim and trim is always more attractive than obesity, but girls who already feel flawed and inadequate, and starved for attention and affection, are quite apt to get overdosed on these images and messages. As you read in Chapter 5, personal attractiveness arises as the result of a variety of components. Anorexics and bulimics become narrowly focused on one – their size, as gauged by their weight. Ironically, that obsession eventually results in destroying the very thing they are trying to preserve and enhance, since nobody who has the gaunt physique of a concentration camp internee is physically or sexually attractive. Furthermore, in their obsession with their size, they ignore of all the other things that enhance one's charm and physical appeal, which actually exacerbates the problems they think they are struggling to fix.

If you are one of the rare boys who are anorexic or bulimic, or are a boy with an anorexic or bulimic girlfriend, that is the message for you. These eating disorders are merely bad habits, brought about by neurotic thinking, much of it probably being done by the mind subconsciously. The cure is to quit letting the mind free run, taking control of what is going on between the ears and thinking rationally about relationships and attractiveness.

Skinniness

Boys, especially young boys, are often *spare* – a better word than *skinny* – meaning free of excess or surplus bulk. The reason for this is simple; boys are apt to be keenly interested in lots of "boy things" and physically very active. Eating is not usually high on their agenda; in fact, mealtime is often skipped or hurried through as an unwelcome interruption.

As boys approach adolescence, they too are subjected to idealized images of body type and build. As a boy, I was quite slim. Charles Atlas advertisements appeared in all the comic books and in any magazine that boys might be interested in. He was supposedly "the world's most perfectly developed man." The classic ad depicted a bullying hunk at the beach kicking sand in a skinny boy's face and running off with his hot-looking girlfriend. Next picture: having completed the course, the now muscular skinny boy knocks the bully on his ass, recapturing the admiration and affection of his old girlfriend. I saved up and secretly sent for his body-building course. What I received was an amateurishly assembled collection of poorly printed pages illustrating and explaining breathing and isometric exercises, and recommending regular enemas. *Regular enemas?* Yikes! As bizarre at it might seem today, enemas used to be thought of as a good way to modify a child's naughty behavior. As a child I had learned to quickly answer "Yes" when my annoyed mother asked, "Have you had a b-m (bowel movement) today?" I skipped the Charles Atlas enema bit, which might explain why the course never worked for me. I remained a "97-pound weakling."

In spite of the marketers' efforts, the idea that muscular guys are more attractive to women never catches on, because it simply is not true. Women are not that superficial. But neither are men, really. If given a choice between a "Barbie Doll" and a skinny chick, the stereotypical guy would be expected to go for the babe with the build. Guys behave that way publicly, merely because they have learned that is what is expected of them. But when it comes to serious relationships, they look a lot deeper. Unfortunately for girls, before they have had much experience with boys, they can only believe what they see – their public behavior – and that instills in them the idea that good looks and a hot body are absolutely essential. Luckily, boys are not usually handicapped in this way.

If you are skinny, and that does sometimes bother you, you should understand its positive aspects. First, it suggests that you probably have healthy interests, and are energetic and active. Second, being slim is not detrimental in any way when it comes to relationships, with either sex. Thirdly, it is not likely that you will remain that way forever. Perhaps you have already heard of the "middle age spread." That happens to both men and women. Starting out slim will give you a big advantage when you get to middle age and begin having to fight "the battle of the bulge."

Finally, here is a hopeful thought for you. Although I was skinny as a boy and during all of my teenage years, I began to fill out and become muscular in my late twenties. In my early thirties, high school girls – whom I was familiar with because I was still single, spent a lot of time at the beach, and patronized restaurants where they waitressed – referred to me (behind my back, of course) as "body beautiful." I was not trying to look good; I was just eating regular meals and having a lot of fun tumbling on the lawn, swimming, and playing Frisbee with the wind. Perhaps that was actually the onset of the "middle age spread," but for several years I was, indeed, looking almost as good as Charles Atlas, and without having to beat my brains out with exercises, or having enemas. Maybe that will happen to you too.

Overnutrition

Americans with eating disorders are more likely to be fat, rather than skinny. Obesity is now recognized as a major health problem in the U.S., especially overweight in children. About one out of every five children is overweight, and they carry that condition into their teenage years and beyond. In adults, every fourth person is too fat, and that is rapidly approaching one of every three.

Being overweight is unhealthy physically. That is not seen as an urgent issue by young people, since the physical problems usually do not appear until middle age and beyond. However, the emotional problems arising from being fat work the other way around, impacting the self-esteem of young people much more severely than adults.

The general sense is that obesity is unattractive, suggests a lack of self-control, and signals probable emotional issues. That being the reality, fat kids have good reason to regret being the way they are, to feel diminished in the eyes of others, and guilty for not having the willpower to do anything about it. Eventually the Monster comes into the picture, trotting out the various ego defenses and causing the already overfed to eat even more in an attempt to lower their blood pressure and somewhat satiate their anxiety. "Fat" becomes "full figured." Gluttony gets blamed upon unusual body chemistry or genetics.

The facts of the matter are simple. The body requires a certain amount of food and drink for normal growth and maintenance. Beyond that, it is a matter of intake vs. outgo. Physical activity, in work or play, requires fuel. If an additional amount of intake is provided to supply whatever is being burned up by such activity, the body's physical equilibrium will be maintained.

If the intake is insufficient, it will begin to consume itself by converting whatever it has in storage into the needed fuel. Hence the emaciated condition that results from starvation, and the body's ultimate death after there is nothing left anywhere in storage.

If, on the other hand, you keep dumping more fuel into your body than it is burning up, it will store up what it can, and crap out the rest. "Store what it can" is the operative phrase here. In most cases, bodies have no sense of what is enough when it comes to storage. They just keep making more and more space available, and no matter how big they become, they are still always able to produce space for more. The heaviest man in medical history, an American who died about twenty-five years ago, weighed 1,400 pounds before being forced to lose 924 pounds, the biggest weight loss ever recorded.

If you are overweight, you have three options. Either get out of the eating habit, get into the exercise habit, or do both. Sitting around pouting and blaming is not going to change your weight, or your own or anyone else's opinion of you. That is the bad news.

The good news is that overeating and under-exertion is often, if not always, a result of neuroticism. Neurotic thinking produces self-defeating behaviors. If you take what you are learning about that in this book to heart, the chances are that your bad eating habits will begin to change as your thinking and behavior become less neurotic. Expanding interests in other areas will divert your attention from the kitchen, and leave less time for meals and snacking between meals.

To help things along and possibly expedite the process, have a look at your lifestyle. You probably do mostly sedentary things like cruise the Internet, play video games and watch movies – things that do not interfere much with eating and drinking. Begin replacing these habits with others not so conducive to consuming food and drink. It is not easy to eat when hiking, swimming, tumbling, or even just lying in the sun on the beach. A habit that is fun and gets you seriously huffing and puffing at least once a day, like throwing the Frisbee, or even racing up some hills or several flights of stairs in a tall building, will prove very beneficial indeed.

Do not force yourself into physical activities that are not fun. That is self-defeating, and never works in the long run. As long as you can stand it, you will probably lose a few pounds. But because the activity is boring and a lot of work, you will not be able to stand it for long. Once you quit, you will go right back to your previous bad habits, and quickly gain back everything you lost. Then you will feel even worse.

By the same token, dieting is also usually a waste of time, and is probably not necessary anyway. Rather than making big changes in what you eat, just learn to eat less of it. You are probably in the habit of overeating at meals, and will not really have to deprive yourself in order to consume less. Rather than heaping your plate, take smaller portions; you can always have another helping if you want. But also stop gobbling and eat more slowly, giving your body a chance to appreciate that you are in the process of satisfying its appetite. Chances are, you will then find you do not really want a second helping.

That leaves between-meal treats. Snacking, especially before bedtime, is a really bad habit. You can find all sorts of advice elsewhere on what to do about that – such as snacking on fruits and vegetables instead of cakes and candy, drinking a full glass of water when you feel hungry, and so on. My advice is to simply bite the bullet and get out of the habit. There is nothing wrong with having a treat now and then, especially when it involves some social interaction. But having to be munching on something all the time is just another bad habit – not much different than smoking.

Finally, here again, nothing succeeds like success. When the weight begins to come off, you will begin to feel much more energetic and light on your feet. As others notice your improving appearance, the compliments will be highly motivating. These things will result in an increased interest in habits that make you feel better, look better, and feel better about yourself.

The Monster (neuroticism, in other words) feeds on negative feelings – shame, guilt, inferiority, and all the rest. Each time you accomplish anything towards overcoming a bad habit, it will render a sense of pride and achievement, enhancing your feelings of self-worth. That deprives the Monster of nourishment. By doing that, you cause the Monster to become anorexic, and it *will* eventually die.

Chapter 8
Venery

Venery has various definitions, but as used here it refers broadly to the gratification of sexual desire. If you are into or beyond puberty, you are well acquainted with sexual desire, and a quick and convenient means of gratifying it.

This is not going to turn into a sex-ed session. There are plenty of other books and Internet resources dealing with that. If you are beyond the sixth grade in school, you have probably already been taught the anatomical and reproductive facts. What follows is an intentionally explicit conversation about male sexuality and its development, discussed from a practical and empirical point of view. It is not intended to be shocking or controversial, but merely to address the issues that boys and young men find emotionally or psychologically confusing or disturbing.

"Dirty Boy" – Troubled Boy

When I was a boy, had anyone accused me of masturbating, I would have vehemently denied it. Nevertheless, the truth was that it had really become a troubling habit.

I felt dirty and guilty about that. In the 1950's, people still talked about all the bad things that happened to boys who played with themselves – I would eventually go blind, it would make my legs weak, it would ultimately ruin my ability to enjoy natural sex with women, it would result in sterility by depleting my limited supply of semen or overtaxing my testicles, it would eventually affect me mentally – and all the rest of that foolishness. And then, of course, there was the biblical stuff like the story of Onan (Genesis 38:9), which raised the possibility of lightning striking me dead some night as I lay there helplessly, but furiously, masturbating.

Nevertheless, I just could not keep my hands off myself. Some days I did it so often my male member would become irritated and sore. Other days I would worry about my nasty habit all day long – trying to think what I could do to make myself stop doing that. At the end of the day I would crawl into bed and pray to God to help me keep my hands off my privates. But of course the more I thought about not doing it, the harder I would become, and I could not get to sleep with it standing at attention and throbbing impatiently with every heartbeat. Then it would always happen, no matter how hard I tried to avoid it. Sometimes while lying there in the darkness vigorously "choking the chicken," I would cry in frustration, having helplessly caved in to that hellish temptation yet again!

Sexually oriented literature of any kind, clinical or pornographic, was hard to come by back then here in West Michigan, the Christian Reformed capitol of the world. Most of what boys learned was information passed down from older boys, and that consisted mostly of lies about their sexual romps with girls. Most never came any closer to that than their secret sessions with "Rosy Palm and her five lovely daughters." The definitive sex book at the time was still Dr. Hendrik van de Velde's *Ideal Marriage*. Originally published thirty years before and banned by the Catholic Church, it included some things about women that our mothers did not want us to know, but also much misinformation, such as an assertion, that men, like male dogs, can occasionally get stuck inside their woman.

From the little non-religious literature I was able to find, I discovered that I was not the only one with the habit, although the discussions always ended up moralizing, teaching that masturbation, if not actually sinful, was at least "defiling the temple of your soul," or represented the wanton destruction of a boy's pristine virginity. I read about boys who, in attempting to cure themselves of the habit, bandaged up their hands at night, twisted rubber bands around their penis to prevent erections, and modified bird cages to fit over their midsections while they slept to prevent their hands from finding their "maleness," as the literature of the day often referred to it. One source suggested that living as a eunuch was preferable to dying as a sinner, and elsewhere I read about a boy who, in a fit of frustration and guilt, castrated himself.

This went on for a few years – probably from about age twelve to fourteen or fifteen. I finally read enough about it to dispel all the old wife's tails and come to understand that masturbation was not just for "dirty boys" like me – that it was a natural thing that all boys do. Some of the literature even claimed fantasizing and masturbating played a healthy role in the development of a boy's sexuality. I figured out that there were not *nice boys* and *dirty boys*, but boys who masturbated a lot, and boys who were liars.

Doing What Comes Naturally

Unless physically or emotionally crippled, masturbation is an essential part of the human male experience, from the time the boy is first able to ejaculate, until the man is finally shoveled into his grave. The boy learns how to pleasure himself in a variety of exciting and satisfying ways. When he becomes a man, he might discover that the touch of other hands brings pleasurable feelings far beyond what he was ever able to achieve with his own.

Boys are sexual creatures right from the beginning. Every toddler eventually discovers his external organs and plays with himself when the diaper comes off. It is a completely natural outcome of the diaper-changing process, the clean-up ritual producing good feelings and raising an erection. Later on, little boys play show-and-tell with other little boys and girls, often even touching each other – and it is all only about pleasant physical feelings, plus perhaps a touch of excitement from the risk of naughtiness.

Maturation changes things. An extremely powerful psychological component evolves as a part of a boy's sexuality. Almost anything can turn a boy's thoughts to an erotic theme. Erections can be produced instantly at any time and in any place just by thinking about it, or by trying not to think about it. Physical stimulation is no longer required.

A boy's life becomes rich in sexual fantasy. Sleep is often interrupted by dreams of sexual activities so vividly experienced that orgasms result. In fact, boys from their mid-teens to early twenties are usually capable of bringing themselves to orgasm by "mental masturbation;" by just concentrating on an erotic fantasy – "Look, Ma. No hands!" – a "wet daydream," so to speak.

In time, the fantasies grow ever more elaborate and bazaar, and even unspeakably macabre. From time to time the themes vary, involving sexual activities with girls, other boys, women, men, animals and even objects. They can involve warm fuzzy feelings of physical attraction and love, or black lust arising from fearsomely sadomasochistic imaginings of sexually related physical abuse, mutilation and even murder.

The physical activity escalates as boys experiment – catheterizing themselves, inserting objects into their anus, filling their bladders to the bursting point by drinking and retaining fluids, flooding their colon and intestines by administering enemas with homemade appliances. Those who become well enough endowed and who have the flexibility engage in self-sucking. Others invent machines to pleasure themselves mechanically. Still others experience high erotic rushes from flirtations with danger and even suicide.

Masturbating with others is not uncommon as boys begin to develop into men. Their partners are most likely to be their very closest buddies, relatives, or family members, where confidentiality is assured. The activity arises from the frequency of arousal, some claiming that testosterone levels in teenage boys peak seven times a day. Other factors are curiosity and pride – comparing notes about their newly developing and often mysterious sexuality, and showing off and comparing their developing physical attributes – activities which both easily lead to arousal. If situations are such that boys have safe opportunities to masturbate together frequently, the sessions are very likely to eventually become more daring and intimate, resulting in petting, kissing, mutual masturbation and eventually oral sex. Such activity is ordinarily exciting and pleasurable, and can easily become a habit.

Unfortunately, with today's sexual hysteria, if such activity comes to the attention of others, the boys will be labeled and stigmatized as *homosexual* or *gay*, even though at this stage their activities are merely experimentation or adventurous escapades. The resulting shame and guilt is almost always severely destructive to the self-esteem. When this comes in the midst of a boy's struggle with his personal identity crisis, he might very well arrive at the conclusion that he is not a normal male – that he is in fact gay. Having decided that, he might feel excluded from any possibility of ever being happy in a normal relationship – married with children, in other words – and that can be emotionally very painful.

The Heterosexual Myth

I do not believe in the concept of homosexuality as it is generally understood in the United States.

Nature does indeed sometimes get mixed up regarding gender when creating new life, with the genitalia of newborns occasionally being somewhat confused. These anatomical birth defects, generally referred to as *ambiguous genitalia*, are rare – probably about one in 1,500. They are mostly not profound, and can usually be surgically corrected very successfully. The stereotypical *hermaphrodite* of jokes and slurs – an individual, usually female, with fully functional male and female organs – is so rare as to be mostly a myth. According to Anne Fausto-Sterling, Professor of Biology and Gender Studies at Brown University, the presence of both testes and ovaries are usually found in only one out of 70,000 newborns.

Sexuality is not only a matter of physiology. More important than that are its psychological and emotional aspects. Since hormones and enzymes are originally involved in the physiological development of gender, which does not always come out perfect, it seems safe to extrapolate that there would be variability in the psychological and emotional components too. But your chances of meeting a person who is gay because of genetics are probably about as good as your chances of meeting a true hermaphrodite – about one in 70,000.

As a result of genetics, you will encounter boys who are fair and slight, and girls who are hairy and muscular. For whatever reasons, boys may be somewhat, or a lot, effeminate and girls, tom-boy-ish. "Gay" and "butch," you suppose?

Not hardly! Nobody has yet figured out what is responsible for a person's sexual preferences. Effeminate boys and masculine girls are no more likely to be "queer" than he-men and glamour queens. During my life, I have had the privilege of being acquainted with several men and women who considered themselves gay and lesbian. In none of these cases did anyone ever have any reason to suspect their same-sex preferences. They were all quite ordinary by all outward appearances, except that they were all highly intelligent, successful, affluent, and very nice people.

If sex was strictly about making babies, then your urges towards other males would seem insane. But sex obviously has purposes well beyond the simple act of initiating the reproductive process.

For one, physical intimacy is the ultimate means of expressing love. Thus far, nobody has been able to explain how physical attraction works, or what love exactly is. These are simply "I know it when I feel it" experiences. A normal male ordinarily experiences physical attraction towards eligible members of the opposite sex, because that is what we are culturally programmed to do. However, nature obviously trumps culture, because normal males, from time to time, are apt to also find others physically interesting, their age or gender notwithstanding. Because of cultural taboos, few men will ever admit to such feelings, and most will angrily deny that they have ever experienced them. But we know from news reports about instances of *pedophilia* and *gerontophilia*, and from Internet pornography, that this is not only so, but also rather common.

Physical attraction leads to relationships that can become increasingly close and affectionate, ultimately turning into what we understand as love. As such relationships blossom, lovers ultimately reach a point where the words have all been said over and over again, and no longer suffice for expressing the depth of their feelings. At that point, we can only resort to physical intimacy as a means of expressing what words are no longer capable of saying. Love always produces a very strong urge to be close – often expressed as a desire to become as one – and sexual intimacy is the only remaining means of becoming that close.

For two people who are truly in love, sexual intercourse is inevitable. Those two people may not necessarily be of opposite gender, or well matched in any other way normally considered culturally appropriate. Again – who can tell us what love is and how it works?

Until someone can, who can explain, other than in cultural terms, which relationships are unnatural and possibly harmful?

As mentioned above, a young man's sexual preferences are usually instilled by cultural conditioning. Little boys are teased about little girls; older boys are encouraged to date girls their age, and so on. Adults never tease little boys about kissing other little boys, or suggest that older boys should be anything more than buddies. In spite of that, a man's sexual preferences may vary from time to time during his lifetime. A man who has never before consciously experienced any strong feelings towards other males – or who has always succeeded in suppressing such feelings – might very well find himself at middle age or beyond obsessed with the idea of experiencing a close relationship with another male, and fantasizing about its sexual possibilities.

Denial and Acceptance

Both boys and men are apt to engage in *gay bashing* – uttering vulgar slurs about people they suspect to be gay, while vehemently and sometimes angrily denying that they have any such interests or inclinations themselves. This adolescent behavior is a dead give-away for men who are not sure of their own sexual preferences. In other words, if you choose to behave this way, you will be making it quite clear to more mature and sensible people that you are disturbed by your own homosexual thoughts and urges.

As a boy, I was physically quite attractive. I was trim and handsome. I used to love spending time at the beach, and was always well bronzed. By virtue of my avoidant personality, I was almost always alone, and probably somewhat lonely-looking. Every once in a while, I would be hit on by another, usually older and smarter, guy. In the beginning, I was so naïve that I would never get the situation figured out until I was in some guy's hotel room or in his car, with him beginning to make sexual advances, like running his hand up my thigh inside my Bermuda shorts. Then I would really feel stupid, and would nervously utter something that was really stupid, sounding much like what a girl in the same situation would be apt to say. After the fact, I would realize that they had dropped so many hints on the way to making their dreams come true that I had no excuse for not knowing where things were going – except for the fact that I was an unstudied naïf from a provincial little town who was now learning about life in the big city. These guys were always nice, and behaved like gentlemen. Looking back, I regret that cannot say the same for myself. I was always nervous, clumsy and ungracious in those circumstances.

Towards the end of the academy award winning movie *As Good As It Gets*, the initially mean-mouth gay-bashing Melvin (Jack Nicholson) eventually says to his gay neighbor Simon (Greg Kinnear), who had just expressed his deep respect and affection, "I'll tell you, buddy, I'd be the luckiest guy alive if that did it for me."

Unless you are utterly repulsive, it is very likely that someday some guy will find you physically attractive and sexually interesting. When that happens, if you are not interested, smile politely and use Jack's line from the movie.

Sensuality

When you make love with someone you truly love, and who truly loves you, you will experience sex at its very best. That probably smacks of moralizing. However, this is simply a fact of life. Of the many possible modes your sexuality has of expressing itself, that kind of love-making results in the highest degree of pleasure and fulfillment. That does not mean it is the only morally acceptable or physically healthy means of expressing your sexuality.

There are many ways to enjoy sexual arousal – so many and so varied that there is no one word that works perfectly as a caption for this discussion. I have chosen *sensuality* arbitrarily – it seemed like the most generally applicable concept.

The Monster at Play

As you probably already know, sexual arousal does not always arise from an opportunity to engage in sexual intercourse with another person. Here are some examples:

1. You will often wake up in the morning with an erection, and you will sometimes decide to enhance the already good feelings by masturbating. As you do that, your mind will turn to erotic thoughts of some kind or another, causing you to become more highly aroused, but this activity did not begin because you were initially turned on psychologically. Waking erections in the morning are more a matter of male physiology; a matter of cyclic testosterone levels.
2. You will often catch site of someone or something that somehow strikes and erotic chord within your mind, causing you to become sexually aroused.
3. You will occasionally find yourself browsing through sexually explicit pictures in magazines such as Playboy, Hustler, and so on, and viewing pornography on the Internet. You will usually do this privately with the intention of raising your level of arousal to the point where you can very enjoyably masturbate to orgasm.
4. Sometimes you will feel somewhat as if you are in love with yourself, finding your own body "sexy" and enjoying good feelings as you touch and massage yourself and permit your fingers to wander to "forbidden places."
5. You may also frequently find yourself very excitedly engaging in some of the lustier activities previously mentioned – doing things that you would never in a million years admit to anyone.

For young males, sexual arousal is not always voluntary, and can at times be rather inconvenient. Uncontrollable sexual excitement is the curse of your teenage years – and also the blessing.

When I was in high school, I would sometimes sit at my seat fearing that the teacher would call upon me to stand at the front of the class to work out a problem on the chalk board or to read my paper, because I knew I would spring a "hard on" just as soon as my name was called. And it seemed like every time, my name was indeed the next one called – and I would indeed instantly become erect. Other times while sitting quietly in class trying to keep my mind on my studies, I could not prevent it from wandering into strange fields of erotic fantasies. The more I tried not to think about it, the more excited I would become, until I began to get that familiar feeling of testicles ascending. I would try to sit perfectly still, lest any slight rubbing of my pants on the swollen end of my penis would get me off. But it was no use. It would happen anyway. On the way to my next class, I would have to walk the halls from class to class, nonchalantly holding my books in front of my pants, embarrassed that everyone probably knew why I was doing that.

Could these sorts of things just be the Monster at play? If so, maybe the Monster has an impish and fun-loving side, and is not actually *all* bad.

Your Privacy Policy

As you grow older, your sex life will become increasingly enjoyable. As it becomes more willful and controllable, it will also become more meaningful and fulfilling. But you will never again experience the heights of sexual excitement of your teenage years, and the thrill of being carried off in a chaotic and uncontrollable jumble of erotic urgency. Your *coming of age* years are indeed very special. Instead of worrying about what is becoming of you sexually, and punishing yourself with feelings of shame and guilt, accept the fact that your emerging sexuality is a normal part of becoming a man – that this brief but marvelously exciting time in your life should be honored by creating and saving up many fond and wonderful memories.

The situations and experiences described above are all highly private things that human males experience. They are a normal part of male sexuality. Nevertheless, you will be secretive about these things, for some important reasons.

1. Common sense about cultural conventions and attitudes force prudent people to guard their personal privacy, in order to preserve their image and reputation. Almost all of the situations and activities mentioned above result in masturbation culminating in orgasm. It is sanctimonious nonsense of course – an obvious double-standard – but the general view is that "real men" do not masturbate; that masturbation is a sure sign of emotional immaturity, and perhaps even suggests a deviant obsession with sex. That is not an image any man wishes to acquire.
2. When it comes to sex, familiarity does breed contempt. What becomes common – common knowledge or common practice – soon ceases to be exciting and pleasurable. Comparing notes with others is not apt to improve things for you.
3. It is never appropriate to "kiss 'n tell." Sexual activity is eminently personal and private. Telling third parties about your relations with someone else is a good way to offend your partner and violate the trust they placed in you.
4. There is a profound difference between fantasy and reality – if you attempt to act out your sex fantasies in real life, you will usually find the real activity far less erotically exciting than the fantasy, if not downright repugnant. Talking about them produces almost the same results as attempting to make these erotic dreams come true.

5. Finally, there is an old adage that says a guy who talks about sex all the time is a guy who is not getting any.

Your secrecy about what you are thinking and doing is therefore perfectly justified, but will nevertheless tend to produce acute feelings of shame and guilt, and those feelings are invariably very destructive of self-esteem.

Ah-hah! The Monster strikes again! Fight back with some rational thinking.

1. What you do by yourself, in the privacy of your own room, is nobody's business but your own. This applies at any age, from the time you become erotically capable to the time you die, and regardless of your situation – married or single; walking, creeping or crawling; blind, crippled or crazy.
2. What you do with another consenting human being in private is also nobody else's business. If you are involved in a committed relationship with another person, the expectation is that the other consenting human being will be that particular person. In our culture, we honor monogamy, and disparage clandestine relationships with others as "affairs" which betray the sacred trust upon which committed relationships rely. But within such relationships, what the two of you do is strictly between you.
3. Your sex fantasies are nobody's business. During your lifetime, you will think all sorts of insane things, some of which will seem scary even to you. It happens to everyone. There is no reason for you to suspect that you are not normal or perhaps are going crazy. Thoughts are not sinful or illegal – you will not go to hell or and cannot be arrested for what you are thinking.

Addicted to Sex?

How much sex is too much?

According to some old Kinsey Institute studies of "normal" males, from age twelve to nineteen, a boy's thoughts turn to sex every five minutes. That diminishes with age – for men in their forties it was every thirty minutes. For boys, that would amount to 480-times a day; for the men, 48-times a day. How many times do others suggest, "Cripes, is that all you ever think about?" That probably strikes a guilty chord when you answer, "No!" But you can see from the Kinsey research that you have nothing to feel guilty about. In fact, you should be happy you are able to answer, "Yes!", thereby affirming that you are as normal as other males.

All this is popularly attributed to testosterone, which surges in men every fifteen to twenty minutes all day long. About eight years ago, one obscure researcher claimed that it spikes seven times a day in the teenage years. That stuck in my memory because just before that report came out one of our son's buddies boastfully claimed to be the masturbation champion among his peers, doing it seven times a day, on average. The correlation was interesting, but the jury is really still out on testosterone, the question being whether testosterone is responsible for, or the result of, what is going on in your mind.

The truth is that people are all different, and the circumstances of individual lives vary widely. Boys come short to tall, slim to hefty, slight to muscular, fair complexioned to ruddy, twinks to bears, gentle to coarse, and so on. They also come with widely differing sexual preferences and appetites. "Normal" sensuality can be defined only within this very broad and diverse range.

In Chapter 11 you will read about *the bell curve*, which is a way of viewing the *normal distribution* of things. In this context, if the left end of the curve represented ultra-conservative boys and the right end the ultra-kinky, the theory would predict that 95% of the boys you meet would fall under the middle 40% of the curve. To the left would be the 2-1/2% who, for some reason, rarely "suffered lust," up to complete abstinence of thought and deed. To the right would be the other 2-1/2% of boys whom most would think were unusually over-sexed, up to the really weird. The curve's bell shape accounts for widely varying values either side of the midpoint. In other words, your ideas and activities could be very different than someone else's, yet the both of you would still fall within that middle "normal" range.

A more sensible approach to evaluating your own sensuality is this:

1. If what you are doing is physically painful or injurious to yourself or someone else, that falls far to the right of "normal." Sex is supposed to be exciting and feel good. If you're your excitement arises from causing pain or injury, you will need to deal with the personality issues that are forcing you over the top in that direction. This can be a touchy subject. For example, boys sometimes do things that seem exciting at the time, but turn out to be painful. For example, if you decide to catheterize yourself, that will be highly erotic and thrilling – until the first time you pee after withdrawing whatever you stuck into yourself. You will probably chalk that terrible burning pain off to collateral damage and decide not to achieve a high that way again, rather than conclude that you need therapy. Another concern is fantasy. Daydreaming and doing are two completely different things. The fact that you might engage in sadomasochistic fantasizing does not suggest that you are really interested in, or even capable of, doing such things.

2. On the opposite extreme, if you are so fearful of eroticism or find sex so repulsive that you rarely engage in such activity, or feel totally filthy and disgusted with yourself when you do, it is again time to recheck your premises. Sex is a totally normal and very rewarding part of the adult experience. It is not dirty, or sinful "lust of the flesh." Because of all the hype, boys are often afraid of their ability to perform as lovers, but good

performance comes naturally with experience, and groping through the process of learning by experience can be a lot of fun, especially when learning with a loving and committed partner.

3. Eroticism is highly stimulating, very pleasurable, and absolutely free. It has no unpleasant side-effects, nor does long-term overindulgence produce any physical harm. Unlike candy, pop, or ice cream, it never leaves a bad taste in your mouth, and you never get tired of it. Unlike alcohol or drugs, you never become habituated such that you need it in ever increasing amounts – any sex is good sex. But simply because it is so enjoyable, sex can easily become a habit. However, there are lots of good things in life. If you are spending most of your free time exploring and experiencing your body's erotic capabilities, you are missing out on lots of other good things that life has to offer. That might be okay for a while when you are young and this is all new, exciting and intriguing. But as time goes on, you must broaden your interests, for your sake and the sake of others, such as your family, assuming that someday you will marry and have children of your own. There's a quaint old saying, "An idle mind is the devil's playground; idle hands are the devil's tools." There is probably a lot of truth in that, to the extent that when we have nothing else to do, the idle times are often filled with erotic thoughts and sensual activities. Perhaps you have noticed that the opposite is also true. When you are absorbed in other activities that are interesting and fun, or consuming in some other way, your thoughts never drift towards sex. Therefore, engaging in other activities does not represent a trade-off. You do not have to think about giving up part of your erotic life for other interests, because eroticism is somehow self-adjusting. Your mind will regulate your eroticism to

accommodate the available opportunities. Sexual arousal will be blocked during other times, to allow you to participate in other enjoyable and worthwhile activities.

Addiction is defined as "the state of being enslaved to a habit or practice or to something that is psychologically or physically habit-forming ... to such an extent that its cessation causes severe trauma." On carefully parsing that definition, I guess I would have to concede that "sexual addiction" could be a real thing – mostly because of the last part. Giving up sex would certainly result in severe trauma for most men.

Of course, so would giving up food or breathing.

Chapter 9
Abuse & Neglect

In a perfect world, families would all be loving, nurturing and protective places for children – and adults. In the real world, families vary from those which approach the ideal, to those which fall far short.

Here again, the bell curve, the standard normal distribution, is a valid way to view the situation. Ideal families are very few and far between, as are those which are absolutely horrible. In the middle we have all the rest. Although the current neurotic endemic probably skews the center of the normal curve somewhat towards the "less than ideal" side, the vast majority represented by the "normal" area are well-meaning people who struggle with their humanity day by day, trying to do the right things, but obliged to live with the pain of being imperfect.

I have never met a parent who did not deeply love the children they brought into the world, or who did not earnestly wish their children would have a wonderful life. I have never met a parent who did not feel that they were doing the best that they could, under the circumstances. I have often met parents who did not much like other people's children, and suspected those children could look forward to a troubled life because of parents who were not doing their best. Meanwhile, most grown up children neurotically fault their parents, believing that their childhood should have been, and could have been, as idyllic as portrayed in fairytales and Disney movies. All these feelings tend to get extrapolated such that children as a class are thought of as innocent and special, and ought to be sheltered from the realities of life.

Human relationships are messy. On a personal level, our feelings toward other people are unpredictable, running from hot to cold depending upon some mysterious personal criteria our minds have somehow conjured up, and with ups and downs within the close involvements we have with others. In spite of this, we insist upon making things even messier by imperiously seeking to impose our personal ideals and beliefs upon everyone in general, sometimes through social pressure, and sometimes through the force of law.

Nature's fundaments building block, the atom, has a nucleus at its center, with electrons orbiting in "shells" at varying distances from the nucleus. Outer shell electrons are not very rigidly associated with the nucleus and, depending upon the atom, can easily be influenced to leave. This is the principle of electric current, with voltage being the pressure that influences electrons to become free to happily bounce from one atom to another within a conductor. Inner-shell electrons, however, are so intimately attached to the nucleus that a huge amount of pressure is required to force them out of their orbit, and then all hell breaks loose. The energy released by ripping the particle away from its rightful place results in smoke and fire, damage and destruction.

And so it is with human relationships. When something intervenes to break up a close relationship, all hell is likely to break loose, and the result is always damaging and destructive. This is especially true when the relationship involves a child and his family.

Child abuse and neglect is a complicated subject. What actually constitutes abuse is often open to question, and what to do about it is even more debatable. When the discussion moves into the realm of sex, the debate becomes much more complex and heated.

The discussions and debates always involve only adults, although those most affected by outcomes are children. As a young person, you are very likely to become caught up in this controversy as a "victim." As an older teenager or young man, you could also easily be accused as a "perpetrator."

This lengthy chapter is offered to empower you in either circumstance. Hopefully, it will enable you to prevent any involvement in the first place. But should either misfortune happen to you, this knowledge will help you control the pain and suffering it will bring to you and your family, and minimize the permanent damage it will leave in its wake.

Politics vs. Family

Until very recently, governments kept hands off when it came to relationships. Somehow the human race struggled through millions of years of survival and growth anyway. The reason was that typical family situations always fall near the center of the normal curve. The family has always been a place where related people, through inscrutable bonds, are committed to loving, caring for, nurturing and protecting each other. Families have always muddled through as best they can, with all outcomes being imperfect, but more or less acceptable.

As do all of man's dreams and schemes, the principle of *popular sovereignty* and the invention of *representative democracy* as a form of government have evoked the law of unintended consequences. In the beginning, while societies were primarily aristocratic, those who were best born, or best favored by fortune, were considered properly qualified for elective office by virtue of their position, which was taken as evidence of their superior intellect. Candidates were appointed by a few powerful men in political parties. Resting on their reputation, candidates felt no need to campaign, or even that campaigning was beneath their dignity. Winning the office was an honor. Not winning was not a personal calamity or disgrace.

With the growth of an educated middle class, the process changed. Anyone could run for elective office. Political campaigns turned into popularity contests, with the winning candidates being those who did the best job of marketing themselves. Campaigns became essentially a sales pitch, with candidates ticking off all the good things they would do for those whose votes they sought. The good things were called *issues*. Legitimate issues sometimes presented themselves. But, issues were also often raised by the candidate or by his party, to pander to zealous factions, or to raise and trade on fear. Candidates who were good salesmen, were sometimes able to sell voters on the virtue of the opinions they personally held. Otherwise, smart candidates learned how to judge and embrace the currently predominating opinions of voters.

One of the more infamous examples of this was the prohibition of alcohol consumption in the U.S. per the Volstead Act passed in October of 1919. Religious factions had long condemned drinking, and from time to time it was outlawed or regulated in various places. In 1874 a new movement began, called the "Women's Christian Temperance Union," or "WCTU." Through high profile activism involving mostly women and children, the WCTU succeeded in promoting a variety of feminist and child welfare issues. Other more zealous organizations developed out of this movement, such as the "Anti-Saloon League," and by the dawn of the twentieth century, drinking had been promoted to the high status of being the chief cause of all of humanity's ills. Silly as this assertion seems from today's perspective, zealous special interest factions and pandering politicians sold the public on it, and after some thirteen years of ineffective enforcement and criminal chaos, the nutty experiment was finally suspended.

Over the past few decades, child abuse and neglect has been similarly elevated to a *cause célèbre*. Initially gaining a foothold by presenting the exceptions as the norm, mission creep has broadened the scope such that what have traditionally been considered normal and acceptable in family dynamics, has now become grounds for government intervention.

Neglect

Neglect refers to a failure to adequately provide for a child's welfare, mostly in terms of health and safety. This is obviously an extremely arbitrary matter, since by the standard of the wealthy, every poor family could be accused. Interventions are common, approaching two-thirds of all reported cases of child abuse. But prosecutions usually arise only from the most egregious cases, or in connection with the accidental death of a child, with a *res ipsa loquitur* case asserting that had the child been adequately watched over or properly supervised, the accident would not have happened. The absurdity of such proceedings is that while accidents are technically always avoidable through the exercise of greater care and diligence, they can and always will happen because human beings are fallible. Tragic as the loss of a child's life always is, the pain of such a loss is certainly apt to be prosecution enough. A shameful truth about our justice system is that such cases are usually brought only against those on the low end of the socio-economic ladder.

Emotional Abuse

Abuse comes in three flavors: emotional, physical and sexual.

Emotional abuse is less frequently charged because of the word *emotional*, which is relative, and raises questions about the victim's capacity to tolerate adversity.

We all know that life is sometimes very trying and difficult, and quite often it is that way because of people we have to put up with. All children, at some time or another, complain about being picked on. As a formal charge, emotional abuse is a pleading usually brought on behalf of a child by an adult, but often sounds like the same "picked on" complaint – someone is treating the child in a way that is detrimental to his self-esteem, or makes him feel unhappy.

Indeed, children do sometimes need special protection from such unfairly abusive treatment. On the other hand, difficult children or wimpy children might very well attract abuse through their own self-defeating behavior. *They* might therefore benefit more from personality adjustments, or the development of a little more backbone, than from a judgment in their favor.

Such charges are most likely to arise in connection with divorce custody disputes, than in the ordinary course of life. However, in a recent example, a mother brought suit against her son's kindergarten teacher and the school board, because the boy's teacher had called for a vote among his classmates on whether or not he should be kicked out of the class. The teacher's purpose was to show the boy that his bullying and disruptive behavior was making him unpopular with everyone. The mother claimed emotional abuse, petitioning for compensatory damages and the firing of the teacher. While the teacher's approach was probably unusual, and perhaps even clumsy, it was certainly much less than criminal. Moreover, the mother might better have devoted her resources to discovering the reasons for her son's antisocial behavior.

Nevertheless, as things are today, such cases can be brought, and they are not usually treated as frivolous. They presently account for a little less than one-tenth of all reported cases of child abuse.

Physical Abuse

Physical abuse, *which* accounts for about one-fifth of all child abuse reports, can also be a messy area.

Traditionally, parents have believed in spanking. More recently, others have become adamant about having corporal discipline or punishment cited as criminal physical abuse. For example, the *U.N. Study on Violence Against Children* set a target date of 2009 for the world-wide outlawing of corporal punishment, among other things, including in the home.

One way to make sure that you are wrong when you express an opinion is to insist on its being absolute. Parents and children are all different, and the ways they interact with each other depend upon widely varying relationships. What works for one family might not be the best approach for all others. Moreover, what works for one child within a family often does not work for his siblings. There are no absolutes when discussing human beings. Therefore, neither side can be right.

The U.N. study is mostly the work of independent human rights expert Paulo Sérgio Pinheiro, a retired college professor from the University of São Paulo, in Brazil, who addresses his attention to all forms of violence against children, wherever it might occur. Nobody would object to an *agenda* of creating a kinder, gentler world for children. But as a matter of common decency, children have no more right to that than adults, and as a matter of common sense, children will never be spared from the various forms of grief that Professor Pinheiro cites until all adults share the same privilege. It is silly to believe that can be accomplished simply by passing laws. Violence is the product of neurotic thinking and behavior and, so far, nobody has undertaken to cure neuroticism by making it illegal.

I the real world, it might very well be a good thing for children to experience the realities of abuse and neglect. The world has always been a dangerous place, and there is nothing to suggest that will change any time soon. It is a fine thing for an individual or a people to aspire to something better, while remembering the West African proverb often mistakenly attributed to Teddy Roosevelt:

"Speak softly and carry a big stick; you will go far." The successful person needs to know how to judge all sorts of human behavior, and to respond effectively. Raising a child in a highly sheltered and idealized environment might prove to have been the epitome of abuse and neglect after that naïve and vulnerable young person is thrust into the real world.

Sexual Abuse

Although sex abuse statistically accounts for only about a tenth of all reported cases of child abuse and neglect, the results of such allegations are probably far more damaging to both the parties involved, adult and child, than any other kind of accusation.

Sexual abuse is the easiest case to make against anyone because of our hysteria over anything having to do with sex and children, and the laws that arise from it. Child protection laws require a presumption of guilt, rather than our traditionally valued presumption of innocence. Investigations are mandatory, even if the original report comes in the form of an anonymous letter or telephone call. When cases go to court, if the allegedly abused child is willing to testify against an accused adult, the adult will almost certainly be found guilty. Even if accusations do not result in a trial, the child protection process will certainly make the accused miserable for several months. Unfortunately, it is often also very disturbing to the child involved in the allegations.

Statistics on child sexual abuse are always suspect, since they are often gathered, compiled and reported by people with an axe to grind. For example, one independent study conducted by an organization interested in the relationships between addiction and mental health determined that *male* pedophiles are typically eight-tenths of an inch shorter than average men, and attributed that to mothers who smoked during pregnancy, suggesting that mothers who smoke during pregnancy might produce sons who ultimately become sex offenders. Government statistics account only for reported cases; nobody really knows how many cases go unreported – which is likely when whatever is going on leaves no physical injury or marks.

Nevertheless, it would appear that reports usually involve children between ages eight and twelve, with the average age for boys being about ten. The adults involved are usually immediate or extended family members, else neighbors or close family friends. Only rarely are they persons unknown to the family. Once having been initiated, such relationships last an average of four years; however that probably refers to relationships that end because of intervention by someone having reported it to the police or the child protection system.

The Mythologies

By and large, pre-teen kids in our culture are treated as asexual. This does not really make any sense, because eroticism is ubiquitous in our culture. Sex is big business. Discount department stores openly offer sex toys, condoms and personal lubricants on the shelves in their pharmacy sections. R-rated movies usually have at least one scene explicitly *depicting* the act of sexual intercourse. Everybody knows that sex sells. Magazine ads and television commercials feature suggestive skin-shots and other sexually evocative content, often including children – but always with plausible deniability, of course. Primetime television programming and radio shock-jock shows abound with sexual content, often insinuated, sometimes quite explicit. Pornography abounds – a $10-billion business involving many of the nation's largest, most prestigious corporations.

The news media, also called the "infotainment business," rarely passes up an opportunity to exploit stories involving sex and children – racy *"ain't* it awful" stuff that really pumps up the ratings. Reports of adult males penetrating young girls rather quickly become hackneyed, so the stories progress to ever more titillating paradigms.

Recent headlines featured what goes on at a remote and private compound in Texas, where lecherous old polygamists impregnate multiple twelve-year old wives and groom their four-hundred young children to prepare them to carry on the tradition. Then there was the explosion of stories confirming the old suspicious cliché about the priests and their altar boys. Reversing the roles, the stories about a hot young teacher and her thirteen-year old student lover went over great, as did the one about the choir director and his twelve-year old Lolita. There was even a story about a Wisconsin farmer sexually abusing his cow!

And, of course, there are all those scary fables about the Internet being a festering pit of smut and vulgarity crawling with perverts and pedophiles, although quite often the "victims" are undercover cops, evidently having nothing better to do than play cyberspace entrapment games.

Although children are bombarded with all this background noise about sex every day, adults pretend that it all goes right over their heads, and that children have no curiosity about, knowledge of, or interest in sex. That is quite ridiculous. Kids already know a lot about sex, even without all the marketing and media hype. They always have.

The Realities

Not too long *ago*, an eleven-year old neighbor boy, quietly and with lowered voice, furtively told me, "We know a whole lot more about a whole lot more than you think we do."

That did not surprise me, since my memory is still excellent. When I was a boy, there was no television and no Internet. Radio was closely monitored by the Federal Communications Commission, and any reference to the body's private parts, sexual lovemaking, or the results thereof (e.g.; *"pregnant"*) was considered "dirty talk," which was absolutely forbidden in broadcasting. As for magazines, the best we could hope for was the occasional artistic nude, in *Photoplay* or *Popular Photography*, and even then, the pictures were always posed or touched-up so as to obscure the content a boy would be most eager to see.

In spite of my severely disadvantaged situation, I easily picked up a *rudimentary* working knowledge about sex. My sex life began at age eight. By today's paradigms, I suppose I could claim to have been molested, and more than once.

The original "perps" were an older boy and girl. We were all Coast Guard kids, the older boy and his family having recently arrived from Miami, his father having been reassigned to duty aboard the local Coast Guard icebreaker. We all lived in our own little world at a vacated World War II Coast Guard Training Camp. There were all sorts of buildings – barracks, a chow hall (the "galley"), garages, a firearms/ ammo *storage* shack, a pump house, a quartermaster's shack with mailroom, a dispensary, a PT obstacle course, and even a brig with explicit hand-drawn dirty pictures in the furthest cell towards the rear. At the time, the Coast Guard used many of the buildings for storage – ropes, buoys, helmets, life rings, brass bells, ships-bells clocks, engine room telegraphs, rifle range ammunition, tear gas capsules, all sorts of office supplies, and so on. What a great place for kids! There was not a single building that we had not been able to somehow get into.

The older boy, Buddy, talked a lot about "fucking" – daring to say that forbidden and most dirty word of all in a vulgar-sounding way that was excitingly new to me. His older sister, Betty, was a sexy, well-built redhead, and had easily hooked a new boyfriend soon after their arrival. She and the boyfriend "fucked" everywhere – in the woods, on the Training Camp's elevated boxing ring, sometimes, if the parents were not home, in their family quarters at the training camp, or his mother's third story apartment over a downtown beer tavern. Buddy and I sometimes sneakily spied on them, hoping to catch them in the act.

He told about sometimes secretly watching his parents do it, and frequently finding his mother's panties between the sheets when making the beds, *which* was his daily chore. I was more than a little jolted when he claimed that my parents "fucked" too – that all grownups did it. But then, I suspected he lied a lot; he also claimed that he had been the leader of a gang in Miami, with a henchman called "Fart Face Fowley." I doubted that was true, although I could not say for sure.

But I was pretty sure he was lying about *all grownups* "fucking." If my mother had ever heard me say that awful filthy word, she would have washed my mouth out with soap. I had never heard any grownups talking about doing that, or using that word. Even my dad never said it – well, only once in a while when he was *really* drunk and *really* angry. No, *my* parents would not do that; only us dirty Coast Guard brats.

When I found out that Buddy was "fucking" the older girl, I was a little put out. After all, I was part of the gang too. I felt like they had left me out because I was just a little kid. The truth was they had been keeping that secret from me because they were afraid I would not be able to keep my little mouth shut – that I would eventually tell on them. I would not have done that; after all, I never squealed about all the other bad stuff we had been doing. My Dad, a Coast Guard Chief, had only found out about the tear gas when we came home nearly blind, with burning red and profusely tearing eyes. But that really was not only my fault. They were throwing the capsules too and making the gas fizz into the air.

When I found out about them, the game plan changed. They decided that the best way to make sure I would not talk was to make me guilty too, so I was *forced* to become a regular participant. It did not take much force. Doing what the big kids were doing, and having them do it to me, was fun and exciting – except for the girl's frequent complaining about my immature little dick not comparing to Buddy's more manly member.

All that happened during the magical summer when I was eight, going on *nine*. Was I being molested by this pair of older kids? Maybe so, but what a wonderful memory!

I can also remember lying in bed with an older cousin when I was eleven, with him teaching me the fine art of "jacking off," as he called it. Since I had yet to experience the thrill of orgasm, I did not quite get it, but he was quite intent on teaching me everything he knew, and it did feel good. In hindsight, I expect that he was getting it off by getting it on with a younger boy there in the darkness of his bedroom. Ohmygosh! I guess I was being molested again, this time by an older, sexually mature, cousin. Be that as it may, I sure did not feel molested at the time. I felt excited and secretively dirty – and I loved every minute of those adventures!

When I was twelve, I did the same thing with Bobby, an older boy I worked with at the local country club – except that Bobby and I usually did it hidden in the broad leaves atop an elaborate grapevine covered trellis. I had yet to *develop*, so was absolutely astounded at the unbelievable size of Bobby's shaft. He was sixteen, but I saw him as just another boy – until he opened the front of his pants. Even more impressive was his shooting distance. Since I had yet to experience ejaculation, watching him was a real eye-opener! I suppose, again, that by today's standards, Bobby would qualify as a teenage gay pedophile – yet another dreaded child predator. But these outings with Bobby and his huge male member are also fond, fun and funny memories, nevertheless – all part of my coming-of-age story.

By the time I was thirteen, I had finally begun to develop, and I finally knew what it felt like to get it off. Then my mutual masturbation partner was a sixteen-year old neighborhood boy. We fooled around a lot in the reeds down by the nearby river, and in his bedroom even with his family at home downstairs. He was obsessed with the idea of me performing oral sex on him. I was not absolutely opposed to doing that since it was a really daring and forbidden thing, but I could never work up the courage. The biggest problem was that I did not like the looks of *his* package. For one thing, he was redheaded, and his "carpet matched the drapes," so to speak. Red public hair seemed revoltingly unusual and unattractive to me, for who knows what reason. But the larger problem was that he was the first boy I had ever seen who had not been circumcised. I could not stomach that at all! When he pulled the foreskin back, the head looked like gooey fresh meat – something like guts. I was not about to put anything like that into my mouth. So I passed up my big chance to learn all about oral sex. But otherwise, he and I had lots of risky, risqué, exciting and fun times together, enjoying our dirty little secrets.

No, no, no. I hardly needed to be clued in by our eleven-year old neighbor that young *boys* know a lot about sex. Gee, maybe I was just a really dirty-minded little boy with lots of dirty minded friends and relatives.

Or maybe not. Regardless of all the conventional wisdom, I assert that my experiences are probably about average. I suspect that most parents somehow *forget*, or willfully suppress, their early sexual experiences, and it never dawns on them that their children are sexual creatures until they are sixteen or older and begin unsupervised dating.

By today's standards, in any of the situations you have just read about, I would *have* been automatically declared the victim, cruelly molested by an older boy and, in that one magical summer, also an older girl. The boys probably would have been arrested and charged with child sexual abuse – and maybe the girl too.

Had that *happened*, I would have been scared to death, worrying that the law would next come down on me, knowing that I was just as guilty – but happy that, so far, I had not been found out and was not also in jail.

Then the social worker – a so-called "child protection specialist" – would have come into the picture to work me up as a cooperative witness. Lobbying me intensively about how sick these perpetrators were, how much they needed our help, and how unfortunate it was for me to have been so wrongly victimized, I would have rapidly gotten the drift. I would no doubt have quickly understood that everything would be okay for me as long as I just played along. I would not be going to jail. I would not have to live with the shame of being a dirty boy. I would indeed be protected, playing the role the system was offering; the role of the innocent and naïve kid. The role of *victim*.

I would have been dead wrong.

Informed Consent

When it comes to theoretical discussion about child sexual abuse, the operative question is one of *informed consent*. How old does a child have to be to make decisions about his personal sexual activities? I was comfortable with that from age eight, and the results of the choices I made were perfectly harmless.

But I was comfortable doing the things I did with familiar others who were not too *much* older than I. What if the others had been adults?

Society seems, until very recently at least, to have had a sliding scale with respect to informed consent. The level of alarm has varied according to the absolute age of the youngest participant, and then according to the difference in age between both participants.

An infant is obviously not physically capable of resisting or intellectually capable *of* consenting. But then how far up in age does that go? In the U.S., the *age of consent* varies from fourteen to eighteen, with most states at sixteen. Worldwide the range is from twelve to twenty-one, with the average again being about sixteen, but also with lots of conditions for special circumstances, such as the difference in ages, whether the younger member is being taken advantage of in some way, and so on.

What is so magical about the age of sixteen? The answer, of course, is, "nothing." There are plenty of people over the age of sixteen who are not *intellectually* and emotionally capable of making sensible decisions about anything, and especially about sex. By the same token, there are people much younger than sixteen who are.

After age fourteen, I had opportunities, through thinly veiled solicitations, to do the same things with a couple of adult males that I had done before with *people* closer to my own age. But I never got involved with an adult. Being sexually intimate with someone that much older, male or female, did not interest me at all; in fact, I found such suggestions pathetic, and was annoyed that they thought I might be willing. I can still remember why. All of my earlier sex playmates were friends. Those relationships developed around what we had in common intellectually and emotionally, and provided a zone of comfort and trust. The adults were not friends. I sensed that their only interest in me was erotically-based, so I would have simply been used to gratify their lust towards a sexually attractive young boy. I am not sure I would have been able to enunciate that feeling as lucidly then, but I am sure that was what I was thinking. I always refused such advances, and the adults involved never pressed.

So that raises the question: what if the sexually attracted adult had been a trusted friend?

From the time I was eleven until I was eighteen I worked all summer long for a young bachelor. He was in his early thirties, and was physically handicapped, having lost the better part of one leg to a Nazi artillery shell in WW-II. He had never married, never showed any serious interest in women, or ever acknowledged that marriage and family were options. I spent all summer, every summer, with him, working six days a week and usually fourteen hours a day. It was more like a life than a job, and I was happy to have the opportunity to spend so much time away from the home my siblings and I called "the hell hole." He also paid me very generously - $75 a week was very good pay for a boy back in the 1950's – and there were other benefits besides that, including discounts on sports merchandise and outright gifts of money and stuff.

After closing the shop at night, he and I would often go out for dinner at a fine restaurant, or to the local drive-in theater to watch a movie and dine on hotdogs. Sometimes we would go to his apartment. It was upstairs in an old converted Michigan mansion; our purpose for going there was so that I could help him carry things – usually his laundry, groceries and household supplies – up the steep and narrow back staircase that led to his small studio apartment. I would also help him arrange things, make the bed, and so on.

At the time, I do not remember ever having heard the words "homosexual" or "pedophile," and if he had any such proclivities, he never gave me any reason to suspect it. It is possible, I suppose, that he might well have had, and I was too naïve to catch any hints.

It was a much different time; a time when eligible, but unmarried men were respected as eligible bachelors, rather than suspected of being queer – a time when a companionate and mentoring relationship involving a man and a boy was considered admirable.

But, when I think back about all the private time he and I spent together, it is quite clear that with today's homophobia and hysteria about sex with children, most people would certainly have made up their minds *that* he was gay, and obviously getting his money's worth out of his cute young hireling. As a matter of fact, in today's climate, it would be foolhardy for a man to carry on such a relationship with a boy. The risk of being suspected and reported for child sexual abuse would simply be too great.

One cannot ever rewrite history, or say what might have been. But upon revisiting that long-time close relationship – one that was almost a father-son affair – with a handsome, kind and clean-cut man a little over twice my age, and considering the unhappy situation I faced at home during all *those* years, I can see how we could easily have become sexually involved. I could never be sure, of course, but I suspect that had I been confronted with that possibility, I would have found it very difficult to refuse, and might very well have become a willing partner.

Was I writing this for parents, or even the average adult audience, my next line would probably be: "Thank God that never happened!" But I am not sure that, had it happened, it would have resulted in a lifetime of shame and regret.

Ohmygod! A *sexual* relationship between and adult and a youth? That is a terrible thought! That can never be right!

Once again – when dealing with human beings, absolutes are *never* valid. People, the *situations* they find themselves in, and the relationships that develop, are far too widely variable.

Getting back to my eleven-year old neighbor boy – on second thought, he might indeed have had a point. He and his peers probably are more knowledgeable than older people suspect. At his age, I certainly had a good *working* knowledge of the physiological aspects of sex, but knew little or nothing about the feelings that would come with increasing maturity – feelings of erotic love and reptilian lust. Because that is now in plain view, whereas it was carefully concealed from children of my generation, today's kids are much more knowledgeable in that respect and are, no doubt, quite interested in putting that knowledge to use.

Our laws dealing with informed consent were written many years ago, reflecting the situation as it was understood to be at that time. Even as recently as my generation, young teenagers where I grew up were, compared to today's kids, laughably naïve about sex and eroticism. Since the law was established well before my time, by extrapolation we might assume that kids were even more clueless then. Since today's children are obviously much more comprehensively informed, it *stands* to reason that, under whatever criteria was used to set the age at sixteen several generations ago, they must now be capable of informed consent at a much earlier age.

Government abhors sexually controversial issues, and in any case, is never eager to critically revisit its acts and amend old laws to reflect contemporary realities. Laws about informed consent are therefore not likely to change any time soon. Attitudes can change, however. Things might work out much better all the way around were we to acknowledge the reality that human beings are sexual beings, beginning at birth, rather than at age sixteen or some other arbitrarily designated age. Children who grow up understanding their immature but evolving sexual nature and being expected to make responsible and age-appropriate decisions regarding its expression, would be far less vulnerable to exploitation and, as adults, might be much less apt to think of children as sex objects and potential partners. Today's hysterical paradigm throws away lives by branding adults as criminal sex offenders, and permanently damages children by subjecting them to severe emotional trauma involving overwhelming waves of guilt and shame. A more appropriate paradigm would be more understanding of unusual, but consensual, relationships, while treating non-consensual, but non-violent, episodes as inappropriate and ill-mannered, but not criminal.

"Pedophilia"

The word *pedophilia* was first found in ancient Greek poetry, referring to relationships between adolescent boys and adult men. These relationships are *thought* to have been part of a boy's education and coming-of-age process, and included erotic love, openly expressed sexually, between the man and his boy. Greeks of the time considered it normal for any man to be drawn to the beauty of a boy. Families hoped for beautiful, sexually attractive sons, since they might ultimately catch the eye of a wealthy, influential and loving mentor and patron. Men have been erotically attracted to boys down through the centuries, and in many cultures. For the ancient Greeks, man/boy relationships were not only considered an essential element in their culture and *important* to a boy's proper upbringing, but even as prestigious situations when a boy was fortunate enough to become well placed. In most of today's cultures, such relationships, assuming sex, are illegal, and "boy lovers" are objects of derision and scorn.

The concept *paedophilia erotica* as a *psychological* disorder was coined in 1886 by the Viennese psychiatrist Richard von Krafft-Ebing in his writing *Psychopathia Sexualis*. He defined the term as referring to any sexual interest toward pre-pubescent youths of either sex, 'the interest not extending beyond the first signs of pubic hair.' Today, the medical profession sees pedophilia as a mental disorder, which is characterized by a preference for, or obsession with, sexual urges towards children, whether actually acted upon, or merely existing as fantasies.

Seen as a mental disorder, research is ongoing looking for whatever it is that causes pedophilia. Current theories range from biological to psychological, but *since* no cause has as yet been determined, there is no known treatment or cure. This leads law enforcement and child protection workers to assert, without any valid evidence, that pedophilia is an incurable disease of the mind, that child-lovers are incorrigible, and unless permanently confined, will always strike again.

The Monster as Matchmaker

Nobody can say exactly what it is that makes one person see another as sexually attractive. It would appear that certain visible physical and behavioral attributes cause the mind to access memories which relate strongly and emotionally to that particular individual, tagging them as a person of interest. Obviously, this is not strictly a matter of physical *beauty* since, were that the case, there would be no hope for the plain looking or ugly. Our minds evidently develop some sort of mate selection paradigm, which is part of the evaluation process we usually refer to as "first impressions." This begins very early in childhood, perhaps initially serving friend-selection needs, but going emotionally well beyond that right from the very beginning.

I remember the first time in my life that I was very strongly attracted to someone with a desire to be something more than just friends. She was a skinny little blonde girl, who was not particularly cute, but had *mysteriously* captured my heart. That happened even though I had never spoken to her, and I understood that she was way out of my class – she came from a prominent and affluent family, was smart and always well groomed – I was a poor boy, dumb, usually in need of a haircut, and dressed in plain and practical clothes, homemade or mail order from Montgomery-Ward. She sat far away, on the opposite side of our *first-grade* classroom. That's right; we were only six!

Six years later I fell in love again – this time for real and this time very painfully – with a farm girl who was an absolute little snot. She went out of her way to ignore me, refusing to even so much as acknowledge that I existed. *She* and I were only twelve, but she had a fourteen-year old boyfriend who made love to her under an overturned rowboat down on the rocky Lake Michigan beach near their farm. When her younger brother told me that, I was heartbroken and devastated! I wanted to trade places with that boy so badly that I could think of nothing else. I poured my heart out in love letters that were terribly mushy and as suggestive as I dared be, and which I suspect her parents intercepted and disgustedly discarded without her ever seeing them. I was critically ill with love-sickness; I wanted to die! She too was blonde, but this time a shapely and energetic "five-foot-two, eyes of blue" nature girl type. She had totally captured my heart, in spite of treating me like crap. In reality, I barely knew her.

Even after all these years, I have no idea why I was so strongly attracted to these particular girls.

Again, it is not just a matter of physical beauty; that is an advantage, of course, since it works to catch one's eye and gets the first impression thing off to a *good* start. However, you have probably already had the experience of being turned off by a beautiful person the moment they opened their mouth. Others whose physical appearance is not so eye-catching are apt to enjoy an opposite result. Although they do not quickly hook your attention because of their good looks, they quickly grow on you as you become more familiar with their other qualities. Either way, everyone seems to put out vibes of some sort which some other person is bound to favorably receive. Regardless of your physical beauty, or lack thereof, there will be some who will think you are the greatest thing since sliced bread.

My guess is that over time, the mind builds within itself an array of weighted images relating to all the physical, behavioral, emotional and intellectual attributes it has thus far experienced. Images that evolve in conjunction with pleasant experiences are thereafter recognized by the *mind* as good, and vice versa. When you meet a stranger, your mind scores as much of the package it can see, or sense, against these mental models, and if that overall score happens to exceed a certain threshold it has somehow conjured up for itself, it singles out that person for special attention. If the same thing happens in the other person's mind, a relationship is seeded.

The process then continues with increasing depth as the two of you come to know each other better, and to the extent that the scores continue to build on the positive side of your mutual lines of good/bad discrimination, an increasingly stronger friendship will develop – perhaps *proceeding* all the way up to a love affair and a permanent life partnership.

The mental imagery is not only rated "favorable" and "unfavorable," but is also weighted, such that some aspects have a much heavier impact upon *the* score than others. It is often said that, "If you like a person, they can do no wrong; if you do not like a person, they can do no right." That is not absolutely true, of course, but the saying does reveal that practical people recognize that relationships are not the product of rational thinking. The saying suggests that when our mental rating system perceives some very high positive hits in the presence of only a few slightly negative aspects, the resulting score will be so highly positive that the negative aspects become negligible.

Experience and common sense teach us that this is actually relative. The higher the *positives*, the more negligible the negatives, until one encounters the situation of lovers, who apparently become totally oblivious to each other's flaws and shortcomings – "… Love is blind …" wrote William Shakespeare in his classic play, *The Merchant of Venice*.

So here we are again, right at the heart of Cognitive Behavior Theory. The images the mind draws upon to size up others are cognitions – things it thinks it knows as a result of previous experience through perception, reasoning, or intuition. As CBT teaches, cognitions are most often *formed* subconsciously, and are not automatically tested for validity or reasonableness, either at that moment or later. Many of them are therefore screwy.

For example, as a boy I had somehow gotten the idea that smallish, blue-eyed blond girls were superior to any other girls. I have gotten over that. On the other hand, I have never been a "tit man." Unlike the stereotypical male, I actually find big boobs to be ridiculously useless appendages and repulsively cow-like except, of course, when found on nursing mothers. I cannot imagine why I would think that; perhaps as a baby I sometimes felt smothered when nursing and developed a fear of the tit. Who knows?

Until we learn a lot more about the mind, we will have to satisfy ourselves with answers like this. That means we also have to accept the apparent *reality* that this function of the mind, although subject to rational review, is ordinarily not under conscious control.

From this perspective, you can understand that human beings always size others up as prospective companions, ranging from friends to mates. That process involves all sorts of physical, emotional and sexual criteria, unconsciously dredged up from the depths of the mind as imagery which represents what the mind believes to be good and bad. The objects of such attention include children, and it is not unusual for adults to encounter children whom the mind identifies very favorably. Adults know this from their own experience in life, and from literature passed down through the ages. Part of this is quite natural; children are often very pretty, or physically attractive in some other ways that rapidly catch the eye. We acknowledge these feelings with comments like, "Gee, what a darling child!" or "What a fine-looking young man!"

The line between physically attractive and sexually attractive is very fine indeed, and is obscured by a muddle of emotion. It is very easy to cross the line into what is currently generally considered forbidden territory. When adults find themselves obsessively attracted to adolescents or younger children – when their feelings go beyond simply noticing that certain youths are physically and sexually attractive, to emotional urges focused upon such children, I suspect this is just another manifestation of the rampant neuroticism that affects everything else in life. Such feelings do not indicate that they are suffering from "pedophilia" or any other specialized mental or emotional disorder, which explains why researchers cannot discover a cause or a cure.

The children involved are usually pre-teens, suggesting a possible connection to archaic memories of the sublime sexual excitement we all experience during that time of life, while on the verge of becoming sexually capable adults. On the other hand, the focus of such interest is sometimes much younger, but that does not seem surprising either, given our understanding of CBT, and my assumptions about how that figures into the way our relationships with others come about.

Researchers tell us that an incredibly rich emotional life is what distinguishes human beings from other animals, and which is largely responsible for our success as a species. When they characterize human emotional development, the sequence is quite well defined from infancy into *the* middle childhood years, but after that their descriptions of the process become increasingly generalized and fuzzy. Their assumption is that, in any case, the process ends in young adulthood, with all the emotional skills and abilities needed to independently and effectively cope with life then being in place.

Observation and common sense teaches us that under normal circumstances, the images, or cognitions, that regulate the development and growth of one's relationships ordinarily change in tandem with emotional growth. Thus, throughout your childhood, your interests were narrowly focused upon your peers. As you become more emotionally mature, the scope of your interest will broaden. Thus, as a first-grader, a kindergartener seemed like a baby, and a second-grader, much too old. But at eighteen, your interests are likely to include people from fourteen to the early twenties.

The development process that changes us from children into adults levels off as our teenage years come to an end, and so does our emotional development. Somewhere in our mid-twenties, the process is finally completed, *and* we are supposedly a finished product – a full-fledged adult. Within the adult universe, emotional intelligence is no longer proportional to age, so we are emotionally compatible with most other adults, and age is no longer a determining factor when choosing friends and lovers.

However, experience in real life also teaches us that human beings vary widely within a normal distribution. While the vast majority will be found at or near the center of the curve, or "the normal," a small number of others will be far out on one extreme or the other. Thus, emotional intelligence does not always track intellectual intelligence and physiological development, so we occasionally encounter children who are eight, going on twenty-nine, and adults who are twenty-eight, going on nine. We call the former a prodigy, and the latter, a Peter Pan. In my experience, the curve seems to be highly skewed towards the Peter Pan side.

It seems like there is always at least one boy in everyone's coming-of-age experience who is not comfortable with boys his own age, and seeks out the companionship of younger children. As he increases in age, he seems to keep falling further and further behind emotionally, until as a young adult, his preferences have only caught up to his late childhood or early teen years.

I grew up with one such boy, who married a much younger girl and had a couple of children, but was not able to grow out of his preference for younger companions. His marriage did not last, and because of his companionships with boys in their early teens, it was whispered that he was a boy lover. Most people assumed that included sexual relations with the young boys although, to my knowledge, no such *accusations* were ever formally made. That situation continued well into his adult life, evidently ending about the time he became a grandfather. Today, his friends and companions are all what everyone would consider age-appropriate, and he appears to have become the most wonderfully loving and generous grandfather a boy could hope to have. Thus we might say that as far as his relationships were concerned, his emotional growth was slowed and fell behind, but did eventually catch up, moving into the "normal" range.

In another case, during his pre-teen and early teen years, another boy gained a reputation among the younger neighborhood boys for compulsively finding opportunities to show them his dick, with most agreeing that he was quite well hung. He finally wound up serving three years in the state prison for exposing himself to a five-year old boy. Nothing has been heard of him since, but being slim, blonde, boyishly cute, and somewhat simple-minded, his sentencing was probably well received by some old lifers in the state prison.

Normal people experience all sorts of sexual fetishes during their adult lives – *obsessions* with unusual possibilities for experiencing sexual excitement. Since these obsessions are kinky at best, but more often closer to what others would publicly declare as filthy, taboo, or even macabre, they are kept secret.

Such fetishes often involve children. Adults, at any level of emotional maturity, *understand* that such interests are popularly considered inappropriate, to the extent that actual sexual involvements are forbidden by law. The prudent therefore limit the satisfaction of such obsessions to secret flights of fantasy, since you can't go to jail for what you're thinking. The more daring, however, find sources of sexually explicit texts, photographs and videos featuring children. Those obsessed to the point of reckless attempt actual encounters.

When adults attempt to turn their sex fantasies into realities, most discover that the realities are, at best, much less erotically stimulating or sexually *satisfying* than they had hoped and, at worst, are regrettable and sometimes even revolting. This is especially likely when a fetish-driven adult attempts a sexual encounter with a child, because the fantasy attributes adult-level eroticism to the virtual child, which the real child does not yet possess. The real child therefore reacts much differently than the virtual child in the fantasy, and the episode turns out to be a huge bummer for both.

Nevertheless, successful adult-child relationships can and do develop, and are often carried on for a long time. There are probably a lot of different reasons for a child and an adult to become sexually involved. Contrary to popular stereotypes, which choose to depict the children as asexual, exploited, and victimized by sexually depraved adults, common sense would suggest otherwise. An adult who is acting purely out of fetish-driven lust would most likely find the experience unsatisfying, as suggested above. That there are usually emotional needs being met on both sides – such as the need to be loved and respected, to be needed and wanted, and to be intimately close to another human soul – is evidenced by the facts that (1) the relationship is continued successfully, and (2) that kids do not usually tell, unless they have some ulterior motive – such as becoming angry or resentful towards their adult partner, or having been found out.

A More Rational Paradigm

After years of observation and contemplation, my conclusion is that there is little *intrinsic* wrong in such relationships when they do occur. Consensual sexual activity is no more physically harmful to children than it is to adults. The real harm, to both the children the adults, is emotional. That harm results from our cultural attitudes, and the taboos they engender, which have given rise to laws, notably our so-called "child protection" acts.

The wrong falls on the child protection side of the picture, which is truly more predatory *than* the sexual predators it is bent on exposing and jailing. When the result of such investigations and prosecutions include emotional trauma for the child and the destruction of families, it is impossible to argue that it is all for the good of children.

A couple of thousand years ago, the Jews of our religious ancestry had all sorts of attitudes, taboos and laws regarding ritual purity, most of which have long since been discarded. Nevertheless, back then they provided plenty of grief for a lot of Jews who were otherwise innocent and decent people – even for Jesus of Nazareth, who was seen as the *baseborn* progeny of an illicit sexual relationship. History will someday teach that this is essentially our situation today with respect to our ideas about child sexual abuse – much ado about nothing, fostered by subjective moral and religious opinions which cannot be objectively substantiated, but which go unchallenged because of an overwhelming fear of stigmatization, or even retribution.

We have laws that deal with assault, forcible rape, and various shades of homicide, and they apply regardless of the victim's age. Do we really need to single out children as a special class of victims?

If a child is coerced, or talked into engaging in sexual activity with an adult, and is not happy with the result, perhaps that would better be dismissed as a learning experience. As we grow up, it seems that there are lots of *things* we have to learn the hard way, and that often involves our having been taken advantage of. Such experiences are embarrassing; nobody enjoys being made a fool of. But they are also very effective as a quick way to replace naiveté with wisdom.

And what if it turns out that the child has no complaints? Who can rightfully intervene claiming that if they have no complaint, they should, or if they do not at the moment, they certainly will sometime later in life. *This* is not necessarily true. It cannot be repeated often enough: when talking about human beings, there are no absolutes. By that principle alone, there must be at least some sexual relations between adults and children that are harmless or even emotionally beneficial to those involved.

It is probably difficult for most people to imagine how a relationship between a middle-aged adult and a ten or twelve year old child could be meaningful and pleasant for either, although such relationships sometimes obviously are. But what if the child is a fifteen-year old girl, and the adult, her eighteen or nineteen-year old boyfriend? These relationships are much easier to relate to and accept. But in fact, this is the situation in many actual prosecutions, and the boyfriend wrongfully winds up on the sex offender registry and branded for life.

I am not sure that children are so valuable as to merit protection at any cost, or so innocent and helpless that in cases such as these, victimization must always be presumed. Be that as it might, our way of looking at *this* reality of life is clearly counterproductive. In my experience, I have never seen a child protection prosecution that actually produced a "happy ever after" situation for the child. By rendering permanent damage to children's egos and destroying their families, our child protection systems are actually child destructive.

From this point of view, the children really *are* the victims. Unfortunately, the child protection system is so firmly entrenched, with so many having a vested financial interest in what has been described as "the child protection industry," I am sure that it will take a long time for reason to prevail. And so it will be up to you and your generation to finally rid our society of this hysteria, this modern witch hunt, and replace it with attitudes that are more rational. I predict that the millions of children who have been victimized by the child protection system in my generation will, in your generation, come together as the driving force that will ultimately bring this to pass.

CPS Realities

If you have been forcibly raped, or beaten to the point of suffering bodily injury, the first consideration is that nobody, neither child nor adult, should suffer that kind of abuse, and nobody in their right mind ever administers such abuse.

Fear mongering to the contrary, perpetrators are rarely strangers, are not insane, and are not afflicted with permanent psycho-emotional aberrations such as "pedophilia." They are merely neurotic, but to the point of having lost control of themselves emotionally and/or erotically. Regardless of the particular circumstances of your situation, they need help to regain control, and in the meantime, you need help to keep you out of harm's way.

Since it is more than likely that the perpetrator will be a member of your immediate or extended family, or a close friend of your family, it will be in your best interest to seek assistance from someone without a vested interest. Go to a competent family law attorney immediately and explain your situation. Attorneys never charge a fee for the first visit. If you are under the *age of majority*, the lawyer will not be able to represent you without the consent of your parent or legal guardian, or assignment by a court.

Unless you or another person is in dire immediate danger, that "someone" should not be the police. Nor should it be any professional other *than* a lawyer, because most professionals – ministers, teachers, school counselors, and doctors – are required by law to invoke the child protection process by reporting their suspicions to the police or the state's child protection agency.

Once such a report is received, child protective services are required to launch an immediate investigation. That usually begins with an attempt to *privately* interview the child or children in question. If school is in session, a CPS worker will show up at the school, probably accompanied by a police officer, and ask to see you privately. School personnel are required to grant access to you; they are also required to then immediately notify your parents or guardians, but usually do not. You should know that if approached in this matter, you are not required to cooperate, or say anything. Even if you feel that you have nothing to say because the accusations are groundless, you should remain silent until having discussed the matter with a lawyer. This will require a lot of courage on your part, because CPS investigators are experts at getting people to talk, and the situation, including the presence of a uniformed police officer is made to be intentionally intimidating. Nevertheless, you need say nothing more than state that you will have nothing to say until you have had an opportunity to speak with an attorney.

Regardless of the usual sales pitch, the primary focus of the child protection process will be on the accused perpetrator, rather than the victim. Most of *the* effort is directed towards arresting and prosecuting violators. That is rarely ever in that adult's best interest, and if that adult is someone close to you or your family, as most are, it will very likely prove not in your long-term interest either.

You should understand that once into the child protection process, the matter will be out of your hands. What you think about your ability or your right to make informed decisions for yourself, or whether criminal charges should be filed, will not really make any difference. Your state government has already done your thinking for you. Were you to formally assert, for example, that sex with the adult was all your idea; that you got them drunk and high on weed to break down their natural inhibitions so you could have your way with them – it would not make any difference. The adult would still be prosecuted, found guilty and sentenced. The law makes no allowances for consent on the part of a child. You might be lip-lashed or required to undergo some counseling, but you would otherwise walk away free.

As suggested above, if you become involved in such a prosecution, you will be in the position of being able to make or break the case. If you are willing to testify that the defendant did indeed do the things the prosecutor has charged, guilty or not, the accused will simply be screwed. There is almost no way for a defendant to refute such testimony when a child is willing to take the stand and willingly support the prosecution's case. On the other hand, should you absolutely refuse to cooperate, and there are no other alleged victims or anyone else able to offer any credible, first-hand testimony, the judge will have little choice but to dismiss the case.

From this you can see that if you become involved in such a case, you will be highly pressured by the prosecution to cooperate, and CPS *workers* will be very keen on bringing you around. CPS workers are specially trained in what has been called by the late Richard A Gardner, professor of psychiatry at Columbia University "the progressive elaboration of the accusations."

For example, a case involving a small child at the center of a vicious custody dispute might begin with the father's being accused of touching the child's genitals while bathing him. Although the child initially cannot remember such an incident and has no complaint, with the coaching of CPS workers and prosecutors they are helped to "remember" that particular episode, and then even provide new and ever more dramatic material as time goes on. For example, the intensive interrogation itself becomes a real eye-opener for the child, introducing him to *concepts* he had never before known. And then, in a sick parody of Lewis Carroll's Queen of Hearts from *Alice's Adventures in Wonderland*, the prosecution proposes that the allegations must be true – how else would the child know about all these nasty things! In this way, even those who were never molested can be seduced into corroborating such abuse. Even if having second thoughts after having made their statements, children recognize that recanting will involve stiff rejection from the professionals, who will have made it clear that denial will result in significant criticism and even public humiliation. At that point it is easier to go along with the prosecution than stand up and tell the truth.

In his book *Sex Abuse Hysteria ~ Salem Witch Trials Revisited*, Dr. Gardner wrote –

> "Although children who have been genuinely abused have certainly been victimized, those who have been subjected to the kinds of interrogations and validations described (in his book) have also been victimized. In both cases their innocence and naiveté have enabled exploiters to use them for their own personal ends. It is safe to say that both forms of victimization can result in lifelong psychological damage; but it is difficult to know which type produces more trauma ... many of these children will forever believe that they were sexually abused and some will become psychotic. If my predictions prove true, then these victims of false accusations will probably end up more traumatized ... than those who have been genuinely abused."

This is why I strongly suggest that if you feel you are a victim of child abuse, and there is *no* imminent danger of physical abuse to you or anyone else, you should seek the help of an attorney first. It might be very difficult for you to feel any compassionate concern for the person who meted out the abuse, or perhaps even for your family, at a time when the hurt and hateful feelings are still fresh. But taking this approach will most likely prove to be not only in your family's best interests, but also in your own, if it ultimately protects you from the psychological abuse described above.

It is a fact that few families survive such cases. Divorce and a breakup of the family is the usual outcome when criminal charges are filed, regardless of whether the case ever actually goes to trial, or of the verdict if it does. A big part of that can be attributed to the process that comes into play under the child protection and victims' rights laws, but it also results from public sentiments arising from the commonly held attitude that regardless of the outcome, the fact that accusations were made and charges were brought is proof that something must have happened – "where there is smoke, there is fire."

Preserving Your Family

Even when accusations are true, and people have been hurtfully abused, individuals can change, relationships can recover, and families can go on happily into a future together. This is what you will be trying to achieve by soliciting the help of an attorney before reporting such matters to anyone else. It is almost never the outcome once the Child Protection Act is invoked and that process runs its course. That should therefore be your last recourse.

In the heat of a crisis, you might not feel very charitable towards people who have selfishly taken advantage of, or meanly hurt, you or someone else. In such situations, it is human nature for one's thoughts to turn first to pay backs. Others will also probably be advising that you need to be tough on those whom you feel are to blame – that they need to be punished or "helped." At such times, you will need to find the strength of character to rise above all this and think about the long-term. Two popular American proverbs apply.

The first is this: "There, but for the grace of God go I." We have already talked a little bit about human fallibility, and there will be more on that in Chapter 11. In a nutshell, nobody is perfect – *nobody*. The day may come when you too will find yourself in a tight spot; in fact, that is not only possible, it is quite probable. In that day, you will be no more of a villain – no more sick or evil – than those whom you feel have wronged you.

I have never known a person who was wicked, evil or no good. I suppose they exist, but in my sixty-seven years, I have yet to meet anybody like that. When well-meaning, but imperfect, people err, causing unhappiness, harm or injury to others, pay-backs are never an appropriate response. Maybe your Grandma has told you, "Two wrongs never make a right." Revenge never fixes anything, or helps victims feel better. In fact, as the product of hate, revenge only contributes to the erosion of one's own self-esteem.

When police, prosecutors or CPS workers attempt to proposition you with the assertion that an accused person needs help, what they usually have in mind is arrest, prosecution and sentencing. In Michigan and most other states, we still refer to the prison system as the Department of Corrections. But since the advent of get-tough-on-crime politics in our country, "corrections" is out; punishment is in. With increasingly harsh sentencing, our prisons have become warehouses for throw-away offenders. When it comes to sex offenders, the concept of paying one's debt to society and having a chance to start over with a clean slate, has been totally dispensed with. Once convicted on a sex charge, the punishment goes on forever; beginning with a prison sentence, then having to live as a registered sex offender, which results in permanent disgrace, the severe limiting of one's opportunities, and being continually suspect and closely watched.

No religion condones this kind of treatment, and neither does our U.S. Constitution, which prohibits cruel and unusual punishment. Such mistakes are invariably the result of neuroticism, and the self-defeating thinking and behavior that spring from it – a common condition in our culture, and one that is correctable. If there is indeed any evil, it is in the hearts of those who condone a system that seeks to permanently destroy persons for having made a mistake.

The second operative proverb is this: "Time heals all wounds." As unlikely as it might seem during a crisis, and as earnestly as you might wish to hate, you can be sure the bad feelings will not last. Hateful feelings never flourish unless continually nourished. People usually choose happiness over hatefulness, hence the truth of the proverb.

Successful marriages are good examples. The key to remaining married is to keep the original vows in mind – "for better, and for worse." During any marriage, there are lots of "for worse" times; times when husbands and wives hate each other just as passionately as they, at other times, love each other. Although the problems that cause the bad times are often dire and always seem insurmountable, they never really are if partners do not want them to be. If they can avoid the urge to impulsively destroy each other through divorce, the fire that was there when the vows were made will rekindle, causing the problems to melt away. Things can work out because people always learn from mistakes that make them unhappy, and are motivated to change as needed to prevent such unhappy situations from happening again. It just takes time.

Safe Sex

This is not about STD's or unwanted pregnancies. It is about keeping you out of prison and off the black list – the sex offender registry.

You are far more vulnerable than you think, especially when you come of age. Once you are at or above the age of majority – the age at which the law considers you to be an adult, which is eighteen for boys in most states – anyone who wants to cause you a lot of misery need only pick up the phone, call the police or the child protection service in your state, and accuse you of sexually molesting someone under the age of consent. If the underage person wishes to cooperate, you will be found guilty as charged, even if there is no truth to the charges whatsoever and you are perfectly innocent.

The reason is this; child protection laws reverse the principles we have always believed were there to protect us from just this kind of unfair prosecution. The child protection law requires that you be considered guilty until you can prove yourself innocent. Your accusers do not need to prove that you did what they alleged; the law requires a presumption that they are telling the truth. You will be required to prove that you did not do what you are being accused of. That puts you in the position of having to prove a negative, which can be very difficult to do, especially if there are circumstances that can support the allegations – such as a close relationship between you and the alleged victim, ample opportunity for you to have committed the offense, and so on.

Furthermore, the credible testimony of a child in such cases always trumps that of an adult, and the younger the child the better. If a child is willing to testify against you and is able to utter a marginally believable story, you had better be able to prove that you were hundreds of miles away at the time, in jail, or in traction on a hospital bed. Else you will very likely be going to prison.

Of course, you are a boy, and in your teenage years you will frequently become horny as a housecat. Whether it is politically correct or not, boys will be boys, and you might very likely find yourself playing around with other boys, including younger boys. If you are all under age, your vulnerability might be lessened somewhat. On the other hand, where there is a large age difference – say you at fourteen or fifteen with a boy of eight or ten – prosecutors have gotten into the nasty habit of getting their backs up in righteous indignation, and convincing courts to try minors as adults.

If you must mess around, your partners had better be close friends who are not likely to rat you out. Mutually assured destruction, "MAD," is a much better strategy. You had better have something on your young consensual partners, their parents, or someone else close to them that will assure against their attempting to use the child protection system against you. A certain amount of hanky-panky is common in any family, and behaviors that families usually feel are innocent fun are often deemed inappropriate and suspicious *grooming* by child protection people. Talk things over with anyone you might be involved with sexually and arrange for your mutual protection by sharing family secrets, making the purpose clear: that what goes around, will come around.

Threats of violence are, of course, totally inappropriate. That strategy usually does not work, and the fact of having made such threats will certainly work against you should you find yourself charged under the Child Protection Act.

A lot of people will go right through the roof when they read that advice. However, this is reality. Boys *will* be boys, and that is not criminal. The law makes no allowances, however. Under the law, "boys will be boys" is always inappropriate and, if at all possible, a criminal matter. If you have the unhappy experience of being charged, the prosecution will have only one thing in mind, and that will be to win a conviction. Regardless of what you might be told in an effort to dupe or bully you into cooperating with your own prosecution, they will not be out to do you any favors. Your best defense is always an aggressive offense. You will need to become as tough and mean as those who are trying to destroy you.

I agree: it is a real shame that this is what our system has come to. But it is what it is, at least for the time being. You can only win the game if you play by your opponents' rules, not according to your own concepts of fairness and decency, or the way you think the justice system should work.

Setups

Another very common threat to boys involves girlfriends who set them up. These are sometimes girls who wish to escape from unhappy families, and intentionally attempt to get pregnant so that their boyfriend will then have to marry them, and they will then live happily ever after. In other situations, an insecure girl decides that the best way to capture and hang onto the boy of her dreams is to get into his pants and have him knock her up. Worst of all is the risk of a girl who is already pregnant by a boy who refuses, or whose parents will not permit, to marry her, so urgently goes after someone else, anyone else!

You and I both know that if some girl who, to your mind, is anything less than totally repulsive unzips you pants and begins playing with what is inside, you will soon be under her spell.

Boys and young men are usually egoistic, so they are more likely to believe that they screwed the girl, rather than admit that it was actually the other way around.

I once hired a nice young eighteen-year old kid, just because he was a nice young kid. He was gentle, good natured, very good looking, and I really liked him. His father had died when he was little so, for a while, I became sort of a father figure to him. One late afternoon he seemed reluctant to leave after work and when I asked why – what the problem was – he sadly spilled the beans that *he* had gotten his girlfriend pregnant, had no idea what to do, felt terribly guilty, and was ashamed to face his mother and the girl's parents. I already knew that was not exactly true. A young female employee in my group had already told me that the boy's girlfriend had, several weeks before, told a mutual friend that she intended to make this boy hers, and was going to lay him as many times as it took until she got pregnant. It was a setup, pure and simple. I did not have the heart to tell him that, so shared other realities instead – that shotgun weddings are far more common than most people like to admit, and often turn into lasting marriages – that he had nothing to be ashamed about if he really loved the girl, and so on.

Shotgun marriages are in fact very common. That only makes sense. When people are in love, lovemaking is all but inevitable. In fact, I have always thought that those who claim to be in love but are able to practice abstinence are not really in love at all.

The risk for young boys is that, contrary to common belief, girls usually have the upper hand in such situations. Most boys can very quickly and easily be brought to a very high level of sexual excitement, and will then be powerfully motivated to do the wild thing, whether there is any love involved or not. Even if a boy has enough character and will power to hesitate, a girl need only question his manliness by inferring that he is afraid to be a man. It is very difficult for a boy to put it back in his pants and walk away fearing that others will hear that he had a chance to get some, but chickened out.

The vulnerabilities are two.

First, you might get roped into a marriage that turns out to be miserable. That is almost guaranteed if you marry a girl because you think you got her pregnant, and were never really in love.

Second, and worse, you might refuse to marry a girl who claims you are the father of her unborn child. If the girl is under the age of consent, and you are over the age of majority, you will automatically become eligible for rape charges. Your only recourse then is to marry the girl, else deny you ever touched her and hope that DNA testing proves that the baby is not yours.

If you agree to marry your underage sweetheart, the law will usually be willing to look the other way and keep hands off, so that is the quick way out. However, it is usually not the best way out for two immature teenagers and their little baby. As hard as such decisions are, biting the bullets and arranging for an early abortion or subsequent adoption is almost always a better choice.

A smart boy should know how to avoid a setup.

Smart teenage girls are usually more mature than boys several years their age, and are apt to be more interested in a secure future, than in a quick solution to an immediate problem. If a girl is too eager or too easy, you should wonder why.

Boys and girls are sexually quite different. Boys become aroused suddenly, and become dis-aroused just as suddenly – especially young boys. A boy's level of sexual arousal collapses immediately upon ejaculation, and unless doped up on Viagra (or watermelon), he will remain sexually disinterested and incapable for at least an hour or so. A smart girl understands how boys work, and can easily avoid intercourse, if she wants to, by forcing ejaculation before things come to that, either by masturbating the boy or servicing him orally. A girl whom you are not really in love with, but who insists on intercourse, might have something more in mind than a quick roll in the hay.

Help for CPS Advocates

Those who object most trenchantly to criticisms of the child protection system are usually people who have already been victimized by it during the prosecution of someone accused of criminal sexual conduct. Having been used and abused by the system in its attempt to prosecute the accused perpetrator, victims are then abandoned and left to somehow cope with the huge burden of guilt and shame that it dumped upon them.

Most cases of child sexual abuse do not involve forcible rape or psychological coercion. Instead, most involve accusations of non-violent molestation, where the victim does in fact actively or passively consent. When such accusations are actually untrue, very young victims often find it difficult to convince professionals that nothing ever actually happened, and are eventually duped into cooperating with the prosecution. Where there actually was sexual contact, victims are often willing participants, else were not moved to object strenuously enough to activities they were not comfortable with, found distasteful or knew to be wrong. For such "designated victims", truths of this nature carry with them an inescapable feeling of culpability.

Furthermore, such cases are usually instigated by a third party; kids usually do not tell unless found out or they become angry and vindictive for some reason. Keeping the secret reinforces the inner sense of complicity that arises from not having adamantly refused to participate, or having actually been willingly involved.

When disaster strikes and the relationship is declared criminal, with all the blame heaped upon the other party, kids will usually accept the role of victim, in an attempt to salvage what they can of their self-esteem and reputation. But no amount of persuasion can ever really make them truly accept that they bore no responsibility, and that none of what happened was their fault.

Most often, the other party is a close family friend, relative, sibling, or parent – someone the child and other family members loves and often depend upon. Permitting outsiders to heap all the blame on that person further reinforces the child's feelings of guilt and shame. Meanwhile, resentful family members and friends exacerbate that by distancing themselves, hinting at blame and fault, or by being openly antagonistic and accusatory.

Most young people are not emotionally capable of coping with such a dilemma effectively. Few will be equipped to appraise the intimate relationship philosophically, and judge the child protection system objectively. The choices therefore become limited to two, both of which are neurotically self-defeating. On the one hand, they can choose to give in to their conscience, accepting that they are just as responsible for what happened as the prosecuted adult, but are even worse for having eagerly accepted the victimization lie to save their own hide, while permitting their partner to be savaged. The other choice is denial; to suppress their feelings of culpability by accepting everything professionals have been trying to sell them about their being too young to be responsible in any way, the other person being a sick sexual predator, and so on. This choice almost always engenders a compulsion in later life to zealously promote the witch hunt as a means of continually justifying a choice their heart knows to be wrong. Thus, former victims sometimes become the most notorious scaremongers, suggesting that sexual predators lurk wherever children play. They often become the most earnest advocates for the child protection system and the harshest possible sentences for convicted offenders.

Chapter 9: Abuse & Neglect

If this describes you, there are three good reasons for you to change your mind.

First, guilt and shame can never be successfully suppressed by denial. If you feel bad about having been duped into cooperating with the child protection system, that is fine. You should. However, we all make lots of mistakes in life, and that will probably not be your last. Punishing yourself forever will not change anything for you, the person prosecuted, or anyone else. Accept your regrets, make your apologies and whatever reparations you can, then move on.

If you feel bad about having willingly engaged in sex with an older partner, or for not having prevented that from happening, those feelings are not necessarily valid. Were it not for the fact that you were underage, what was going on between the two of you would have been nobody else's business. Such relationships usually do not just happen out of the blue, but rather because they fulfill needs. Think about what you were getting out of it, what was in it for the other person, and what harm was actually done, beyond the emotional harm you suffered from the matter having come to the attention of others. Perhaps for you it was just exciting and fun, or perhaps you gained from it feelings of closeness, affection and being needed that were otherwise missing in your life, or perhaps it just felt right to be submissive and give pleasure to someone you loved, and who was very important to you. You might decide to regret it ever happened, but otherwise conclude that you really have no reason to feel terribly ashamed and guilty.

Second, as you probably learned from your experience, the child protection process did not actually help anyone involved. It left you emotionally damaged, and your partner permanently stigmatized. In helping to perpetuate the hysteria about child sexual abuse and advocating for the child protection system, you are helping to visit the same unfortunate outcomes on others. Whether or not you can admit that, you cannot lie to your heart. Deep down inside, perhaps quite subconsciously, you will sense that what you are doing is falsely and hypocritically ingenuous. Your bad feelings therefore will continue to accumulate, driving you to become ever more extreme and confrontational – and miserable. Thus your behavior is classically neurotic and self-defeating.

Finally, I believe that non-violent sexual relations between children and adults should be considered unusual and inappropriate, but not criminal. When children are willingly or passively accepting of sexual attentions, it is likely the result of their being deprived of the kind of attention and affection that every child deserves and needs in order to become an emotionally healthy human being. When a person of age engages in a sexual relationship with one who is not of age, the probable cause is their neurotically retarded emotional growth, which renders them more comfortable and confident when interacting intimately with a child, than with a more mature person. Both situations can usually be fixed by recognizing them for what they are, making the appropriate adjustments for the child, and helping the adult to develop missing emotional skills. Moreover, these voluntary fixes can usually be achieved more rapidly and much less expensively than anything achievable through the coercive and punitive child protection system, which almost never produces a happy outcome.

If you are in need of a cause to justify yourself, would it not be better to work towards helping emotionally deprived children get the love and attention they deserve, and emotionally immature adults catch up to where they had ought to be? The rewards of seeing people succeed in these ways will easily eclipse any satisfaction you might experience from exposing and securing the conviction of a so-called sexual predator.

Chapter 9: Abuse & Neglect

Conclusion

It seems ironic: eroticism, sensuality and venery bring some of life's greatest pleasures, yet are responsible for the largest share of human suffering and unhappiness. The fact is, of course, that the bad things result when our neurotically risqué or over-the-top sexual thinking or behavior endangers someone else, or collides with society's neurotically driven attitudes about sexuality and sexual relations.

To the extent that you can break the habit of neuroticism and replace it with rational thinking and behavior, your chances of becoming involved in sex-related problems and prosecutions will diminish.

Chapter 10
Depression & Suicide

One of the worst bad habits of all is depression. As usual, there are all sorts of theories about the causes of depression. Mine is that depression is the pain that results from beating yourself up by stubbornly insisting that things have to be the way you wish they were, rather than the way they are.

I come by this opinion honestly, as a result of my personal experiences with depression. My childhood, from age four to the time I finally left home at age eighteen, was far from idyllic. In fact, it mostly sucked. We still refer to our childhood home as "the hell hole." I have written more about that elsewhere; here I need only explain that I grew up thinking our family was shamefully terrible, that it was the only one in the world like that, that I deserved better, and that someday it would all change for the better – we would all be nice, well adjusted, perfectly happy people, just like the idealized families portrayed on the old *Donna Reed Show*, or *The Walton's*. What was worse was that I let that bad situation become defining of me, and in the back of my mind I had the sense that I could never be happy or amount to anything until my dysfunctional family got all straightened out. That involved six other screwed up people – a father, a mother, two sisters and two brothers – so, of course, that was not likely to ever happen.

My bouts with depression began somewhere very early in my teenage years. As also mentioned elsewhere, I often thought of suicide, and even made several attempts to go through with it, but never had the guts to complete the process. While in the Air Force, I would often get off work on Saturday mornings, sack out in the barracks, and stay that way until it was time to go back to work the next Monday afternoon. Depression is a treacherous thing, maybe somewhat like drowning. They say a person who is drowning, once they get past a certain point, goes into a "rapture of the deep" – a sort of macabre euphoria that urges them to go deeper, rather than attempt to save themselves. Depression produces a sick sort of obsession with itself, causing a person to secretly want to get deeper into that self-abusive state, rather than lift themselves out it. Whenever I was depressed, I knew full well what I was doing – that I was willfully making it ever worse. In the beginning, I think I probably thought that people would see how miserable I was and would feel sorry for me, and when they failed to respond as I had hoped, the only alternative was to become more and more miserable until someone finally did. Later on in life, I think that changed to an obsession with the idea that I did not deserve to be happy; that I was such a loser, I deserved to be miserable. I knew better than that too, of course, but depression will not listen to reason. It is a profoundly neurotic game where rational thinking is not allowed.

In my mid-twenties, the onset of depression began to be preceded by severe tension headaches. The back of my head and upper neck would hurt so bad that I would become almost totally disabled. Whenever that happen, I could not work, concentrate on anything, or even sleep. One evening, alone in my apartment in Anaheim, California, it got so bad I began to fear I might die or go crazy there all by myself. Mustering up all the energy and courage I could, I managed to drive four or five blocks to the nearest drug store and bought some Excedrin – the most powerful non-prescription pain-killer that was available at the time. I then went immediately to a nearby Carl's restaurant where I was a regular customer and gulped down two pills with a glass of water. As it happened, some of the other regulars were there – an Chinese man in his fifties, Charlie Wang, who claimed to have been part of the Flying Tigers mercenary force during WW-II; Kish, a young student from CSU-Fullerton who cashiered at the place; and some others. So I joined them, ordering a coffee and a piece of boysenberry pie alamode to go with it. Within only a few minutes, my crippling tension headache miraculously vanished. I concluded that Excedrin was the best thing that ever happened! It was a long time before I figured out that it was the companionship, not the Excedrin.

Ironically, while living in California, I had little to be depressed about. I was young, slim and trim, and good looking. I was working on my own as a field engineer for a company located in Holland, Michigan, so was free to set my own agenda, without bosses and home-office nuisances to put up with. I was well-paid, and the company also provided a car (a rented Hertz Mustang), paid for my apartment, added an extra per-diem amount to my salary because they thought that the cost of living in Los Angeles was a lot more than in Holland, Michigan (it really was not). To boot, I also had an unlimited expense account! My company-leased apartment was in a place called "The Waterwheel," a beautiful complex with a huge A-frame common area at its entrance and lovely gardens within its inner courts. The gardens ended at a large sculptured swimming pool, fed with freshened water by means of the water wheel on a full-size replica of a picturesque old gristmill. The place had its own restaurant/lounge facility just outside the complex, patronized by "beautiful people," many of whom were swinging singles from the apartments. Just down the road in one direction or another were Disneyland, Knotts Berry Farm, Marineland of the Pacific, and similar attractions. A little further into town were Hollywood, Sunset Boulevard, the Hollywood Wax Museum, Universal Studios and all that. Weekends I was free to do as I wished, which usually meant camping/fishing/hiking adventures in Baja, deep sea sport fishing out of

San Diego, or just lying on the beach at Malibu or Zuma, or perhaps going down to Newport Beach. My work would sometimes take me up to San Francisco, where I loved driving up and down the hills in town, walking around Chinatown, having lunch at Alioto's out on Fishermen's Warf, or sometimes driving down to Santa Cruz or Monterey/Carmel.

I had little to be depressed about, indeed! What a foolish young man I was!

My habit of being depressed continued for many years. I spent a lot of time being sorry for myself because I was a lonely bachelor. I would see families with children and think that I had a right to feel bad, because that would never be me. By then I was in my thirties, and thought that opportunity had been missed, and was now forever gone. But then, at thirty-seven, I finally did fall in love and get married, and the children began coming immediately. That eliminated that excuse, but I remained depressed on and off nevertheless. That bothered even our children. Our eldest child, a daughter, would sometimes come to where I would be sitting alone in a pout and shake me saying, "Stop it! Stop it!" She was probably only six or seven at the time.

Then there was a family crisis. I wound up as the defendant in a criminal matter. The prosecution really did not have a case but, as is their usual practice in such situations, dragged their feet for several months, trying to wear us down financially and emotionally, while also doing the carrot and stick game – threatening the direst outcomes, while also offering plea agreements. We decided to make it as tough on them as possible, sticking to our guns and demanding a full-blown jury trial. During all those trying months, extended family and close friends deserted. By the time our trial day finally came after waiting almost a year, we had been totally abandoned, save for one elderly couple whom we had come to know through church activities. Otherwise, even our church "family" had abandoned us – and worse. I had been serving as an elected board member at the time, and the board – my fellow ruling elders, which in our church is called the "Session" – voted to dismiss me, their reason being that I had become "too angry." They were right about that. We had been unfairly accused by people we had tried to help, who were themselves convicted felons and drug addicts, and people from the church who should have been able to figure that out and come to our support – people who had known our family since its beginning – were some of the very people in the local prosecutor's office and circuit court who were engaged in the process that was trying to destroy us!

When the trial was called and I took my seat in the defendant's chair, I looked at my wife and oldest daughter sitting elsewhere, and they looked terrible – literally like death. I turned around to see who was sitting in the gallery. There were only two people there; one who had been involved in the State's "investigation" and was probably there to testify, and the other, surprisingly a very prominent woman from our community, and our church – a person whom I had known since I was a boy, she the rich girl and me the poor boy from the wrong side of the tracks. There was nobody else. No other friends; nobody from either side of our family. Later on I learned that my mother was, at that very moment, right across the street from the courthouse, sitting with friends and working on church Christmas Bazaar projects. Her excuse turned out to be, "Oh, I don't know anything about those sorts of affairs, and wouldn't have felt comfortable there."

This experience finally brought home to me in a very lucid way the realities about the family that I had grown up in. We were never a family, and never would be. My parents had been totally neurotic and dysfunctional, and had raised five totally neurotic and dysfunctional children. We were just seven individuals living together, each one struggling to survive emotionally, and doing little more than that – merely surviving. There was little love, little joy, little camaraderie, little caring and concern – very little of anything that ordinary people have in mind when talking about family. For us there was mostly just anger, jealousy, resentment and sadness, and later on, as adult "children," occasional attempts to play family, namely at awkward holiday gatherings.

That was a moment of epiphany – as the dictionary says, "a sudden, intuitive perception of or insight into the reality or essential meaning of something, usually initiated by some simple, homely, or commonplace occurrence or experience." I suddenly realized that being born into that mess had not been my fault; just my bad luck. One cannot choose one's family. I also saw that what had happed in that family was not my fault, and that the misery and sorrow of that beginning did not have to be defining of me. At that moment, I decided to let it go, and kissed my family of origin goodbye forever.

That was in November of 1991 – almost seventeen years ago, as I write this. I have *never* suffered a moment of depression since.

Lots of people suffer from what we used to call "melancholia" and "the blues." I suggest to you that if you suffer from depression, it is likely the result of something you are doing to yourself, rather than a condition you inherited or bad brain chemistry. I suggest you think about accepting and making the most of the life you have, rather than stubbornly insisting that life meet you on your own terms.

Medical and religious writers usually suggest that depression is sometimes normal and helpful, usually referring to situations involving grief over the loss of a loved one. I assert that this is neither normal nor helpful. We are all dying; it is only a matter of time. Our bodies are vulnerable, and life is a dangerous place. When death comes early of unnatural causes, the unexpected loss will be acutely, and momentarily, regrettable to some, but will become a permanently disabling tragedy or disaster only to those who wish it so. Bodies are also subject to eventual wear out, becoming no longer capable of supporting life. At sixty-seven, my death could no longer be seen as a sudden and unexpected loss. The only tragic thing about it would be the fact that I wasted so much of my life in neuroticism. Regardless of the circumstances of a loved one's death, life goes on. It is a fine thing when a person who dies lived the kind of life that leaves fond memories in their wake, but otherwise all who pass are soon forgotten. That is as it should be, since life is for the living to explore and celebrate, not for worshiping the dead. When the death of a loved one leads to endless mourning, that is depression, and it is being caused by the same old thing: angrily and stubbornly refusing to accept things that you cannot change. That is not helpful.

Psychologists and medical experts disagree on treatments for depression. Some insist on drugs, some on therapy, and some on a combination of drugs and therapy. Research has shown that antidepressant drugs are really no more effective than placebos (sugar pills.) That did not surprise me, since when I tried Prozac it did nothing for me but lighten my wallet and create a note in my medical records that impaired my insurability. On the other hand, what the research indicated was that sometimes placebos worked as well as the real thing. That is a good example of the power of your mind; if it believes that the pill you are talking will work, it will work. From that point of view, perhaps all the marketing hype that supports the popular antidepressant drugs is actually a good thing.

If you can accept this, you can believe that your mind is quite capable of forever ending your habit of depression, all by itself, without either drugs or therapy. It is only a matter of figuring out what it is that is bugging you, then thinking about that particular matter in a more rational way.

This is, of course, usually more easily said than done. You will not be able to work on this while you are depressed because your mind will not want to get better. Meanwhile, when you are not depressed, you will not feel like messing up your happy situation by delving into these sorts of issues. In any case, it is often hard to figure out what it really is that is eating away at you, since whatever it is, is often masked behind an array of secondary issues.

Outsiders are often able to see through these much more easily than you, because of your emotional investment in your long-standing habit. For this reason, it is often very useful to have a coach to talk with at length about your history, feelings and whatever ideas you might come up with. If you have the money or health insurance, that could be a professional CBT or REBT therapist. It could also be someone who is struggling with the same bad habit that you are, the two of you committed to pulling each other up by the bootstraps. But it could also be a respected elder in your family, a member of your faith's clergy, or anyone else who is willing to listen with sensitivity and intelligence, talk to you candidly and truthfully, while staunchly respecting your privacy.

Frank Sinatra and Sammy Davis Jr. were long-time best friends, both completing their fabulous careers as featured acts in top Las Vegas casinos. Sammy, who was prone to debilitating bouts of depression, once shared that Frank had many times kept him from going off the deep end by simply holding him and reassuring, "Just hold on Sammy. It'll pass."

I almost always avoid supporting an argument by religious-speak, but in this case the following is worth repeating:

> "God, give us grace to accept with serenity the things that cannot be changed, courage to change the things that should be changed, and the wisdom to distinguish the one from the other."

Often mistakenly attributed to the scriptures, St. Augustine, or others, these lines were authored around 1940 by Reinhold Niebuhr, a protestant theologian teaching at Union Theological Seminary in New York. His words very concisely capture the dilemma of depression.

Suicide

Threatening suicide all the time is another bad habit, and one that is really annoying to others. So you feel like ending your life. Go ahead! It is your life, and you can do with it whatever you want.

Suicide sometimes makes sense.

A favorite eighty-year old aunt recently died. She had been admitted to surgery for an intestinal blockage, but during the procedure was found to be hopelessly full of squamous cell cancer. Before being released, complications set in and she was rushed back into surgery. She never regained consciousness, and died the next day. She was lucky.

My Dad died of the same thing just before his sixty-fifth birthday. He had been diagnosed as a terminal case, twelve months before. After having been pestered by a family member, his surgeon blurted out, "Look. Your father's a goner! It's not a question of *if*, just a matter of *when*. People in his condition usually die within four to ten months!" Unfortunately for my Dad, it took him about twelve months to die. Before that finally happened, the cancer spread to his brain, affecting his balance and emotional stability, and he knew it. So besides the physical pain, he suffered the terrible emotional agony of knowing that his life was over, of waiting day after day for the end to finally come, while fearing the further emasculation and degradation that tomorrow might bring. Of those three hundred and some days, there were only two or three that were worth living. Otherwise, nothing happened during that long goodbye that made it worthwhile for him, or anybody else – except for the medical providers who were able to milk his case like a cash cow for about $400,000.

Michigan pathologist Jack Kevorkian served eight years in prison for promoting the rights of terminal patients to die the "good death," otherwise known as *euthanasia* or *physician assisted suicide*. We get upset to that extent about the exact circumstances of death brought about through compassionate but unnatural means, yet we, or at least many of us, eagerly promote indiscriminate killing by "shock and awe" – the much more dramatic and exciting U.S. style of modern, high-tech warfare.

In my observation, the words of Reinhold Niebuhr are particularly applicable to this situation. What sense does it make to force anyone to carry on with life, when it is clear they have no life to carry on? From my Dad's experience, I learned that it is extremely difficult, if not impossible, for anyone else to make the final decision for someone who is evidently at the end of their life. But if that person is capable of it themselves, it is not right to deny them, or to disrespect them after the fact.

But that's just my opinion.

As mentioned elsewhere, during the early years of my life I became a highly practiced student of suicide. In spite of engaging in many elaborate set-ups, I was never able to go through with it. I am not exactly sure why. I think that for the most part, being well into the habit of being depressed, I just wanted the emotional misery to end, and could not figure out any other way to make that happen. But then, when it came right down to it – when I was just about at the point of no return – something inside me would hint that I was smarter than this, and should be able to figure out a more sensible solution. Closely connected with that was the fact that I was very sensitive about what others thought of me, and I felt quite sure that were I to kill myself, they would surely conclude that I was a dumb horse's ass after all.

I know – that does not make any sense at all. Why would I care what others thought? I would be dead!

I am sure that I sometimes thought that committing suicide would send a message to my parents and everyone else about how miserable I was. But then, again, what good would that do. I would be dead. And knowing my parents, I figured they were really too wrapped up in their own unhappiness to care about mine anyway –

that they would more likely be angry with their dead son for disgracing them in that way.

The last time I ever considered suicide was just after being arrested and charged with a felony offense, as mentioned above. I walked across town in the middle of the night to the local Grand River waterfront, and stood there on the edge of the pier for a long time in the misty darkness, staring into the cold, black water. I was fifty-one years old. It seemed like no matter how hard I tried to *be somebody*, nothing ever came to no good in my life.

With the exception of her mother, my wife's family had, from the time she and I were married fourteen years before, busied themselves trying to convince her that she had made a big mistake. Surely they were now gloating, and she now finally had reason to wish she had never met me. It was probably true; she would be better off without me.

But then, there were our four young children. A parent's suicide is often stigmatizing. Children sometimes think it is somehow their fault – that they were bad, or not loveable enough. Others sometimes get the idea that suicide runs in the family and, once that happens to one of the parents, the children are always at risk. Mothers and wives forever worry about sons and husbands whose fathers killed themselves. Married daughters worry that perhaps someday their husbands will decide to leave them that same way. With me out of the picture, what would become of those four treasured children? Besides all that, they were too young to understand what was going on, and still loved me – still needed me. In spite of all my faults, I was probably still better than nothing.

I turned my back on the river and walked slowly back home, having no idea what the future might hold for my family and I, but determined to play whatever cards I was dealt as best I could. I had no clue that the key to a happy rest of my life lay just ahead.

I am not here to convince you not to kill yourself. If you are so miserable that you can no longer stand living, and you have convinced yourself that your problems will plague you forever, go ahead and end your life.

But I can assure you that nobody will feel sorry for you. At best, people will think you died of a terminal case of neuroticism. Those who are more charitable might wonder if you actually had a brain tumor. Those closest to you are more likely to be embarrassed and angry at you than sad about your passing. If your intention is to disgrace them and piss them off, that is a good way to do it. But then, what good will that do you. You will not be around to enjoy it.

And then there is the possibility that a different life is just around the corner for you and you might not even know it which, as you have just read, was the case with me. It does happen.

Thinking about suicide all the time is just another bad habit, usually arising from another bad habit, depression, which, in turn, arises from neuroticism.

So there you have it – the Monster is even capable of killing you.

Chapter 11
A Practical Faith

Regardless of what you think you believe, or do not believe, religion and religious diversity is a reality you will encounter wherever you go, and regardless of whom you chance or choose to associate with.

When dealing with human beings, it is always a mistake to define a person according to stereotypes. This is especially true when it comes to religious beliefs and practices. Within any particular religion, believers will vary all across the spectrum, from those who are seriously devout and strict, to others who only loosely associate themselves with their faith, who are familiar with, but rather ambivalent about its basic tenants, and would rather play golf. In the middle are the bulk of believers; people who honestly attempt to apply the valued precepts of their faith to everyday life in the most practical way possible, while still remaining within the bounds of real world conventions and expectations.

Chance vs. Choice

Mark Twain described this majority wisely when he said, "In religion and politics, people's beliefs and convictions are in almost every case gotten at second hand, and without examination." He had a knack for packing a wealth of meaning into a paucity of words.

First, whatever your tradition is, it probably came to you second hand through your parents, as a part of the culture you were born into. That is ordinarily how religion is passed on down through the generations. Along the way over those generations, religion becomes enmeshed as an integral aspect of cultural traditions. If you wish to truly know and understand a person from another place, you will need to know something about the religion practiced in their culture. By the same token, to critically or cavalierly dismiss another's religion is to dump on many important, and probably dearly valued, aspects of that person's culture. This applies not only between major religions, but also between minor subdivisions of the same religion.

Second, children are inducted into their parents' tradition when very young, often at infancy. They are then instructed in that tradition for a dozen years or so, after which there is usually a ceremony of some sort in which they formally espouse it as their own chosen tradition. That is usually not really a *choice* however, since there was no real examination of alternatives. Indeed, early religious training and indoctrination usually teaches that there is no other choice – that all other traditions are bogus.

The Sensible Middle Ground

Whatever your tradition, I strongly suggest that you embrace its mainstream, and avoid its extremes.

In the fields of mathematics, statistics, and engineering, there is a thing called the *Gaussian Distribution*. Carl Friedrich Gauss was born in northern Germany in 1777, the son of a common stone mason. In spite of his lowly birth, he turned out to be a genius; a child prodigy, noted for his astounding precociousness, even as a toddler. He made ground-breaking mathematical discoveries while still a teenager, some of which you have, or will encounter in your own studies of math and science. One will be the *standard normal distribution*, often called "the bell curve" because of its general shape. Gauss came up with this in the 1820's.

The whole idea is this; if you were to graph all the known values of any particular variable, the resulting plot would take the shape of a bell, the big hump in the middle representing the preponderance of normal values, collapsing rapidly on either side, reflecting how the values drastically fall off towards the most extreme deviations.

The center of the bell curve, its *mean*, is assigned the value of "0," and the most extreme values on either side are designated "-5" and "+5," representing *deviations* from the mean. The exact shape of such curves varies, depending upon the values they represent – some very narrow and highly peaked and some more broad. But in any case, the majority of the values plotted will fall within the range of "-2" and "+2." According to the *empirical rule*, which is also called the *68-95-99.7 rule*, more than two-thirds of the values plotted will be found very close to the middle of the curve (between -1 and +1), 95% of the values plotted will fall under its middle 40% (-2 to +2), 99.7% under its middle 60% (-3 to +3), and the remaining 20% extremes on either side (left of -3 or right of +3) accounting for less than 0.3% of the values plotted – less than three out of every thousand.

Religion, through its penchant for elevating prophets and martyrs, tends to draw people towards the extremes, especially towards the fundamentalist end of the curve.

A sure way to get yourself singled out as an opinionated kook, and possibly even become a threat to others, is to adamantly profess the dogmas of a particular religious fringe, earnestly, but foolishly, asserting that you are right and everyone else is wrong.

It is equally silly to dismiss religion in general as pure superstition or outright boloney. Much of it is, of course. The earliest faiths were based purely on fairy tales and magical thinking, and even today, the predominant religions require their followers to believe in metaphorical "truths" and vague metaphysical concepts.

Thinking again about Gauss' curve – if you are out there beyond the "±3" fringes – ultra conservative (fundamentalist) or ultra-liberal (atheist), you will find that to be a lonely place. Statistically, you will not find more than one or two people in a thousand who share your point of view. If your thinking is quite different than that of the mainstream, there is a very slight chance that you are indeed a philosophical prodigy – right up there with Socrates and a handful of others that the human race has produced over the past few thousand years. It is more likely that you have personality issues that are causing you to be different as a strategy for getting attention or recognition.

Controversial author and philosopher Ayn Rand left us with at least one very useful and memorable quotation: "Whenever you think you are facing a contradiction, *check your premises*. You will find that one of them is wrong."

Human Fallibility

This is a good time to revisit what you learned about the fallibility of human thinking in Chapter 3.

Religion is mostly a matter of faith, which Paul of Tarsus, the founder of Christianity defined as, "… being sure of what we hope for and certain of what we do not see."

This certainly raises questions! What do "sure" and "certain" mean?

All religions urge the use of these words in their absolute sense – you may not be "pretty sure" or "almost certain," else you will be seen as harboring doubt. That, in the eyes of organized religions, is never a good thing. In most civilized places today, doubt is just something you would be better off not talking about among members of your faith family. In other places and in other times, admitting to anything less than sureness and certainty sometimes gets, and has gotten, people branded as infidels, heretics, or even blasphemers, then beheaded or burned at the stake.

When I was a young teenager, probably about twelve or thirteen, having just studied how the scientific method worked, I was quite cocky about being able to figure things out. When it came to religion, I could see no alternative to absolute belief. I reasoned that since we in our faith believed we were right, therefore, logically, everyone else had to be wrong.

It was easy to see things as black or white at that age. I suspected that the adults who were running the world were stupid, lazy or preoccupied, because it was quite clear that any problem could be correctly solved and any question correctly answered simply by gathering all the facts, then sorting them out to see what obvious answer would be magically revealed.

In the musical *The King and I*, Mongkut, King of Bangkok, had never in his life had his wisdom questioned – until the arrival of a young English widow whom he brings to his country to tutor his many children, begotten of his several wives. Gradually and painfully, he learns about human fallibility. In his song he laments:

> "When I was a boy
> World was better spot.
> What was so was so,
> What was not was not.
> Now I am a man;
> World have changed a lot.
> Some things nearly so,
> Others nearly not.
> *Is a puzzlement ...*

> There are times I almost think
> I am not sure of what I absolutely know.
> Very often find confusion
> In conclusion I concluded long ago.
> In my head are many facts,
> That, as a student, I have studied to procure.
> In my head are many facts,
> Of which I wish I was more certain I was sure!

Is a puzzlement ...
There are times I almost think
Nobody sure of what he absolutely know.
Everybody find confusion
In conclusion he concluded long ago.
And it puzzle me to learn
That tho' a man may be in doubt of what he know,
Very quickly he will fight ...
He'll fight to prove that what he does not know is so!
... Is a puzzlement!"

You have probably told someone, "Well, you have a right to your opinion." You probably did not really believe that – you were just trying to avoid any further argument, and probably because you were not that sure of what you knew. But everyone does indeed have a right to their opinion. The reason is *fallibility*. Our minds are awesome, to be sure, but they are not perfect.

Your mind uses a cognitive process to make sense of its inputs and organize data in your memory. All of the information it receives through the senses is filtered through preexisting data for meaning, importance and to fill in vague or missing details. It interprets things as best it can according to what it already *knows*.

Even when confronted with the same scene and from the same vantage point, the reports of eye-witnesses can be expected to differ significantly, especially with respect to details. What they can report will not be as factually reliable as a video of the event. Their report will instead be a description of the picture that was formed in their minds, as their cognitive processes shifted into gear to make sense of the inputs being received.

Consider, for example, two young men watching a sports event. A play is carried out, it scores, the crowd cheers and boos, and then the game continues. Both men witnessed the action from the same perspective, however one is a regular fan who is well familiar with the sport, and the other is attending such an event for the first time in his life. You can easily imagine how these two otherwise equal men would give two significantly different accounts of what they just saw happen.

An English friend once told me about having taken his visiting mother to a baseball game. Having never seen the game before, he explained each activity to her so she could grasp what was going on. The batter swung at the first pitch and missed, "That counts as 'strike one,' Mother." The second pitch sped by without any response from the batter, yet the umpire again screeched "Steee-ryke!" "That's because the pitcher succeeded in accurately throwing the ball over home plate, Mother, so it counts as a strike, regardless of whether swung upon, or not." She nodded, apparently understanding the concept. The next pitch missed the plate, and was ignored by the batter. The umpire, turning his head to his right, rubbed his nose with his right hand and picked his crotch with his left, but said nothing. Mother shot an inquisitive, if somewhat embarrassed, glance: "That's called a ball, Mother. Ball one." And so it went through the count; "1 ball, 2 strikes," then "2 and 2," hit foul – still "2 and 2," then ball three, "3 and 2." The pitcher wound up again and threw well off the mark. The umpire stepped back as the batter tossed the bat and began to jog slowly towards first base. Mother jumped up yelling "Run swiftly! Run swiftly!" Tugging her back down into her seat, my friend explained, "Ah, no Mother. That's called 'a walk.' He doesn't have to hurry because he has four balls." Rising back to her feet, Mother yelled, "Walk proudly! Walk proudly!"

Okay, well that is British humor. The English would get a giggle out of that. I did, in fact, hear that one from an English friend years ago, and I thought it illustrated my point perfectly.

Emotion is also a powerful modifier of data. Assuming an altercation between a little old white lady and a young black gang-banger, witnessing this event through the stereotypical background noise in their mind (elderly white lady – motherly, weak and vulnerable; black boy – delinquent, angry, threatening), a typical white observer would be apt to assume, and report, that the boy was the villain, without actually having seen or heard anything that would rationally support that assertion.

If you are not comfortable with that example, consider two people having witnessed a serious traffic accident – one of whom has been recently involved in such an accident and the other who never has. Although disturbing to both, you might well presume that the one will report what he observed as a much more traumatic event, and with much more detail.

Your opinions therefore merely reflect your view of things, based upon information you receive, as filtered through your prior knowledge and preconceptions, and as colored by your emotions. It is very likely to differ from the opinions of others, just as theirs will differ from yours.

In small matters, this should never be a problem. People of ordinary intelligence and goodwill make allowances for each other's having different takes on things. In fact, this is often seen as an asset when we team up to approach issues together, with the understanding that two heads are always better than one.

It becomes a problem only when a person, as a matter of pride, or to avoid embarrassment, stubbornly clings to their views even when they know them to be weak or incorrect, or when a person ignorantly refuses to consider any possibility that their thinking could be flawed. That kind of intransigence is always self-defeating, and sometimes even becomes dangerous.

Understanding that your cognitive process is fallible is the best you can do towards limiting your vulnerability to this aspect of your human nature. From this perspective, you can accept what you think you know or believe, as the best you can do under the present circumstances, while maintaining a willingness to openly review the situation, should new information suggest that revisions might be in order.

This is often a difficult stance when it comes to religion, since many religions forbid it. Stories which are passed down over the generations as oral traditions eventually get written down, are compiled into scriptures and are translated into modern languages. Religions attempt to get around the fallibility issue by claiming that their scriptures contain the word of God or, at least, the writings of men inspired by God. But whatever the case, the fact remains that these holy writings are finally the work of men. We know that the cognitive process is fallible in all men, yet we are ordered to believe that in the particular case of the scriptures, its authors, compilers and translators were somehow always able to rise above that aspect of their humanity.

You can probably surmise what my opinion is. However, faith is a highly personal thing. Its value as a code that provides guidance and a personal moral compass varies according to the strength of your convictions. If you mindlessly take your marching orders from someone else – "Don't let me think – just tell me what to think." – by definition you have no real faith at all. You are simply brainwashed, else are marching to the beat of the loudest drummer because you do not have the strength of character to stand up for what you really believe. You must therefore decide for yourself what to believe, and whether or not it makes sense to abide by a doctrine of infallibility. Towards that end, let us briefly review the leading world religions as they stand now, at the beginning of this twenty-first century.

The Common Roots

According to those who study antiquities, the very earliest religions appear to have focused upon fertility; human and agricultural. The ancients apparently understood their own vulnerability and mortality quite clearly, and conjured up various deities with the power to regulate things humans otherwise had no control over. The invention of these gods provided some sense of security. By pleasing and appeasing these gods, believers hoped to be favored with safety and abundance.

The evidence indicates that the earliest gods were actually all goddesses. This suggests an ignorance of the human reproductive process – the ancients not having caught on to the connection between sexual intercourse and childbirth. Women were highly esteemed as the givers of life, and that view was extended to all forms of rebirth, including the natural seasonal cycles of flower and fauna. The subsequent appearance of phallic symbols (representations of the erect penis) suggests that people eventually did learn what caused women to become pregnant and produce children. Religions then developed elaborate seasonal fertility rites – sexual spectacles evidently designed to please the gods by demonstrating the believers' willingness to do their part, with the hope that the gods would then respond in kind by providing plenty by way of crops and game. Unhappily for women, their stature then declined. They became merely the medium through which the produce of the male seed was realized.

Sacrifice was also common in early religions, as a way to show the gods how highly they were esteemed. This was simply a gift-giving exercise, the value of the sacrificial item, or its cost to the giver, reflecting the depth of his reverence for, and fear of, the god in question. Obviously, there was not much of any greater value than human life, and especially the fruit of one's own loins, so this ritual eventually involved the offering up of one's own children, usually infant children.

There are about twenty-one major religions in the world today, but more than two-thirds of the world's 6.6-billion people associate themselves with the major God-fearing faiths:

Christianity	2,100-million
Islam	1,400-million
Hinduism	900-million
Sikhism	26-million
Judaism	13-million

The two leading religions, Christianity and Islam, are remnants of the same legendary tradition, which began about 4,000 years ago in Ur, a small town on the Tigris and Euphrates rivers in what is now southern Iraq. Ur was the birthplace of Abram, later known as Abraham, who is considered to have been the father of Judaism, Christianity and Islam, in that order.

According to legend, Abraham migrated northward into the land of Canaan, which is what we now refer to as the nation of Israel and the disputed territories. God is believed to have appeared to a childless Abraham, declaring that he and his numerous descendants would be his "chosen people," and would ultimately become many nations. According to Jewish tradition, he also promised that the land of Canaan would forever belong to those peoples.

Abraham eventually had two sons, Ishmael and Isaac. Ishmael, the first, was born of the maidservant Haggar, acting as concubine since Abraham's wife Sarah was well beyond childbearing age. Some thirteen years later however, Sarah miraculously gave birth to Isaac. Sarah then insisted that her natural born son should be the inheritor of the birthright, which would otherwise traditionally fall to the firstborn son. As the story goes, Abraham therefore reluctantly banished Haggar and Ishmael into the desert. However, God placated Abraham and Haggar with a promise that their son Ishmael would become the father of twelve princes. Eventually, Ishmael did indeed have twelve sons. Jacob, the son of Isaac, also had twelve sons. The sons of Ishmael are believed by some to have become the root of the twelve ancient Arab nations, while those of Jacob became the roots of the legendary twelve tribes of Israel.

These tribes eventually dissolved and disbursed. It is thought that the twelve tribes of Israel generally migrated north and east, into what is now Europe. Meanwhile, the twelve tribes of Ishmael probably disbursed south and west, into territory now generally thought of as the Arab lands of the Middle East.

The advent of Judaism with its belief in one god marked the beginning of the end of multi-theistic systems. What happened to all the earlier gods? According to the old joke, when *Yahweh*, the God of Abraham and the Hebrews, said, "I am the only god," all the other gods died laughing.

More seriously, it is rather easy to understand why the monotheistic Judaism would have easily been widely embraced. For one thing, the various multi-theistic systems involved somewhat complex interrelationships between the gods, and gods and humans, which were often difficult to understand and rather obviously farfetched. Yahweh, on the other hand, was simply seen as having created everything, and was believed to have control over everything. Different cultures had different sets of gods; the Romans had one set, the Greeks another, Persians yet others, and so on. This complicated things when these people intermingled in trade, war, marriage, and so on. Standardization with a "one god fits all" system made things much easier in a world that was already becoming smaller and multicultural. Perhaps most importantly, the famous Abraham-Isaac legend, wherein Abraham was prepared to sacrifice his beloved son Isaac atop Mount Moriah but, at the last minute, was shut down by God, established the belief that this one god no longer found human sacrifice acceptable, thereby putting an end to that emotionally painful and macabre practice.

There is, of course, a great deal more to these stories and religious traditions, but it is helpful to realize that in spite of present day political differences in the middle east, the peoples involved have much in common from a religious point of view. Christians in particular often have the feeling that the Muslim religion is a dark and mysterious faith, and are often surprised to learn that it shares the Old Testament with Judaism and Christianity.

Judaism and Jesus of Nazareth

At the present time, Christianity has the largest following of any religion, with significant numbers on every continent. One out of every three people in the world professes to a belief in one version or another of the Christian faith.

After centuries of struggles with foreign invaders and occasional occupations by foreign powers, both the Israelites and Ishmaelites developed traditions foreseeing the coming of a *messiah* who would ultimately establish the *Kingdom of God* on earth. The expected messiah would not be a god, or a king in the political sense, but rather a great leader. The expression "Kingdom of God" merely referred to a time of freedom, peace, prosperity and justice for all, which would occur in the ordinary course of history. It did not refer to a political entity. Potential messiahs appeared from time to time, Jesus of Nazareth being the last of note in the Jewish tradition.

Jesus' agenda was primarily just that; the realization of Hebrew prophesies predicting the ultimate establishment of the Kingdom of God. Although most of the territory in the region where he spent his life was occupied and controlled by Rome at the time, such movements were not overtly revolutionary in nature. For the most part, Rome was happy to permit the Jews a rather high degree of autonomy, with their own king and complete religious freedom, in exchange for their good behavior. Except for some very infrequent rebellions on the part of Jewish minority factions – which were promptly and brutally put down by the Romans – the Jews satisfied themselves with a belief that God would eventually produce a messiah who would establish a decent civil society, and that God would deal with political oppressors in his own way, and in his own time. Since the activities of Jesus involved only Jewish religious issues, he was more of a threat to the Jewish religious leadership than to the Roman political establishment.

Jesus of Nazareth differed from other potential messiahs by introducing a revolutionary new theory of *purity*. In the Jewish tradition, the concept of purity referred to a person being acceptable in the eyes of God. There were all sorts of situations that would result in a person's becoming "unclean," such as eating the wrong thing, or in the wrong place, or touching a female during her time of menstruation – so many, in fact, that the natural state of persons was "unclean." The remedy for uncleanliness was a rather involved purification ritual, culminating in sacrifice if a particular transgression required it; offering God something of value. Property, perhaps gold or incense, but more usually livestock and grain, would be brought to the great temple in Jerusalem, where officiating priests would send them up in smoke, usually after reserving a share for themselves.

Purity codes were common in ancient cultures. They provided a definition of what was considered appropriate at certain times and places, so as to provide a sense of order and safety in a world that otherwise seemed chaotic. Jewish law established elaborate rules and procedures regarding ritual purity in an attempt to emulate what they believed to be God's preferred ordering of things. This gave people a way to figure out how to fit into that order, so as to remain acceptable in the eyes of God and thereby continuingly eligible to receive his blessings and benefits.

In this sense, the meaning of the word "purity" is somewhat like today's understanding of "righteousness" or "godliness," as opposed to "cleanliness." For example, hand-washing and bathing rituals were about making oneself "clean" in the eyes of God, not necessarily about personal hygiene.

Jesus came to believe that moral purity was more important than ritual purity – that purity came from within, from the heart, not from rigorous compliance in a ritualistic way with rules that were in many cases rather superficial. The rules were given in the Torah, many of them having to do with what people could eat or drink, and who they could associate with and when. Jesus was very sociable, and became quite well-known for being very liberal in these respects. Since compliance with the Torah was not considered optional, his teachings and personal behavior became quite controversial. But to his critics he supposedly responded, "Think not that I am come to destroy the law, or the prophets: I am not come to destroy, but to fulfill. For verily I say unto you, till heaven and earth pass, one jot or one tittle shall in no wise pass from the law, till all be fulfilled."

This actually made perfect sense. Jewish prophecy foresaw the coming of a messiah who would finally establish the Kingdom of God on earth. That apocalyptic event would involve the destruction of the temple at Jerusalem. That, in turn, would greatly modify the ritualistic observances, with all people from every nation and every walk of life then being forever acceptable in the eyes of God, worshiping him together in the temple. Jesus believed that this predicted happening was imminent; that "till all be fulfilled" was just around the corner.

Scholars argue over the issue of whether or not Jesus actually believed he was the promised messiah. Whatever the case, as Jewish religious authorities began to realize where he was coming from, they were not happy. Here was a "mamzer," for cripes sake, Joseph's bastard son, who claimed to have a direct line to God, and who, without needing them as a go-between, claimed to know things that they did not know. This was not only as insult to the Torah; it was an assault on their power and prestige. When Jesus began to make noises like this in his own hometown, they threw him out, and he was forced to flee to Bethesda. He was lucky to get away with his life, since that sort of behavior warranted death by stoning.

Eventually, the inherent threat to the Roman occupation was not lost on Rome and its puppet Jewish king, Herod Antipas. A similar messiah movement, about 170-years earlier, had restored Israel to independence upon ousting its Greek occupiers. The Roman occupation government was therefore increasingly suspicious of Jesus' renown as a healer, and his growing following. When people began to speak of this rabbi as a prophet, and even perhaps the long-awaited messiah, suspicion turned to concern.

Jesus was not a native of Jerusalem. He was born and grew up in a northern region known as Galilee. To the more urbane Jews in Jerusalem, Galileans were considered to be rather crude country bumpkins, as it were, with fundamentalist attitudes that were in conflict with how the huge temple complex was being managed and operated. Moreover, Jesus himself was considered to be a "mamzer" – a child born of a forbidden relationship, or sort of the Jewish equivalent of a bastard child. That automatically placed him in a position of second-class citizenship, as a person not eligible for certain rights and privileges normally accorded to any common Jew. Probably as the result of his Galilean antipathy towards the Levite temple management, his personal resentment of authority arising from his mamzer status, and his ignorance of Jewish-Roman and temple politics down in Jerusalem, he organized a raid on the temple which, by today's standards, would certainly be considered insurgent, and quite possibly a terrorist attack.

When Jews came to the temple, their sacrificial offerings had to be approved by the temple priests. Bringing things from great distances, especially livestock, was burdensome, and when what they brought was not found acceptable, there was no recourse other than to purchase something else locally. If they brought money, it had to be exchanged for silver shekels before it could be brought into the temple. This led to the development of an exchange and marketplace on the nearby Mount of Olives. Naturally that gave rise to exorbitant prices, fraudulent practices and thievery.

Meanwhile, an important group of Jewish intellectuals known as Pharisees, who met regularly in the Royal Portico, an outer court on the southern end of the temple, often proved vexing to the High Priest Caiaphas ("KAY-uh-fuhs"). They challenged his decisions, insisting on strict knit-picking adherence to Jewish law, yet sometimes introduced rites which originated in popular custom, with no foundation in the Law whatsoever.

Caiaphas eventually came up with a cleaver solution to both problems. He decided that the people would be better served by moving the exchange and market from the Mount of Olives into the outer court of the temple – the Royal Portico. To make room for that, he arranged meeting facilities for the Pharisees out at the Mount of Olives. Naturally the Pharisees were not happy about this. Many regular Jews also found it distasteful, if not downright disgraceful and unlawful, to have part of their beautiful temple, the high holy place that represented God's home on earth and the center of their faith, defiled by commerce and the sights, sounds, odors and piles of dung commonly associated with barnyards.

In what proved to be a fatal political blunder, Jesus took it upon himself to round up a band of perhaps a thousand followers, who raided the temple with the intention of clearing out that abomination. It was a high holy holiday season, and the crowds were heavy. There were injuries and fatalities.

The priestly class in Jerusalem consisted of Jewish religious elites known as Sadducees, led by the High Priest Caiaphas. This caste, who controlled the Temple and thereby the Jewish religion, was abetted in that role by the occupation government. It was not difficult for them to convince the Romans that Jesus of Nazareth was a political threat. As was the common Roman practice at that time, he was eventually apprehended and summarily executed.

A Turk Invents Christianity

That probably would have been the end of the Jesus movement had it not been for a man named Saul. Saul came from Tarsus, a city north of the holy land in what is now southeast Turkey. He was the son of an affluent family who, although not Jewish, practiced the God-fearing Jewish religion. The affluent among such families commonly sent their sons to the great temple at Jerusalem to study under the Pharisees, a class of respected lay scholars and philosophers.

Saul evidently did not excel as a student in that setting, and was perhaps dismissed. An Ebionite tradition, on the other hand, suggests an involvement with a daughter of the High Priest, which ended with Saul being contemptuously rejected. Whatever the case, he somehow wound up working for the priestly class of Sadducees at the Temple, a move that friends and family probably would have viewed with feelings of disdain and disgrace. The Sadducees were not generally well thought of in the Jewish community. Presumed to be descendants of Levi, the third son of Jacob, they considered themselves a special priestly caste authorized by Moses; the aloof custodians of the faith and the only authorized intercessors between the Jewish people and God. Since their position was also secured through complicity with the Roman government, and supported in part by taxation, they were generally suspected of collusion and corruption.

Unhappily for the Sadducees, the Jesus movement did not die out with its leader's execution. Some of his followers were claiming that he had indeed proven himself to be the messiah by having come back from the dead. To deal with the continuing threat some twenty years after Jesus' death, Saul was evidently assigned by the High Priest Caiaphas to lead a contingent of temple guards to Damascus to covertly apprehend some leaders of the movement, perhaps Jesus' closest associate, Peter "the Rock." Somewhere along the way, he apparently had a change of heart. According to tradition, the resurrected Jesus appeared to him in a vision, appointing him as special apostle to the *gentiles* – "gentiles" being those who were not ethnically Jewish. This made Saul rather unpopular with everyone other than gentiles – the High Priest, the Jewish community, and the leaders of the Jesus movement.

The name "Saul" would certainly have had negative connotations with the Jewish culture of the time, because of its historical significance – a king of the same name having acted in evil ways towards the legendary David, and subsequently dying in infamy. At some point not long after his vision, Saul's name was changed to "Paul," a Roman name meaning "small" or "minimal," and having no special significance to Jews. Whether done to avoid the negative connotations of his infamous Jewish name, or in an attempt to escape his past, or as part of an effort to ingratiate himself with the original twelve by positioning himself as "the least of the apostles," can only be speculated. Whether his name was changed by God, or by himself, is also purely a matter of what one chooses to believe.

If actually from Tarsus (and there is some skepticism regarding those origins), Paul's tradition would have included Hellenic paganism and Gnosticism, as well as Judaism. He eventually combined components of these traditions with those of the Jesus movement, and introduced a radical new messianic concept – a major departure from Jewish tradition and the Jesus movement. Paul saw the death of Jesus not as an execution, but as a sort of sacrifice in reverse – an ultimate and final sacrifice, wherein God gave up *his* only son, for the ultimate purification of all his children. In this way, he changed the concept of Jesus as messiah – a great leader who had come to bring freedom, justice and prosperity to the nations – to a sort of demigod who came to make personal redemption available to everyone simply for the asking. Paul then preached that salvation was available to anyone who accepted that gesture, and who believed in the eternal presence of the resurrected Jesus.

Up to that point, practicing Jews believed that purity was established by earnestly following the law, and was not generally available to gentiles. Paul's thinking, in combination with familiar pagan and Gnostic concepts, was therefore wildly popular with believing gentiles. It was also highly aggravating to devout Jews, and especially to those in the Jesus movement.

Through a series of compromises, mostly based on Paul's willingness and ability to support the Jerusalem Jesus movement financially while ministering to gentiles in out of the way places, Paul was permitted to operate under the auspices of the Jerusalem leaders. As it turned out, the *Pauline* movement proved highly successful outside of Jerusalem, eventually dominating the Jesus movement in spite of vigorous efforts by the Jerusalem church to contain it.

The eventual Roman response to a Jewish rebellion in the year 66 was the siege of Jerusalem, the eventual ransacking of the city and the destruction of the temple. Thousands were slaughtered, thousands were sent into slavery in Egyptian mines, while thousands of others were disbursed throughout the empire. Thus was the Jesus movement in Jerusalem severely crippled. Paul, physically unattractive and somewhat outspoken, continuing to be personally unpopular with the Jewish religious establishment wherever he went, is said to have been executed in Rome on separate charges about this same time.

Nevertheless, the Jesus movement prospered, with the eventual growth of five powerful and influential centers around the Mediterranean area, at Jerusalem, Antioch, Rome, Alexandria and Constantinople. The Pauline movement, which became known as the Christian movement, continued to prosper in Rome and the Roman provinces. Upon the deathbed conversion of the Roman emperor Constantine the Great in the year 312, Christianity was finally designated the official religion of the Roman Empire.

A couple hundred years later, a schism between Rome and Constantinople resulted in what became the Roman and Greek Orthodox, or Eastern Orthodox, versions of the faith. In a few hundred more years, as a result of papal corruption in the Roman church, Martin Luther's rebellion resulted in another split, which gave rise to a Protestant faction. Various theological and political disagreements within the Protestant faction have given rise to numerous denominations, a process that continues even to this day.

Islam – Back to the Basics

Although Islam is stereotypically associated with Arab regions, it is found all over the world. *Islam* means "to submit." *Muslim*, the word which refers to the Islamic faithful, means "one who submits."

Historically, Islam originated in the seventh century, about 300-years later than the Roman adoption of Christianity. It began in Mecca – on the western side of the Arabian Peninsula in what is today's Saudi Arabia. Theologically, Muslims trace the origin of Islam to Abram, claiming that it restores the original precepts of the faith after centuries of corruption by Judaism and Christianity.

Muslims believe that Muhammad, a 7th century Arab religious and political figure, was a direct descendant of Abraham's firstborn son Ishmael, and the final prophet in a line of messengers from God that included all the prophets of Judaism and Christianity, including Jesus of Nazareth. Muslims believe that Muhammad was the greatest of the prophets, coming closer to absolute perfection and virtue than any of his predecessors.

At the time of Mohammad's birth, the descendants of Ishmael had lost their way, having become fiercely tribal, worshiping many pagan gods, and living under viciously corrupt and morally bankrupt conditions. At age forty, Mohammad began to experience revelations, through which God restored his code of divine guidance and direction for mankind. Mohammad's following was very slow to develop – only about ten converts a year during his first four years of prophesying in the streets of Mecca. Others responded with mud-slinging; literally pelting him with handfuls of mud.

His message was simple: "There is but one god, and Allah is his name." He called for an end to licentiousness and cheating, a respect for order and the mending of people's morals. He challenged the people to turn away from their false gods, to give up their evil ways, and prepare for the day of reckoning. After ten years however, his following in Mecca remained only in the hundreds. Although he was revered by these as God's special prophet, others sought his death and plotted against him.

At age fifty-two, he decided to leave Mecca, and journey some 250-miles east to Medina, in what is now Iraq. In Medina, his message was much more eagerly received. During the next ten years, he developed the rituals and ethics that lie at the root of Islam. His revelations, rituals and ethics were eventually compiled in the Qur'an, Islam's holy book.

Mohammad evidently had some contact with Jews and Christians, since he wrote respectfully of these "people of the book," as he called them. He respected all the important characters from the earlier Jewish and Christian traditions, from Abraham, Moses, Noah, David, and so on, up to and including Jesus, acknowledging all as being great prophets.

Islam was originally extended militaristically. This came about unintentionally, when Mecca launched an unsuccessful attack on Medina. Under Mohammad's leadership, Medina responded by subduing Mecca, and establishing it as a "holy city." From this episode, the concept of "holy war" (now commonly called *jihad*, which actually means "struggle") became part of the tenants of Islam. Mohammad showed great mercy to his enemies, establishing a good and just theocratic government in Mecca. He proved to be an able politician and great leader, and before his death he had succeeded in uniting all the various independent Arab tribes. By the time of his death at age sixty-two, almost all of Arabia was under his control.

Having designated no successor, a scramble for power ensued among the leadership, who were called *Caliphs*. These men were very capable military leaders. Within a hundred years, Islam had been spread by the sword from Persia to Egypt, and as far into Europe as France. The struggle for succession sorted out as a struggle between Caliphs who were blood relatives of Mohammad, and those who were not. This resulted in a split between these two factions. Those who insisted that the leading Caliph should be a descendant of Mohammad became the minority (15%) fundamentalist faction known today as Shiites. Those who felt otherwise constitute today's Sunnis, the more liberal majority (85%).

Islam is probably most like early Judaism in that its religious law rules civil affairs, it insists that its god, Allah, is the only god, and that Allah embraces Islam as the true faith, exalted above all others.

Moslems observe *the five pillars of faith*, which require a belief that there is but one god, and his name is Allah, there must be prayer five times a day, and that one must give alms to the poor, fast during Ramadan, and make a pilgrimage to Mecca. Moslems are also required to observe various other duties and regulations governing the conduct of men and women, from life to death. Mohammad greatly elevated the status of women. Although Islam provides differing codes of rules and rights for men and women, the sexes probably fare equally under these differing systems.

While Islam is theologically tolerant of other religions, the Qur'an requires that government be theocratic, meaning that religious law applies, with no separation between government and the faith – a major difference between it and Judaism and Christianity, as practiced in the United States, and one that sticks in the craw of most Americans, who uphold religious freedom and separation of church and state as among the most revered of our founding principles.

Traditional vs. Transitional

Until recently, not much was known about the ancient Maya culture of Mexico. On the basis of what could be gleaned from remaining evidence, the Mayas were thought to be a highly advanced, artistic and peace-loving people. Then, only about nineteen years ago, a young scholar, David Stuart, unraveled the mystery of Maya hieroglyphics, their highly sophisticated system of graphical writing. Being able to finally read what was inscribed on monuments and tablets presented a whole new and much different picture of Maya history and culture, much of it quite macabre and unpleasant.

And so it goes.

There was a time when the wisest of men, including those responsible for what we find in the scriptures of Judaism, Christianity and Islam, thought the world was flat and lay at the center of the universe, orbited by the sun, the moon and the stars.

When I was a boy, I was taught that the dinosaurs became extinct because of their size – their having become larger than their food supply and their ability to consume it.

As a young man, I was taught by Air Force technical school instructors that transistors were interesting as a novelty, but that PN junctions were inherently too noisy to ever find applications in military-aerospace electronics.

At any particular time and place, we make the best of what we think we know. Then someone discovers evidence leading to a more valid understanding. For a while the custodians of the old truth resist the new, but eventually the new and better ideas prevail. Knowledge improves.

Religion, like every other work of man, is subject to review and revision. I will speak only of Christianity, since that is my tradition and I do not wish to offend any others by seeming to criticize them from a Christian point of view.

Over the past two or three decades, researchers and scholars have discovered evidence to suggest that the scriptures are considerably fallible. Interestingly, many of their findings also provide new historical insights to support some Old Testament legends, although not their literal interpretations. But there appears to be much in the New Testament that is probably best described as historical fiction.

Most people understand that the Old Testament's stories, which often seem quite far-fetched, do not have to be accepted literally. The seven-day creation sequence, Adam and Eve, Noah's flood, Jonah being swallowed up and living within a whale, Moses' parting of the sea – these are obviously legends, folk tales, poorly understood accounts of actual historical events, and so on.

We have learned a lot about the universe since the long-standing Jewish oral tradition was written down. If, as according to the book called *Genesis*, creation happened as a seven-sequence process, the epochs were certainly much longer than a 24-hour day. On the other hand, science often finds evidence to support other Old Testament tails. For example some now suspect that what has been reported in many traditions as a flood that destroyed the world might have been the result of a catastrophic glacial event, wherein the rising waters of the Mediterranean Sea eventually breached a narrow land bridge, allowing a massive spill into what was an expansive fertile valley, but is now the Black Sea.

The New Testament is much more of a problem for the thinking faithful. While Christianity is Jesus-centered, it would now appear that Jesus was a devout Jew, and never expressed any intention of being anything but. The faith's precepts and doctrines are actually the work of Paul, and writers who were his contemporaries or who produced their contributions as much as one-hundred years after Jesus' death, much of it apparently slanted to avoid offending Rome, to discredit Jewish opposition, and to bulwark tenets of the new Pauline faith.

The Gospel of John, for example, includes more direct quotes of Jesus, and more inside information about his life with the original disciples, than any other source in the Bible. John also goes further than any other reference towards presenting Jesus as a demigod. Much of what is in John became central to the faith, such as the oft quoted John14:6 – "I am the Way and the Truth and the Life. No one comes to the Father except through Me," but few scholars view this material as authentic. John the apostle was probably about eight to thirteen years younger than Jesus. He lived a long life, but died in the year 101 CE, about the time this gospel appeared. If actually written by this John the son of Zebedee, it would represent a remarkably vivid memory for of man of ninety-some years. Most scholars consider the authorship anonymous, and the material, which would have been second or third-hand information at best, as not a reliable source of information about the historical Jesus.

The scriptures are also quite probably in error regarding lesser things. The story of Jesus' birth is dearly beloved, but is probably otherwise unimportant, except to the extent that it links him to prophesy regarding the coming of a messiah – that he would be born of a virgin, in Bethlehem, a descendant of the House of David, and so on. You have probably heard the story enough times that it need not be repeated here. Jewish and Christian scholars suggest a different version, which appears to be much more plausible.

Mary was the daughter of Joachim ("JHO-uh-keem'), an "exceeding rich man" in Sepphoris ("SEF-uh-ris"), an upscale town, some three to four miles north of Nazareth being developed by Herod Antipas as the capital of Galilee. Joseph was probably a farmer, and a skilled handyman, who lived in a small town called Bethlehem, which was only about seven miles northwest of Nazareth. It is not difficult to assume that Joseph would have been spending a lot of time working in Sepphoris, a boom town as it were, and that one of his wealthy clients would have been Mary's father. Joseph was evidently a widower, having at least three existing children, James and Jude and daughter Joanna, when he met Mary. The disparity of social class notwithstanding, a romance between the hired handyman and the client's young daughter would have been only too understandably human. However, that evidently led to scandal when the daughter became pregnant.

First there was the issue of her father's position and the family's social class, compared to that of the prospective father, artisans at that time being socially even lower in the pecking order than peasant farmers. Second, under Jewish law, sex outside of marriage was forbidden for persons eligible for a first marriage. With these things in mind, it is easy to imagine why Joseph would have been permitted to whisk the pregnant girl away to his tiny hometown. There has never been any evidence to support the assertion about an Augustinian census decree, which is rather mixed up anyway, since it refers to the Bethlehem of Judea – eighty or more miles to the south along rugged and dusty trails – rather than the little nearby town in Galilee. The legends about the virgin birth, the bright guiding star, the singing angels, the lowly stable, the gift-bearing magi – these are themes that also appear in other traditions, including pagan beliefs dating back much earlier than Jesus' birth.

Recent research indicates that Galilee was not really the backward pastoral kind of place it has traditionally been thought to be. Evidence from digs at Sepphoris indicates that the city was culturally quite advanced, surrounded by smaller towns like Nazareth, which served as satellite communities. Jesus was reputed to be very comfortable as a frequent guest in the homes of affluent and socially prominent people, spoke three languages, and was evidently very well educated. This would seem strange for the son of a peasant girl and a lowly farmer/handyman, but it would make perfect sense for the grandson of a man such as Joachim. His mamzer status notwithstanding, any mother can easily relate to Mary's probably insisting that he be brought up according to the high standards of her privileged family. There is some indication of jealousy on the part of his stepbrothers, otherwise very little is known about Jesus' childhood. Except for a comment about him learning his father's trade as a boy, there is no information about his life from the time of his birth until his early teens. That time might very well have been spent in Sepphoris, under circumstances much different than the simple, impoverished life depicted in Sunday school booklets.

Herod Antipas began the construction of Sepphoris about four years before the birth of Jesus. The city became the largest and most beautiful in Galilee, but was destroyed by earthquake in 363. Serious excavation and study of the site has been going on only since the 1980's – only about twenty years. This is but one example of many instances where newly acquired knowledge suggests new, and seemingly more plausible, scenarios for New Testament narratives.

Those who earnestly defend the scriptures as infallible, refer to this sort of thinking as dangerously liberal, revisionist, or worse. Their arguments, however, are based exclusively upon their interpretation of scriptures, and a staunch refusal to consider the possible validity of any new information. I will leave you to judge that attitude for yourself.

Meanwhile, as the fortunes of mainline Christianity continue to decline, there is growing support for a new approach to the faith.

Fundamentalists and those of the evangelical persuasion, claim this is the result of the perverse liberal kind of thinking illustrated above, having been promoted by "such liberal institutions as Harvard, Yale, Princeton, Duke, Brown, Union, etc.", and thereby having become widespread among the mainline churches. Their back-to-the-bible movement attracts believers who feel more at home with a simplistic, unquestioned and unchanging version of the faith. The evangelical movement itself has enjoyed a certain success as these people leave mainline denominations and gather under new roofs. It is less clear that the movement has brought new believers into the faith.

Others choose the more difficult path of integrating the expanding historical and cultural knowledge of the biblical Christian era with what we are learning in other areas, such as social and cultural anthropology, political science, comparative literature, the physical sciences, and even psychology, with hopes of coming up with an understanding of the faith which is more meaningful and more useful in today's real world.

Up to now, ordinary Christians have been led to believe that Christianity is the only way of salvation, with the faith generally being about sin, guilt, and forgiveness. Their understanding is that Christian living is about obeying rules and reaping benefits, as provided for in the scriptures, the Bible being the only definitive guide to acceptable behavior. The ultimate prize under this paradigm is *salvation*, which refers mainly to what happens after life.

In plain words, we have been asked to believe that Jesus meant what he said when (and if) he warned in John14:6, "I am the Way and the Truth and the Life. No one comes to the Father except through Me." We must therefore "accept Jesus Christ as our personal Lord and Savior" in order to get a ticket to Heaven. Unfortunately, nobody is able to explain exactly what that means. What exactly does one's "personal Lord and Savior" do?

Next, we are told that Jesus died for our sins. That seems a little illogical. Since He died two thousand years before we were even born, God must have known we were always going to be a hopeless case – that even after two thousand years, we would still be in need of that saving grace. So what's the point? Why not have thrown in the towel way back then; but of course, that is what Jesus' closest associates actually did think was going to happen – that the end times would soon be upon them. Christians have been expecting that for the past two-thousand years.

Then there is the ever-repetitive confession of sin/assurance of pardon ritual. Behave badly; but, not to worry. If one is truly repentant and asks, all his sins will be forgiven – removed "as far as the east is from the west." Down here in the real world, when people pull this, we call it *incorrigible* and we eventually send them to our man-made hells (a.k.a. "prisons"). What sense does this make? If you can always be sure you're going to get a free pass, why worry a bunch about your behavior? If you were God, would you not eventually begin to suspect that someone's coming back week after week with the same old confessions and pleas for mercy, probably suggests that they have never really been contrite at all?

And from a psychological perspective, how good is it to sit bowed in a pew fifty-two or more times a year saying stuff like, "My bad! God, I know I am no good – lower than a snake's belly in a wagon track, and totally unworthy of your attention, let alone forgiveness. But in your infinite compassion, have mercy on me (even though you know I am just a liar, who will be right back here next Sunday, hat in hand, saying the same thing)." Most of us already have self-esteem issues. How, exactly, does this help?

Then there are the sacraments, such as Baptism and the Eucharist, also known as Holy Communion or the Lord's Supper.

Infant baptisms are usually cute, and sometimes touching. It is a nice way for parents to show off their latest blessing. That is probably about the extent of it. During the ritual the parents mumble a quickly forgotten promise to raise their child in the faith. Then the congregation promises to also see to it that the child will come to know the Lord – a promise that is perfectly perfunctory and probably taken seriously by neither side. Most people probably see this for what it is; an old initiation rite which harkens back to an even more ancient purification right, and which has become rather irrelevant at today's level of intellectual sophistication.

Communion is supposedly a high holy sacrament, so sacred, in fact, that I feel reluctant to mention it in this vein. Nevertheless, anything ritualistically practiced over and over again eventually loses its ability to excite and awe anyone. The scenario seems as if it was simple enough. Jewish meals always featured at least bread and wine, since there was a common ritual connected to each of these elements, one at the beginning of the meal, and one at its end. At a special meal, which was essentially a farewell, Jesus simply said, 'Remember me, friends,' adding some Dale Carnegie-type memory clues; bread=body, wine=blood. That was no doubt a touching moment for all present. Maybe when they did their little Jewish bread and wine rituals at every meal thereafter, they did indeed remember. What does that mean to us? A little thimbleful of grape juice and a cube of stale bread is somehow the equivalent of that deeply touching moment two-thousand years ago? Does the Jewish bread and wine of old translate, in today's culture, to burger buns and Pepsi such that we should take a moment at Burger King to remember? And if the church really feels that this sacrament is so sacred, what's with the cheap generic reconstituted grape juice? Not even Welch's! No real wine? Who does that pander to?

Well, there is more, of course. Much more. And the institutional answers to these "puzzlements" are always the same – more scripture, more metaphorical and metaphysical jargon, more magical thinking – along with a thinly veiled undercurrent that were we better Christians we would not be bothered by such questions and doubts.

I am quite sure, as are many more notable than I, that this is mostly what keeps people home on Sunday mornings. It is not that they have decided to be atheists, or even agnostic. Rather, it is just frustration with the institutional church, which feels entitled to their continuing support in spite of its never being willing or able to come up with any plausible answers to these simple, but relevant questions.

I suspect the statistics indicating a decline in church membership reflect only that. I am quite confident that there are just as many God-fearing faithful now, as a percent of the general population, as there have ever been, and probably even more. They might have lots of questions and doubts, and only the vaguest notion of what the connection is between God and Jesus, if indeed there is any. But they still *know* that there is a God, if for no other reason than the plainly visible fact that someone or something creates order in what is a profoundly complex and potentially chaotic universe. For lack of any better name, that someone or something might as well be called "God."

There is indeed "good news." The future holds hopeful prospects for these lurkers.

What is being called the *emerging paradigm* offers Christianity as a model that leads people to God, and creates a passion in them for justice, mercy, love – the things God cares most about. Under this new paradigm, faith involves growing in loyalty to God, and trust in God. Rather than an after-death reward for good behavior or long suffering, salvation in this paradigm is thought of as a transforming process that begins on this side of death to bring joy and fulfillment to the living.

Jesus and the Emerging Paradigm

Jesus began a liberalizing movement in the Jewish faith, such as it was during his life and times. He was egalitarian; his Jewish contemporaries affirmed hierarchy. Jesus was kind to wayward women, the poor, and the ill; his Jewish contemporaries scorned them. Jesus focused on ethics; they, on ritual. He preached and lived a politics of compassion; they practiced and enforced a politics of purity. Jesus taught a love of neighbor that extended naturally across ethnic, racial, and national boundaries; they were consumed with Jewish nationalism and a concern for racial purity.

Jesus' attitudes were no doubt formed, at least in part, as the products of his own personal experience with discrimination. To devout Jews, he was a mamzer – an outcast of sorts, or second-class citizen. Whether he intended it or not, Jesus laid the foundation of a faith that made the God of the Jews accessible to everyone, through the subsequent works of Paul, who carried Jesus' ideas to their ultimate implementation, and beyond.

In Paul's mission to gentile God-fearers, the rigmarole of the Jewish traditions – namely, Torah observance and circumcision – eventually fell by the wayside. At that point, the Jesus movement, at least in Paul's implementation of it, ceased to be a faction in Judaism, and began to take on a life of its own, with a name of its own. Jesus' image gradually morphed from that of a Jewish rabbi whom some thought of as a prophet or even the messiah, to a demigod – the son of God himself. The Christian church developed the concept of a trinity; Father, Son and Holy Ghost, with Jesus taking on a highly personalized and sentimentalized role of intercessor – one's personal Lord and Savior. All this was probably a little over the top, since there is nothing in the scriptures to suggest that Jesus of Nazareth ever envisioned such an outcome.

In spite of the attitudes of his contemporary Jews, Jesus' thinking was not revolutionary, or anti-Jewish. Native to ancient Judaism itself was a belief that at the *End of Days*, God would reveal himself in glory. Gentiles would then repudiate their idols and as gentiles (without converting to Judaism) acknowledge and worship the true God together with Israel in the temple at Jerusalem. This arose from the Jewish understanding that their God was the only God, not just the God of the Jews, but the God of all the nations, and in the end, would redeem all who had gone astray.

Jesus and his followers believed that time had come, that the long-expected End of Days was at hand. Therefore, what they were suggesting was not out of order at all – just a little ahead of its time.

If emerging knowledge eventually leads to a rescinding of the Pauline aspects of the faith, and the un-deification of Jesus, Christianity will revert to its roots as an Abrahamic tradition. Jesus of Nazareth will nonetheless continue to be revered as its founder, much the same as Mohammad is venerated in Islam. In that day, Judaism, Christianity and Islam will stand together as three branches of the same faith.

The Kingdom Coming?

The thinking that is being brought to bear on the Christian faith is largely the product of *the information age*. Archeologists may dig, researchers may research, and philosophers may philosophize. Yet the evidence will never be perfect, and the conclusions, no matter how well studied, thought out, and debated, will forever remain speculative.

The difference between now, and the two-thousand years that have led up to now, is that this is no longer happening in a limited and cloistered domain. It is happing in the public domain, where tens of millions have access to the data, and have the option of deciding for themselves what it all means. The final sorting out of any issue will have to make sense to the majority of these stakeholders, and in that, you can be confident that the most sensible and rational thinking will prevail. It always ultimately does. As Abraham Lincoln supposedly said, "You may fool all the people some of the time; you can even fool some of the people all of the time. But you cannot fool all of the people all the time."

Judaism and Islam are no more immune to this developing process than Christianity, and will certainly also gradually change as new information produces new ways of thinking about aspects which do not stand on solid foundations of fact or logic.

The coming revisions will, I am sure, ultimately dilute traditional differences, making at least part of the Kingdom of God a reality – that all the nations will finally worship the one and only God under the same roof. In fact, this is already happening. Protestant-Catholic suspicions and antagonism have largely dissolved over the past fifty years. Christian youth groups are hosted by Rabbis in Jewish synagogues to learn about that faith, and its relationship to their roots. During his first visit to the United States, Pope Benedict recently shared the *bimah* in worship with Rabbi Arthur Schneier at New York's monumental Park East Synagogue – a historic event of deep significance to both Christians and Jews. As an unintended consequence of wars in Iraq and Afghanistan, Americans are rapidly developing an interest in Islam, and that previously unfamiliar sister faith is rapidly being demystified.

The portent of this is profound. History teaches that religion has been the source of much of the world's troubles. Religion has been one of the chief promoters of tribalism and xenophobia, causing strife between people practicing differing faiths, or differing versions of the same faith. But now, as knowledge and belief begin to merge and the differences between cultures begin to dissolve, the tragic pattern of human history will inevitably change.

This new epoch of improved communication and mutual understanding might very well also bring to fruition the remaining aspects of the Kingdom of God – peace, justice and prosperity for all.

Things That Matter

You will not find in this chapter anything to suggest that any particular religious tradition is better or worse than any other. In *things that matter*, all religions, and especially Christianity, Islam and Judaism, have much more in common than in conflict. In offering this chapter, I hope to sell you on two ideas. The first is to keep well away from the extremes – the ultra-conservative or fundamentalist right, and the ultra-liberal or atheistic left. The second is to participate actively in your religion.

Why should you do that?

God is not going to send all sorts of favors and goodies your way because you have decided to become devout and righteous, nor will others think you are a really decent person because you are "walking the walk, and talking the talk." Much of what I have already written in this chapter is intended to discourage you from thinking like that about religion. Faith, when followed in a sensible way, works to everyone's benefit – including yours. It would therefore be silly to stubbornly stick to your fundamentalist, agnostic, or atheistic guns and pass up these benefits.

To understand what I'm talking about, let us briefly review.

Religions arise from man's fear of loneliness and vulnerability. Our religions help us to understand and establish a cooperative relationship with the invisible forces behind nature through a belief in an unseen higher power. Each religious tradition strongly embraces stories, or *mythologies*, which spring from that belief, regarding the behavior of their gods, creation, fertility, the social order and morals, and death.

Myths are not factual. They do not arise from hard knowledge of actual events. They are basic truths which are devised to satisfy our inquisitive nature and fulfill our need for meaning.

Some of our myths seem to spring spontaneously from a standard knowledge base, so to speak, which seems to be shared by all humanity, no matter how distant and different people might be from each other. The truths they communicate are always more or less the same – as generally valid in one setting as in any other. All religions have myths which explain creation, myths about their god or gods, myths explaining how their religion began and evolved into what it is today, myths that explain death, and so on.

Other myths seek to explain and give meaning to natural phenomena and actual events, by spinning them as acts of god. These include stories of such events as a great flood or a military catastrophe that resulted in a people being displaced and forced into slavery.

We devise *rituals* that dramatize the myths we think are most sacred. In the Christian tradition examples are baptism, communion, marriage, burial services, and so on. *Symbols* (e.g., the baptismal fount, the loaf and the wine, golden rings, the cross, stars, menorahs, and more) are invented to represent these concepts and stories visually.

Thus, each religion develops its own unique tradition of faith, pomp and ceremony.

Religion forms culture. Religion's mythology, rituals and symbols produce the culture's laws, ideas, habits, holidays and social organization. You come into life as a child of the culture you happened to be born into, and therefore as a product of its religion.

No human being can know with absolute certainty about creation, fertility, or death. Are we more than the animals? Are we immortal sprits momentarily occupying mortal flesh? What is "spirit"? Where do we come from? How and when does human life begin? What happens when we die? These mysteries are unknowable, so we must satisfy ourselves with our religion's mythological explanations.

You *can* certainly know about your culture's social order and morals. These come about as widely accepted fundamental ideas of what is considered right and wrong. Do not murder, steal from others, or lie to anyone. Do not jeopardize a marriage through illicit copulation. Respect elders. Show compassion and charity to all.

Every religious tradition has such a code and, not surprisingly, they are all very similar. In this context, this is called *religious humanism* and the obeying of these fundamental principles is related to righteousness and the pleasing of God. As a practical matter, however, they are just as valid in a *secular humanist* (non-religious) context. These ideas arise from rational considerations which are easy to relate to self-interest. Even a child can figure them out. To protect yourself from hurtfulness and abuse by others, you agree to not do hurtful and abusive things to them – to treat others as you would like to be treated.

So here you have the first couple of reason to adhere to whatever your faith is.

First, it provides explanations for the unknowable. You might think they are nebulous and questionable, but they are better than nothing, which is what you would otherwise have. What would it be like to have absolutely no ideas at all about creation, life, or death? I cannot imagine what that would be like, because I was indoctrinated into a tradition from the time of my birth, and have no way to erase the myths that I was taught. Your situation is probably the same. You could not be totally devoid of religion even if you wanted to be.

On the other hand, I *can* imagine what it is like to believe the mythology implicitly.

My maternal grandmother never, ever had any doubts about being a child of God, her Father in Heaven, who loved her dearly, who would always care for and protect her and would one day take her home. She never doubted that God always acted for good, whether she understood or not. She lived a hard life on a rather crude little farm in what is now Michigan's historic Port Oneida. She gave birth to nine children, five of whom died young, mostly before age five. Their father, her hard-working farmer husband, also died young, unexpectedly leaving her alone with family and farm.

Yet, I cannot remember ever seeing her cry. I think she probably did because she was a gentle, kind-hearted soul. But she had no need to make a big thing of adversities. If it was death, she *knew* that her loved one had just crossed over to a better place. If it was anything else, she *knew* that "… all things work together for good to those who love God …"

She died at age ninety-nine; just shy of one-hundred years old. She was tiny – barely five feet tall and weighing less than a hundred pounds – but was spry and healthy right up to the end. The day before she passed on, she said to my mother, her youngest daughter, "Well, Myrtle – I think my time has come now." The next day she was gone. It was as simple as that. No suffering. No regrets.

"Yeah, so your grandma was a bible-thumper!" you say.

No, she actually was not. Other than saying grace before meals (which, admittedly, always seemed to us kids as if it would never end), she never talked much about religion. I never heard, or heard of, her witnessing, evangelizing or proselytizing.

I am not suggesting that you should be like my Grandma – I certainly am not. But you can be, if you want to. You do not have to be a freak to believe in that way. She certainly was not, and although I have never been that innocent and devout in my beliefs, I still have a great deal of respect for her, and even envy the way she was able to be.

Up to now, I have always looked upon Grandma Kelderhouse's faith as something that probably came easy to a person who was simple and earthy – much less intellectually sophisticated than I am, in other words. Now I suspect that she was actually a lot smarter than I have been. I have always thought her simplistic beliefs were too – simplistic. What a racket! You rue something bad happening, so you pray God it will not. Then it happens and you simply shrug it off as "God's will." That seemed really convenient all the way around; a no-lose deal for God – a no-doubt deal for Christians.

When I was young, I rather impudently anticipated that I would eventually learn some things, or new knowledge would arise, which would debunk Grandma's simple faith. But now, in my more mature years, I wonder. How does it profit anyone to discount the mythology without having anything to put in its place? Would cluelessness or chaos work better?

For example, maybe all things actually do work together for good – after all, what do I know? Am I an all-seeing eye high in the sky? Maybe God has priorities bigger than me. Maybe something that is a great good for most others, the earth or the universe just happens to be not so good for me – in which case, that would just be my tough luck. Would I expect a loving and caring God to favor me at the expense of everyone or everything else? Yet again, it often seems as if God is, in fact, mindful such situations, caring of individuals, and ultimately makes up for them with other compensations.

From another point of view, maybe God knows that things which seem like such a catastrophe to me are not actually such a big deal. I am now sixty-seven years old, and as I think back upon my life, I can now see that no matter what ever happened, no matter how impossibly tragic or awfully fatal I thought anything was at the time, I somehow always muddled through. What is the explanation? Maybe there was an angel always on my shoulder? Or perhaps I was simply in the habit of unnecessarily awfulizing everything, making every bad situation much worse than it had to be? Had I been a better student of my faith, I could have known the answer all along, since it is taught in the Old Testament book *The Song of Solomon* – "This too shall pass." As a matter of fact, every religion offers this same bit of fundamental wisdom which, as Lincoln put it, 'chastens in the hour of pride and consoles in the depths of affliction.'

If I embrace these fundamental precepts of my faith, I can accept things I cannot change and get on with life. The alternative is the *stercus accidit* philosophy of life, and when stercus does accidit, one usually feels victimized, becomes angry, and eventually winds up chronically pessimistic, hopeless, and often depressed.

When accused of being negative, which I frequently was during the first half of my life, I used to respond, "I am not negative! I simply believe in preparing for the worst, so if anything better happens, I can be happy about it!" In fact, that did not work very well. Preparing for the worst seldom produced better outcomes. I had lots of problems with disabling stress and depression.

I can now see that there is something to be said for religion and its fundamentally positive precepts. It is not just about being good in order to please God and one's religious friends now, and to avoid going to hell later on. Switzerland's Carl Jung (pronounced "Yung"), influential thinker and the founder of analytical psychology, elevated common sense to psychological principle when he said, "People do better when hopeful, rather than when afraid – when looking forward, rather than when looking back." This is perhaps the best reason to remain active in the practice your religion.

We are talking about the "big things" now, not the little, inconsequential things. Recall that religion begins with a perception of an unseen god. A tradition of legendary stories gradually develops – myths explaining that god and natural phenomena. Then come rituals and symbols which produce remindful pomp and ceremony.

And therein usually lies the rub.

Being ever restless and inquisitive, we begin to wander into the realms of the sublime. Seeking more meaning where there is none to be found, we begin to create it. Becoming enamored of our rituals and symbols, and preoccupied with their elegance and formality, we endow them with meanings and significances of their own. We create issues that do not matter.

All religions agree on the things that really matter. Disputes and rivalries between religions arise from the things that do not matter.

Born Again

I avoid quoting scripture, because I feel that the Bible is neither infallible, nor the "word of God." I would be especially reluctant to refer to the New Testament's *Gospel of John*, since its authorship and purpose are generally considered suspect.

However, the third chapter of John introduces a concept to Christians that is common to all faiths, and to the Cognitive Behavior Theory of modern psychology. One has to wonder if the ancients knew a long time ago what CBT has only recently rediscovered.

According to John, Jesus told Nicodemus, a wealthy and popular Jewish Pharisee, "Except a man be born again ... except he be born of water and of the Spirit, he cannot enter into the kingdom of God."

Assuming the quotation is authentic, which is reasonably questionable since John is thought to have been written about 100-years after Jesus' death, recalling that Jesus was a devout Jew and parsing it accordingly, "the kingdom of God" referred to a sort of Utopia – a time and place of legal, social and political perfection, or peace, prosperity and happiness. The reference to water referred to the Jewish ritual of immersion, which symbolized a final washing away of one's past, promoting a sense of readiness to resume a close relationship with the Spirit – God.

Mohammad offered a similar teaching for Muslims: "Fight in this life itself the tendencies of the spirit prone to evil, tempting to lead you into iniquity's ways. Reach the next stage when the self-accusing sprit in your conscience is awakened and the soul is anxious to attain moral excellence and revolt against disobedience. This will lead you to the final stage of the soul at rest, contented with God, finding its happiness and delight in him alone."

In Buddhism, "born again" refers to enlightenment. As recounted in the legend: "And then a great understanding came to him. He saw in his mind all the life of the world and the planets; of all the past and all the future. He understood the meaning of existence, of why we are here on this earth and what has created us – the cause of suffering and the path to everlasting joy." Among other things, through his enlightenment Siddhartha the Prince, who became the Buddha, discovered that the creator or architect was not an external being, but was our own internal nature. This sounds a lot like what Carl Jung thought he had discovered; his "collective unconscious" (or "objective psyche").

Psychology, through Cognitive Behavior Theory, has come around to this same sort of thinking, couching it in secular terms, of course. In its simplest expression, CBT teaches that growing up is bad for self-esteem, producing negative feelings – feeling flawed, unworthy, ashamed, guilty, and so on – feelings which cause adults to behave in all sorts of self-defeating ways. The solution offered by CBT is to recognize what happened while growing-up, then repeating the process, this time infusing the mind with rational complimentary concepts, to offset all the invalid cognitions that reside there as a result of childhood. This is sometimes called *self-reparenting*.

Sounds a lot like being "born again," does it not?

Does God Really Exist?

> Who has seen the wind?
>   Neither you nor I.
> But when the trees bow down their heads,
>   The wind is passing by.
>
> *Christina Rossetti*

"Believe? I cannot believe. I do not believe just for the sake of believing. One must have a reason for a certain hypothesis. When there are sufficient reasons to form a certain hypothesis, I shall accept these reasons, obviously. Then I say, 'We have to accept the possibility of ...' whatever."

Carl Jung

When asked, just before his death in 1961, if he believed in God, Carl Jung's (usually pronounced "Yoong") reply was rather lengthy and profound: "I could not say I believe; I know! I have had the experience of being gripped by something that is stronger than myself, something that people call God."

When he was about thirty-seven, Jung began to occasionally sense a presence – as if he were not alone. Up to this point, although he had had a falling out with his former friend and colleague, the eminent psychiatrist Sigmund Freud, Jung was still highly regarded. As his ventures into the paranormal became more frequent and profound however, many began to regard him as a crackpot. His most frequent "visitor" took the form of an elderly and very wise man, an apparition he eventually named *Philemon*. Here is what Jung had to say about these episodes:

> "Philemon and other figures of my fantasies brought home to me the crucial insight that there are things in the psyche which I do not produce, but which produce themselves and have their own life. Philemon represented a

force which was not myself. In my fantasies I held conversations with him, and he said things which I had not consciously thought. For I observed clearly that it was he who spoke, and not I."

"Psychologically, Philemon represented superior insight. All my works, all my creative activity, has come from those initial fantasies and dreams, which began in 1912. He was a mysterious figure to me. At times he seemed to me quite real, as if he were a living personality. I went walking up and down the garden with him, and to me he was what the Indians call a guru."

"That religious experiences exist no longer needs proof. But it will always remain doubtful whether what metaphysics and theology call God and the gods is the real ground of these experiences. The question is idle, actually, and answers itself by reason of the subjectively overwhelming numinosity (supernaturalness) of the experience. Anyone who has had it, is seized by it and therefore not in a position to indulge in fruitless metaphysical or epistemological speculations. Absolute certainty brings its own evidence and has no need of anthropomorphic proofs (the attribution of human motivation, characteristics, or behavior to God)."

"I find my God in my dreams."

Jung thought he had discovered a hidden aspect of the mind, which he called the *collective unconscious*. This peculiar aspect of the mind contained "a reservoir of the experiences of our species," – fundamental knowledge and universal truths which direct a person's conscious thinking and behavior by means of archetypes (a pattern of thought or symbolic imagery), dreams, and intuition. It was something that every human already possessed as they came into this world, a part of their being as common and essential to their being a whole person as any physical part of their body.

Unfortunately, it contained not only knowledge of good, but also of evil.

Furthermore, he thought that this faculty was not confined to space and time, that it was capable of psychic phenomena – producing visions of the future, receiving messages from spirit guides, and such things. Therefore, it seemed to him that the psyche (one's spirit or soul), being not subject to the dimensions of time and space like the physical body, exists in some other realm about which we know nothing.

In Jung's view, this was the manifestation of God, as we know it, and that this God exists within every human being. With this understanding in mind, he suggested:

> "Man's relation to God probably has to undergo a certain important change. Instead of the propitiating praise to an unpredictable king, or the child's prayer to a loving father, the responsible living and fulfilling of the divine will in us will be our form of worship and commerce with God."

Near the end of his life, Jung felt quite certain that the *evil* aspect of the collective unconscious, which he had by then renamed the *objective psyche*, would soon prove to be our undoing. At first, he foresaw the total destruction of creation, as we know it here on Earth. But prior to his death, he was evidently led to understand that our world would indeed suffer a terrible calamity, but would not be totally destroyed. Limited areas would escape total annihilation. He shared these dark thoughts only with his closest friends and colleagues. For everyone else, he offered these thoughts:

> "As far as we can discern, the sole purpose of human existence is to kindle a light of meaning in the darkness of

mere being. God's goodness means grace and light, and his dark side, the terrible temptation of power."

"Man has already received so much knowledge that he can destroy his own planet. Nothing shows more drastically than this possibility, how much of divine power has come within the reach of man."

"We are the origin of all coming evil. Let us hope that God's good spirit will guide him in his decisions, because it will depend upon man's decision whether God's creations will continue."

Whew! That is some deep stuff!

I feel a little ambivalent about giving Carl Jung so much ink, since modern psychology has moved well beyond many of the ideas he and Freud came up with in the early years. I, for instance, do not accept the proposition that we are born into this life with a canned archive representing all of the experiences of our species up to the point of our birth. I think it is easy to see how what we consider fundamental knowledge and universal truths is simply common sense knowledge, passed along from one generation to another in the normal course.

I have brought Jung along here for two reasons.

First, to illustrate that people have lots of different concepts of God – breathtakingly different, as you can see from what Jung, a widely acknowledged genius, thought. Because of the way he conceived of God, Jung had absolutely no doubt that God exists. He could say quite honestly and earnestly, "I do not *believe* – I know!"

Second, Jung and I have some paranormal experiences in common.

My Philemon

If I were to write about those without any preamble, you would be apt to think of me as many others did of Jung – that I am a crackpot.

Only one of my experiences was as elaborate as Jung's ongoing collaboration with his Philemon. It was the second such experience I ever had. Unlike Philemon, the old man, my spirit advisor was just a boy, about nine or ten years old, and he came for a special purpose. To understand what it was, you will need to know something about my early years.

The home I grew up in was full of anger to the point of rage, resentment, meanness and vulgarity. By the age of ten or twelve, I was emotionally numbed, reclusive, alone and terribly ashamed of myself. I hated my father, my family, and myself, and often wished I could die. Every now and then I'd think of killing myself, and would get well into the process, but always stop short, never having the courage to go through with it. I recall standing on a box in the basement, with a hangman's noose around my neck, and weeping bitterly after another failed attempt. I was so useless I did not even have the guts to kill myself! I was totally frustrated. I eventually found myself hunting my father like an animal with a loaded 12-Guage. When I had him in my sights, I chickened out then too. I stood there stupidly crying. I hated myself even more than him!

Sometime during those years, the boy who was me went away. What remained in his place was a shell of a person. I developed the habit of planning on the worst, so that when anything less than that happened I could be happy. As soon as I graduated from high school, I enlisted in the U.S. Air Force. That was my ticket out. Unfortunately, I was forced to wait several months before the Air Force could finally take me, but in March of 1959 I finally left that hell hole.

For most of my life, I remained a loner – not by choice, but simply because as a child I'd perfected the art of avoiding close relationships. I eventually married, and had children of my own, but there always remained a part of me that was still a loner, a part that needed a certain amount of time in solitude. I had that time at night, after my family had gone off to their beds, in the wee hours after they had all long been asleep. In the peace and quiet of those hours, I could efficiently take care of the day's business paperwork, catch up on correspondence, or study, or read.

One night, in the spring of 1996, while sitting at the computer in the family room where I burned the midnight oil, I suddenly sensed that I was not alone – that there was a presence, as if someone looking over my left shoulder. Assuming it was my wife or one of the kids, perhaps having trouble sleeping and gotten up for a drink or a snack, I was not disturbed and continued with my attention focused on what I was doing. After several minutes of their just standing quietly there at my shoulder, I turned in my chair to see – nothing. There was no one there. Yet, when I turned back to my work, I still had the same feeling that someone was standing just behind me, looking over my left shoulder. From that moment on, wherever I moved to that evening and whatever I did, I could not shake the feeling that someone was following.

The next morning I woke up with the unsettling feeling that it was not just a figment of my imagination – a hallucination caused by fatigue at that late hour the night before. I also soon realized it was still there. Not long after I had gotten up, the sensation reappeared – someone tagging along behind or beside me.

At that point, this was frightening. Was I having a nervous breakdown, or losing my mind altogether? Was I dying – was this was the angel who would take me home, or maybe the devil coming to claim his due. Yet, it did not really feel like that sort of situation. In fact, this presence felt friendly – even comforting in a way. I began getting used to it during the next couple of days, and liked having it around. While doing my best to act perfectly normal, and not mentioning any of this to anyone, in my thoughts I talked to it, and eventually it began to talk back.

"It" was a boy. A nice boy, without an age, of course, but feeling like about ten or twelve. He became my constant companion, getting up with me in the morning, sharing in everything I did throughout the day, and crawling back into bed and snuggling up beside me at night. He was beautiful. He was loving. He was awesome in every way. I was in love.

What would others think were they to become aware of what was going on in my head? Was I becoming a dreaded pedophile – a boy-lover? What else could this be? Although actually an apparition, this boy was entirely real to me and I loved him dearly. In these few days, I had become as happy as I had ever been since the days of falling in love and marrying my wife. My heart was full of joy, and I felt a wonderful peace and contentment.

Then, about two weeks after the boy first came to me, he said, "I have to go now." A prolonged silent dialog followed. I did not want him to leave and begged him to stay with me. For two days I agonized over the realization that this obviously could not go on, that it wasn't real, that maybe I *was* losing my mind – that I still did not want him to go. And he kept trying to make me understand that he should not stay – could not stay.

On the morning of the third day, he hugged me, clinging to me tightly and whispering, "I have to go now, but I'll always be with you."

As I felt his presence begin to fade, the tears began streaming down my cheeks, and I rushed away to a private place where nobody would see me crying – over nothing.

How could I explain this to anyone? Surely they would think I was in bad need of therapy!

But I had a friend in Los Angeles, a very sensitive and intuitive friend. I knew he would listen with an open mind and would believe.

On hearing my story, and because he already knew something of my background, he immediately knew the answer. The boy was me – the me that had gone into hiding so many years ago, and had finally found the courage to come back out. He had come to show me the boy I had really been – a boy who was beautiful, loving and awesome in every way – a boy who bore no resemblance whatsoever to the image of myself that I had carried around in my mind for forty-six years – an image that had spoiled what could have been the best years of my life.

In an instant, I realized my friend in L.A. was right, and I understood what "I have to go now, but I'll always be with you." meant.

Happily, the boy went away but did not go far. I always have the feeling that he's somewhere nearby, and every now and then he comes back for a moment, or a few hours, or a day.

Although that happened over ten years ago, I still have trouble controlling my composure when I revisit what is for me a very emotional story. Although I know there are others who would judge this as the delusions of a crackpot, I still have no doubts about it; sometimes wondering how such apparitions work, but knowing that it was certainly not insanity, or merely a "brain fart." As Carl Jung said, such experiences bring with them absolute certainty, as anyone who has ever been seized with one knows. It is a certainty that comes from within. It cannot be analyzed because the experience is overwhelmingly supernatural, with the mind operating in realms man knows nothing about, as yet, and possibly never will.

So what has this got to do with God?

A devoutly religious person would never doubt a story like this. An ancient might suspect that "the boy" was actually an angel that God had sent to drive out a demon. A more modern believer would interpret it as God, or perhaps Jesus Christ or the Holy Ghost, intervening directly to turn someone's life around. Jung would interpret this experience as proof of the "peculiar mind function" he interpreted as God, and which he believed resides within every person. Whatever you choose to believe, the reality is that, fantasy or not, this was indeed a life-changing experience for me – the kind of thing we believe God is supposed to do – the kind of deliverance from emotional pain and sorrow that we pray for.

If not God, then who or what?

My Indigo Visitor

God made man in his image? More likely, it was the other way around.

We typically picture god as a father image – a wise and all-powerful old man with white hair, a full beard, wearing a white robe, possibly with fire shooting out of the tip of his right hand's index finger. As you can see, others have dramatically different ideas. Were you able to get your mind around Jung's concept of God as an intangible and mystical presence in your mind, a presence that is not confined by the law of physics, therefore giving you access to, and making you accessible to, metaphysical realms and agents not of this physical world?

That actually makes more sense than the image of God as "father." Jung found the concept acceptable because his visions and dreams provided certain evidence to support such a hypothesis, whereas there is no evidence whatsoever to support the familiar imagery of God being physically and psychologically similar to the humans he created – save for the brief and highly parsable comment in Genesis 1:26, "And God said, Let us make man in our image, after our likeness ..." In fact, Jung's ideas in this regard were original only to the extent of relating what many Bible scholars and commentators already thought, to his field of analytical psychology.

Genesis 1:27 goes on to say, "So God created man in his own image, in the image of God created he him; male and female created he them." People who take all this literally, thinking that God has the same physical form as humans, often get hung up on gender, questioning the use of masculine forms in referring to God. This leads to the cavalier modification of old, familiar and beloved hymns, and affected English constructs such as, "For God so loved the world that God gave God's only begotten Son ..." It exposes an ignorance of both biblical meanings and the English language, the masculine form having traditionally been used as the unmarked or *gender neutral* form – the form to be used unless it is known to be inappropriate. It also exposes the penchant for believers to take their attention away from things that matter, to occupy themselves with issues that do not.

Several months after the boy episode, I experienced another strange and upsetting presence, this one gender-neutral and very brief, but no less profound and meaningful.

Alone again, this time in my office in the early evening hours, I was merrily doing some paperwork when the ambiance suddenly and dramatically changed. All of the familiar sights, sounds and surroundings dissolved from my awareness, as if I had been transported to another place, where there was nothingness – just me, and a conspicuous, but invisible, "presence." I actually saw nothing with my eyes, yet in my memory there is an image of a figure that was tall, featureless, and blue – dark blue and indistinct, as if perhaps draped in a full length robe, and chimerically wavering, like a reflection on water or a form seen through heat waves in air

Nothing was said, but somehow I was struck with the realization that I was in the presence of something much superior to me – something more perfectly pure and without fault or flaw than the human mind is capable of fathoming. As often as I have tried to describe this apparition, words have failed. None of the superlatives in the English language seem adequate; all of them seem to apply, yet even in combination they fall far short of the glory of whatever this was.

I felt so small and ashamed, and utterly unworthy to be in the presence of such a figure – yet overjoyed by having, for who knows what reason, been chosen for such a blessing.

A new general view of our terrible world suddenly took form in my mind. All my life I have known the myth about the Garden of Eden, and Adam and Eve. I understood that we humans had become stubbornly self-centered and dark spirited, even sometimes downright evil – that we had fallen far from what we originally were. But until that evening, I had never really realized *how far* we had fallen, or how awful we had made our world.

We are born into the mess our ancestors have created. It is all we know. We become accustomed to living with dark things – our *seven deadly sins*, which lead to hate, shame, and guilt. Success in life, for us, is merely to avoid wretchedness or death. We abide.

The utter perfection that stood before me showed with profound clarity the depths to which we have fallen. So far separated are we from that kind of perfection and purity that our situation seemed tragically hopeless. The chasm was so wide; how could man ever rise back up to approach anything worthy of deliverance?

We abide indeed – like a man fallen into a cesspool who, frightened and struggling, is barely able to keep his head above the stinking muck. He lives, but helplessly, at the bottom of that pit, ever hopeful that someday, somehow, someone will come along and raise him up. And such are we – ever copiously replenishing the contents of the cesspool we are drowning in.

And yet, in spite of it all, God evidently remains faithful to us. Else, what was this standing here in my office, making me to see the difference between what we are, and what we were and could again be?

And I wondered, why me? 'Who am I that these would be mindful of me?' I am nothing. I am worse than nothing, since I am equal among all those who sin and hate, and suffer the consequential shame and guilt.

I sat there in my office armchair and stupidly wept; ashamed and broken-hearted.

As this fantasy faded back into reality, I thought the dark-blue form left with a message: "Well done." I had no idea what that meant. What had been 'well done'? I had no idea then, nor have I come up with any since.

After this episode, I never again wondered whether or not God exists. Call it "God," "Allah," "Yahweh," or whatever, I have to accept the hypothesis that a primordial consciousness and creator, exists. A preponderance of circumstantial evidence supports it.

No, I would not presume to suggest that I had an encounter with God in my office, or the Holy Ghost.

Your Imaginary Friend

Over the years since this experience, I have developed the sense that we are not alone in this life, that each one has a guardian angel who accompanies and watches. Some call this a *spirit guide*. Unlike them, I do not pretend to understand this. All I know is that once in a while my angel or guide intervenes, usually invisibly I suspect, but sometimes coming quite close to revealing himself.

Although it is convenient to simplify by thinking of him as a discrete spirit or an invisible but benevolent spook, I suspect that Jung was right in his hypothesis that these entities arise out of a peculiar faculty of our mind – a function that we, as yet, do not know and understand.

Lonely little children always acquire and imaginary friend. Mine was called "Bill." I wonder about that now. Was Bill really the product of a lonely little boy's imagination? Is he still with me now?

Can he morph into different forms – was it "Bill" playing the part of "the boy" and the "dark blue" ghost?

At some point in your adult life, your imaginary friend will appear before you – in a vision during your waking hours or perhaps as you dream. That experience is something like falling in love – when it is real, you know it without knowing how you know it.

As I write this, I hear music playing in the background of my mind – an old song from *South Pacific*. It seems applicable, even if slightly out of context …

> Some enchanted evening.
> You may see a stranger.
> You may see a stranger
> Across a crowded room.
> And somehow you know;
> You know even then.
> That somewhere you'll see him
> Again and again …
>
> Who can explain it?
> Who can tell you why?
> Fools give you reasons.
> Wise men never try.

Chapter 12
The Good Life

So now you know what your mind is capable of.

It can dream. It can imagine. It can invent. It can solve problems. It has an unlimited capacity for learning. It has all the power and capabilities you might ever need in order to have a vocationally successful, abundantly happy and richly rewarding life.

Our minds are emotionally driven systems. This is a good thing, because it makes us capable of feeling – of being happy, of laughing and loving – of empathizing with others and crying when grieving or hurt. We do not understand how or why our minds do that, but we do know that as life draws to a close, the most memorable times are those where feelings ran the highest and the warmest. It is the feelings that we remember, before the facts.

Our minds are also designed to thrive on happiness and joy. Over time, hurtful things seem to fade away ever deeper into memory, while images of the good things, the things that are dear to our hearts, somehow remain more buoyant, always floating close to the surface. Happiness and joy seems to be what nature intends as the natural state of life.

It is easy to believe that we are like this, through the grace of some wonderfully benevolent intelligent designer. Or perhaps it is just a matter of natural selection, since the sad, the stressed – those who find little in life worth smiling about – often die young.

Perhaps evil, rather than good, is the more convincing evidence of higher powers. Our minds are just as capable of low things, black things – the "seven deadly sins." These are self-defeating things, things that make us unhappy, things that make us feel that life is a curse and not worth living.

From the time we are born, something seems insistent upon creating a Monster within us that constantly promotes ugliness, a painter with a broad brush, tinting all our recollections with guilt, and shame, and sorrow – footnoting every memory with a reminder that we are no good, that we deserve to be disrespected by others, and that we are right in hating ourselves.

After thinking about it for several years, I finally realized why I was never able to find words to accurately describe what it was like in the presence of the "dark blue" apparition. My "Philemon" was evidently the personification of perfection, and what I felt for those few brief moments was what it feels like to be totally free of guilt, and shame, and remorse. It was love, happiness and joy elevated to levels far beyond anything we know or can imagine. It was what it feels like to be totally free of the Monster. It was a glimpse of the ancients' "Kingdom of God," the now hoped for "Good Life."

And thus, our conversation comes to an end. So here again is the big question: What will you be carrying around between your ears for the rest of your life – a beautiful mind or a self-defeating monster? The choice is yours.

Goodbye and Godspeed.

Index

A

academic dismissal, 118
academic probation, 118
achievement, 80
    futility of obsession with, 82
    gift vs. effort, 80
    remedy for anxiety over, 83
    sharing the spotlight, 84
    why admired, 81
addiction
    as scapegoating, 126
    defined, 161
    to sex, 157
affairs, 157
affluence, 73
    and happiness, 73
    and self esteem, 73
    earnings vs. obligations, 75
    living within your means, 80
    the "rat race", 79
age of consent, 177, 194
age of majority, 7
aggressive personality type, 44
agreeableness, 36
ambiguous genitalia, 150
American Psychiatric Association, 42
anorexia, 136
aphonia paralytica, 114
A's (3-A's), 51
    "Why bother?", 86
attractiveness, 59
    and first impressions, 72, 184
    and self esteem, 72
    as influenced by behavior, 60

as perceived by others, 60

components of, 72

enhancement of, 61

physical beauty, 184

autonomic function, 26

avoidant personality type, 45

axons, 23

B

bad breath, 66

bad feelings, dealing with, 48

balance, 46

achieving, 47

or self acceptance, 49

vs. neuroticism, 41, 49

Beck, Aaron - originates CBT, 16

behavior therapy, 14

bell curve, 222

brain

as "mind", 12

capacity vs. utilization, 21

functions, 11

brainstorming, 31

bulimia, 136

C

CBT, 9

and being "born again", 263

origin, 16

celebrity. *See* achievement

central nervous system. *See* nervous system

character, 35

charm, 70

behavior guidelines, 71

child abuse, 164

~*getting immediate help*, 192

and politics, 165

categories, 167

consensual relationships, 190, 191

emotional abuse, 167

physical abuse, 168

safe sex, 199

sexual abuse, 170

spanking, 169

Child Protection Act, 167

anyone vulnerable to accusations, 199

child protection "industry", 192

common advocate motives, 204

compulsory reporting, 193

defense strategy, 201

emotional harm to children, 190

if approached by CPS, 193

impact on families, 196

pressure on children to cooperate, 195

progressive elaboration of accusations, 195

prospects for vitims, 204

seeing a lawyer or attorney, 193

victim culpability, 204

victim grooming, 176

class. *See* charm

coercion vs. persuasion, 130

cognition, 32

and fallibility, 34

Cognitive Behavior Theory. *See* CBT

cognitive process, 226

college

academic dismissal, 118

high school vs. college, 117

independent learning, 117

coming of age, 155

conscientiousness, 36

consent. *See* informed consent

CPS Advocates - changing your mind, 206

crabs, 63

D

deadbeat, 79

death and grieving, 214

debt, 77

a result of inferiority complex, 78

dendrite, 23

denial, 44

dependant personality type, 44

depression, 209

causes and cures, 214

grief, 214

Prozac and placebos, 215

Diagnostic and Statistical Manual of Mental Disorders. *See* DSM

dieting and exercise, 142

dress, 67

shopping for clothing, 68

what to wear, 67

drop outs

    job outlook, 91

    legacy to future family, 121

    rate of, 89

    reasons for, 92

DSM

    on bad habits, 128

    personality disorders, 42

E

eating disorders, 136

Edison, Thomas - on achievement, 80

effeminate, 2, 150

ego defenses, 44, 45

Einstein, Albert

    on "balance", 49

Ellis, Albert

    on neurosis, 4

    originates REBT, 15

    What is a neurotic?. *See* frontmatter

emotional abuse, 167

empirical rule, 223

escapism, 44

euthanasia, 217

extraversion, 36

F

fag magnet, 152

fallibility, 31, 47, 224

    and opinions, 228

    risk of absolute thinking, 87, 169, 180, 191

family, 163, 165, 169

    and the Child Protection Act, 196

    saving troubled families, 197

fantasy

    erotic, 148

    vs. reality, 156, 159

fat, 140

first impression, 51, 182, 184

forbidden fruits, 134

Franklin, Benjamin - Thirteen Virtues, 123

G

G.I. Shower, 63

Gaussian Distribution, 222

gay. *See* homosexual

gay bashing, 152

gender confusion, 149

gender roles, 2

genetics and behavior, 128

gerontophilia, 151

good looks. *See* attractiveness

grief, 214

H

habit, 125

    and culture, 133

    arising from rebelliousness, 135

    avoidance through moderation, 129

    bad, defined, 125

    breaking bad habits, 129

    genetic predisposition, 128

    sex, 160

    vulnerabililty of neurotics, 129

hermaphrodite, 150

higher education, 117

homosexual

    denial and acceptance of interest, 152

    inappropriate labeling of boys, 149

myth?, 149

what determins sexual preference, 150

hygiene. *See* personal hygiene

I

Iacocca, Lee - on boyhood, 4

identity crisis, 37

imagination, 31

inferiority complex, 46

informed consent, 177

    revisiting the criteria, 180

interest, essential for learning, 105

interneurons. *See* neuron

Islam, 241

    five pillars of faith, 243

    Shiites and Sunnis, 243

J

Jung, Carl

    and Philemon, 264

    collective unconscious, 265

    concept of God, 266

    definition of neuroticism, 42

    on belief, 264

K

Kandel, Eric – memory and learning, 28

L

law
>bad law, 166, 169, 181
>Child Protection Act, 167, 170

learning
>and rational thinking. See aphonia paralytica, 114
>as a memory process, 30
>cultivating interest, 105
>early, a natural process, 39
>from texts, 104
>higher education, 117
>improving concentration, 100
>intellectual, 41
>learning and memory, 28
>memory process, 102
>negativr motivators, 113
>reading skills, 102
>role of repetition, 103
>sponge concept of, 40
>the hard way, 113
>unconsciously, 40
>vocabulary, 102

life
>as a gift, 57
>purpose of, 56

living within your means, 80

M

map, body. See somatosensory cortex

masturbation, 145
>and age, 147
>mutual, 147, 149, 175
>real men don't do it?, 156

memory, 12
>and learning, 28
>limits of, 30
>persistency, 48
>virtual maps, 28

mental mechanisms. See ego defenses

mind
>cognitive process, 226
>conscious mind, 26
>disorders, 12
>how it works, 22

inherently fallible, 34, 226

learning to control, 17

multi-tasking, 98

moderation, 125

molestation. *See* child abuse

money. *See* affluence

monogamy, 157

Monster

    capable of killing you, 220

    explained, 17

    learning to control, 17

Muhammad, 241

my Philemon, 268

N

neglect, 167

nerve cell, 23

nervous system, 22

    motor functions, 26

    reliability, 26

    sensory functions, 26

networking, 53

neurobiology, 26

neurology, 11, 26

neuron, 22

neuropsychiatry, 14

neurotic

    defined. *See* frontmatter

    modern meaning, 13

    original meaning, 13

neuroticism

    as a personality trait, 37

    as defined today, 41

    childhood beginnings, 42

    informs culture, 18

Niebuhr, Reinhold – *Serenity Prayer*, 19

O

obesity, 140

openness, 36

opportunity, a dividend of education, 121

overeating, 140

P

paradigm principle, 33

parents, 7, 163, 169

    and this book, 7

partners in creation, 57

paying attention, 97

paying attention to others, 84

pedophilia, 151

ancient meaning, 181
and "emotional intelligence", 187
and sexual fetishes, 189
as a disorder, 182
simple neuroticism?, 186

people skills, 53

perfectionist, 45

performance anxiety. See aphonia paralytica

personal hygiene, 63
and smoking, 66
morning routine, 65

personality, 35
and relationships, 35
development, 35
disorders, 42
nature or nurture?, 38
traits, 36
types, 44

Peter Pan, personality type, 45

physical abuse, 168

physical beauty. See attractiveness

popularity. See achievement
after graduation, 83
in school, 82

predestination, 56

privacy, sexual, 155, 157

prohibition, 132

psychoanalysis, 14

psychology
not a science, 13
theories come and go, 7

psychotic, 13

puberty, 2, 61

R

Rand, Ayn - "check your premises", 224

Rational Emotive Behavior Theory. See REBT

rationalization, 44

REBT, 9
origin, 15

REBT/CBT
and men, 16
common sense approach, 16

reincarnation, 56

relationships
and CBT, 185
children and adults, 186, 190

creation and cultivation, 184

religion

    a simple faith, 259

    agnosticism, 223

    and CBT, 262

    and culture, 257

    and the information age, 254

    atheism, 223

    avoiding extremes, 222

    being "born again", 262

    choice or chance, 221

    christianity

        emerging paradigm, 252

        Jesus - a more rational version, 253

    common roots, 231

    dogmatism, 228

    fallibility of scriptures, 229, 244

    fundamentalism, 223

    historical development, 229

    importance of participation, 256

    is there a God?, 264

    Jesus of Nazareth, 233

    Kingdom of God - a developing reality?, 255

    major world religions, 230

    nuts and bolts of, 229, 256

    Paul of Tarsus, 238

    purity codes, 234

    sacrifice, 230

    spirit guide, 275

    things that matter, 256

    traditional vs. transitional, 244

    typical believer profiles, 221

reparenting, 263

S

safe sex

    "MAD" (mutually assured destruction), 200

    avoiding setups, 201

    keeping yourself out of trouble, 199

school. *See also* learning

    attention problems, 99

    being an honor student, 94

    compulsory education, 120

    developing interest, 97

    education as a gift, 120

    high school vs. college, 117

    how to concentrate, 100

importance of your school record, 94
paying attention, 97
reading skills, 102
relationship with teachers, 96
teachers' pet, 94
value of collegiality, 119
Science of Mind, 27
second decade of life. *See* ten
self esteem, 46
    as a product of childhood, 43
self-made man, 52
senses, 25
    touch, 24
sensuality, 153
    fear or repulsion, 159
    opening night jitters, 159
    safe sex, 199
    what's "normal", 159
Serenity Prayer, 19
setups
    boy's vulnerability, 202
    coerced fatherhood, 201
sexual abuse, 170, *See also* child abuse

a more rational paradigm, 190
sexual arousal, 154
    automatically regulated, 160
sexual attractiveness
    as a mind function, 184
    in children, 186
sexual attraction, 182
sexual desire. *See* venery
sexual preference, 150
    variability over time, 152
sexuality
    feminine/masculine range, 150
    pre-adolescent, 171
    psychological and emotional aspects, 150
signals - in nerves, 23
skinny, 138
smile, 62
somatosensory cortex, 24
spanking, 169
standard normal distribution, 222
styptic pencil, 65
suicide, 217
    physician assisted, 217

synapse, 23

T

ten

    beginning of neuroticism, 4

    childhood before, 3

    how life changes at, 3, 4

    sex abuse, 171

    what young boys know, 5, 172, 180

    why ten?, 2, 4

testosterone, 149, 158

Three A's, 51

tomboy, 1, 150

V

venery, 145

    and privacy, 157

    arousal, 154

    how much is too much, 157

    illicit affairs, 157

    intimacy, 151

    love, 151

    monogamy, 157

    preferences and appetites vary, 158

    privacy, 155

    safe sex, 199

W

War on Drugs, 132

wardrobe. *See* dress

wealth. *See* affluence

wet dreams, 148

X

x-generation, 57

www.ingramcontent.com/pod-product-compliance
Lightning Source LLC
Chambersburg PA
CBHW031235290426
44109CB00012B/307